SAP
NATION

*a runaway
software economy*

VINNIE
MIRCHANDANI
author, *The New Polymath*

SAP Nation

For information about this title or to order bulk copies and/or electronic media, and for SAP and other IT advisory services, contact:
Deal Architect, Inc
P.O. Box 262262, Tampa, FL 33685, USA
www.dealarchitect.typepad.com

Updates to the book at www.sapnation.com

ISBNs: 978-0-9909296-1-1 (soft cover)
        978-0-9909296-0-4 (eBook)
        978-0-9909296-2-8 (Hardback – bulk copies only)

Printed in the United States of America
Cover and Interior design: 1106 Design

This book is dedicated to customers — the underappreciated stakeholders in the IT industry.

Table of Contents

Preface

∿→

I first thought about writing this book five years ago. In February 2009, I was invited to an SAP event in New York City where the company announced Business Suite 7, the latest version of its high-end ERP software that runs operations at many a Fortune 500 company and other enterprises. After the formal presentations, then-co-CEO Leo Apotheker sat down with a few of us analysts for Q&A.

Most of us wanted to talk about the recently announced maintenance price increase, which was proving unpopular with SAP customers, coming as it did in the deep recession. We also wanted to discuss why ECC6.0, their previous version of the ERP software, was seeing slow uptake among customers. But, Apotheker was irritated that none of us wanted to talk about Business Suite 7.

As I wrote the next day:

> "Alternatively defensive and feisty, there was piss and vinegar that I hope Leo turns into action.

It started off with Leo accusing me of spreading "rumors" about SAP overruns and little productivity improvement in systems integrator (SI) work plans over the years. Forget that the legions of staff in the SAP ecosystem and the hundreds of billions of dollars and euros and yens in SAP customer TCO models confirm my "rumors." Have done so for 15+ years now.

To my point that SAP's efforts have done little to improve productivity in data migration, user acceptance testing and other implementation phases around core SAP functions, he proceeded to discuss tools SAP has delivered in many of the areas.

What about the fact that these tools have not driven significant productivity in SI proposals? Leo bravely said, "If we believe [a project] takes 500 days and another partner says it's 5,000 days, I'll do it for 500 and a fixed fee."

To our point that in the field it often appears partner interests trump those of the customer, Leo was at his passionate best: "I've been in the field all my life. That monster out there [the field] is my creature. Loyalty is to the customer. The obligation is to the customer," and "I don't give a s**t if it's Accenture or IBM. I care about the customer."

Unlike some other analysts who were in that room, I am also a consultant to CIOs, helping them evaluate SAP and partner proposals. I had to smile through Apotheker's brave talk.

Then it turned interesting. Apotheker emailed me to say that I should not have published my note — the conversation should have stayed private. That had not been communicated at the start of the meeting. In fact, some of the analysts in the room were live-tweeting the event. My column was already old news by the time it was published.

Nonetheless, I apologized in a follow-up post:

> "We got the chance to ask him tough questions, see him come out swinging, show spunk in the blogger session. We want him to continue to be that way. In return we owe it to him to not have to defend every word he says in that frame of passion. And we can do so while providing our readers the spirit of what is being discussed.
>
> We goofed. Sorry, Leo. I hope we can continue that level of open conversation. On our part, we will use better judgment in how we report it."

Then it turned even more interesting. An SAP marketing executive called to ask if I would talk with Accenture and IBM and explain to them what had happened in the meeting. I grudgingly agreed. The calls never happened, but the damage was done. I was giving Apotheker credit for finally standing up to his partners as I had repeatedly asked over the years, and again SAP appeared to have backed down.

Despite those concerns, I did not write the SAP book at that time. Instead, I have written three books in the last five years, on technology-enabled innovation and the digital transformation journeys of companies. Also, I was convinced in 2009 that

SAP had peaked and customer investments post-recession on their SAP projects would be much more modest.

About that, I was dead wrong.

Earlier this year, I had a chance to build a model of "SAP Nation" — as Chapter 3 details. I was shocked that post-recession customers appear to have spent over a trillion dollars around SAP. This, when SAP's own sales and deliverables have leveled off. When you compare how nicely IT costs via software-as-a-service (SaaS) applications, cloud infrastructures and mobile broadband have dropped in the last few years, you have to ask why those in the SAP economy have not followed that trend. Likewise, when you see all the front-office technology opportunities — in product and customer-facing areas — you wonder how many are being crowded out by the SAP back office. Those vexing questions are what has convinced me to finally write this book.

The book is organized into five sections and four groups of customer strategies.

Section I sets the stage and shows that in spite of the customer and SAP pivots, the SAP economy keeps marching to its own drumbeat. Chapter 1 shows where innovative customers are moving their IT investment. Chapter 2 shows a significant shift in SAP investment away from leadership in business applications to a focus on platforms and acquisitions. Chapter 3 details our model of the SAP economy.

Section II documents the growth of the SAP economy over the last three decades. Chapter 4 covers the 1990s, Chapter 5 the 2000s, and Chapter 6 the current decade.

Section III investigates whether the huge spend in the SAP economy has yielded commensurate payback. In Chapter 7 we see that, in spite of the large investment and decades of experience, the casualties in SAP project failures and write-offs continue unabated. Chapter 8 covers the transformative waves of industrialization, consumerization, externalization and boardrooming of IT that have eluded many SAP customers.

Section IV looks at the root causes of how the SAP economy got to be so massive. Chapter 9 looks at SAP's own mistakes. Chapter 10 focuses on the role of partners in the SAP economy. Chapter 11 examines whether market watchers could have done more to highlight the bloat in the SAP economy. Chapter 12 evaluates why SAP customers have not done more to better manage the economics.

Section V looks at recent SAP and customer trends. Chapter 13 describes customers' shifting IT priorities. Chapter 14 shows a glimmer of hope as SAP moves to newer business models and start-up ecosystems. Chapter 15 presents likely future scenarios for the SAP economy.

My model of the economy led me to call executives at SAP customers — some that I have consulted with and several others. I wanted to hear what they were doing to optimize their SAP spend. Based on their feedback, I have classified their strategies in Case Study Groups A-D in four customer profiles:

- Un-adopters
- Diversifiers
- Pragmatists
- Committed

Each of the alphabetic-section chapters describes various customer strategies — some are doubling-down and investing in SAP's in-memory analytics, some are consolidating SAP instances, others are implementing cloud solutions around SAP, and still others are moving away from SAP. Figure 1 below shows many of the customers we profile across those four categories.

Customer Strategies

Un-adopters	Diversifiers	Pragmatists	Committed
A1 – Flip it off *Inteva Products* *Jefferson County, AL* *Middlesbrough Council*	**B1** – "Ring Fence" with clouds *HP* **B2** – Change Talent Model *AstraZeneca*	**C1** – Keep relationship analytical *CLP Group* **C2** – Keep projects low-hype *DeVry Education Group*	**D1** – Align with SAPs Future *Burberry's* *John Deere* **D2** – Make SAP dance to your business tune *Endo International*
A2 – Freeze and Shrink *Color Spot Nurseries* *United Biscuits* *Embraer*	**B3** – Tiers of Joy *ABS-CBN* *Delta Airlines* *Microsoft* *The Würth Group* **B4** – Best of Breed for agility *Schneider Electric*	**C3** – Rethink the Customer Experience *DigitalGlobe* **C4** – Balance with Open Source and commodity technology *British Gas*	

Figure 1   Credit: Deal Architect

We also profile strategies at companies like Big Heart Pet Brands, BP, Flextronics, GE, Lexmark and Unilever in other parts of the book. The majority of the case studies were developed from interviews with executives conducted specifically for this book. For the others, the material was collated from presentations given by their executives or from content where they are quoted.

One could ask, "What's a trillion dollars when the software runs so much of the Fortune 500?" It is a good question till you shade it against the fact that the Fortune 500 for the *first time ever* reported total profits of a trillion dollars — barely — in 2013.

Earlier this year, I was talking to a German journalist about impressive modern-day factories, and I told him the data centers at Google, Facebook, and Amazon are impressive "factories." These 500,000-square-foot behemoths, servicing billions of users, are supported by a handful of staff with the latest in cooling efficiencies and security features. In contrast, the SAP economy is people-intensive, with labor constituting 70 percent of the costs in our model. It also lags behind world-class benchmarks on most computing, network and other components.

Some readers may argue it's not all about economics; what about speed and agility? SAP's HANA is blazing fast (indeed, it is short for High-Performance Analytic Appliance). True, but that is SAP's future. Only a few thousand of its 250,000 customers have adopted it. The vast majority of SAP's customers are stuck with its older products. At Gartner in the late 1990s, we snarkily compared using SAP to pouring concrete around your feet. Fifteen years later, the expression is still in use!

And speaking of time, the five-year delay in writing this book means it is now aligned with my 25th anniversary of "meeting" SAP. In 1989, while on assignment with Price Waterhouse in London, I led a team to set up SAP R/2 and McCormack & Dodge (M&D) prototypes on our mainframe in our brand-new Docklands data center.

So, the book has turned into a bit of a retrospective for me. For the book research:

- I revisited archives from my Software Intelligence Group at Price Waterhouse that analyzed emerging client/server applications from 1993–1995.

- I reviewed Walldorf (SAP headquarters) visit notes and many research papers on SAP from my stint at Gartner from 1995–2000.
- I unearthed documents from our start-up IQ4hire from 2001–2003 where we had built tools to help customers select systems integration services.
- I dusted off notes from many visits to SAP application management and hosting firms around the world as part of consulting services provided by my firm, Deal Architect.
- I reread my blog entries from Sapphire Now trips and SAP meetings over the last decade.

In a column I wrote for *InformationWeek* earlier this year about *The Digital Enterprise,* a book I helped write for the CEO of Software AG, I noted that "I found a surprising sentiment in most of these conversations: joy. To them, IT is fun and profit-able again." A reader commented on the column "Did we just use the word "joy" in an IT article, Vinnie?"

In contrast, the emotions to describe interviewing for and writing this book would be "bittersweet" and "puzzlement." The walk down memory lane allowed me to connect with a number of colleagues and clients from my past. But, the research also exposed a lot of pain in the SAP customer base. My interviews for innovation books tend to be excited and positive. For this book, many of the conversations were defensive and guarded.

And, I had a gnawing sense of "How was this allowed to go on and on?" The initial IT failure of the Obamacare-related HealthCare.gov got a relentless amount of media, political, and business scrutiny. That was reported as a $1 billion project (even after the overruns). In contrast, the SAP economy has had significantly more write-offs and waste. Why has it not seen anywhere near the scrutiny? How did a vendor, born and raised in German efficiency, with an intense product focus on controlling, costing, and compliance allow this much waste in its own economy? And, how have so many sophisticated customers tolerated the inefficiencies for so long?

Conversely, several customers I interviewed asked "How come so few alternatives have emerged to SAP?" SAP grew prominent by killing off siloed vendors like MSA and Cullinet. It overcame challenges from best-of-breed players like Siebel and i2. The recent wave of cloud challengers — Workday, Salesforce.com, NetSuite, ServiceNow, Plex Systems, Kenandy, Kinaxis and others — are merely nibbling around the edges of SAP. Few have launched a full frontal assault. I have been told that several SAP customers have called and pleaded with these cloud players to expand their functional footprint. Gas car buyers are waiting for electric options, but all they see so far are hybrids, not a full replacement.

Of course, if you were to pose such an excuse to executives at Infor, Microsoft, Oracle, Syspro, Unit4, and others who offer full ERP suites, they would likely say "hogwash!" They would say that's just a convenient SAP customer defense of the status quo.

Even if they stay with SAP, customers have options to optimize their environments, and many of the case studies in the book showcase that ability.

In many ways, the effort to tame SAP and its partners is an epic battle to reshape back-office IT and to refocus resources on product- and customer-centric, front-office digital technologies. As Daru (as he is known) from BP describes in Chapter 1, it's about focus on the "coal-face" — the front office. And, as Bill Ruh of GE describes in Chapter 13, it's about moving from IT to

OT (operational technology). The customer strategies described in the book can also be applied to optimizing other IT costs beyond the SAP footprint.

As I reviewed decades of archives, I found myself admiring the architectural brilliance SAP co-founder Dr. Plattner has displayed over four decades. He was a visionary when SAP developed a real-time system in the 1970s, when most U.S. vendors were in batch mode and companies planned on month-end closing of books. He was farsighted again, in the late 1980s, when he invested in UNIX and R/3 as he saw IBM and the mainframe fading. And yet again, more recently, with HANA.

In fact, the company has had no lack of impressive leadership. You have to respect the global enterprise that SAP ex-CEO Dr. Henning Kagermann helped establish. I have had a chance to watch the even more impressive work he has done after leaving SAP at acatech, the German National Academy of Science and Engineering, as I describe in Chapter 2. Even with his short tenures as CEO at SAP and at HP, you have to respect the enduring customer relationships Leo Apotheker helped build at SAP. And, new SAP CEO Bill McDermott was an entrepreneur even as a teen, and brings a new sense of urgency and optimism.

The fact is that SAP has done many things right, and the book acknowledges those along with the many other things it could have done better. The "done better" part was astutely summarized by my wife, who commented, during an early-draft "readability" review of this book: "This is such a contrast to the Apple experience. Apple must tightly manage its suppliers and the store with all its apps. The only flaw I can think of is the initial problems it had with AT&T around the iPhone. In

SAP's case, the controls around its partners appear so loose. I bet there is plenty of AT&T-type performance."

She is right. SAP has a tendency to write code, and then hand it over to its partners. It fails to think enough about customer deployment issues. Worse, it lets customers fend for themselves in dealing with its partners. Many SAP customers have not done well negotiating with or monitoring hardware vendors, hosting firms, telco carriers, offshore application management vendors, etc. In fact, it has been suggested that unlike Ford, for SAP, "Partners are Job #1." Partner interests, it would appear, trump those of its customers. The sum total of partners' inefficiencies explains much of the excess in the SAP economy.

So, what was my motivation in writing this book? Certainly not to give SAP's competitors something to gloat about. In fact, though Oracle is a sponsor of our blogs (as are Cognizant, Workday, Infor, and several other technology vendors), I deliberately avoided reaching out to executives at Oracle for commentary.

My hope is CEOs and directors at SAP customers emulate Mike McNamara, CEO of Flextronics (see Chapter 1), when he says "keep your hands on the IT wheel." Or, to be like Rajiv De Silva, CEO at Endo (see Chapter D2), who demanded a detailed project review before approving continued funding. In fact, I hope customers/readers pore through all the optimization strategies profiled in Sections A through D and help to reverse the "business as usual" that I estimate costs SAP customers over $200 billion a year.

While some of the case studies in the book are reporting better than 50 percent savings, let's aim at shaving just 10 percent from the SAP economy. What could enterprises do with $20 billion a year? My personal preference is that they use it toward innovation projects that give me fodder for future books! But, seriously, there are limitless worthwhile causes and initiatives for CEOs and boards to pursue. As Albert Camus wrote "In the midst of winter, I found there was, within me, an invincible summer." So, let's look forward to the many opportunities to streamline SAP Nation.

November 2014

Acknowledgements

~~>

I have countless people to thank for contributions to the book. I interviewed or read materials from several hundred SAP customers, executives, alumni, partners and market watchers. Everyone quoted in the book worked patiently with me. Many others provided "background" perspectives. I understand and honor why you chose to contribute that way, and I am grateful for the input and validation.

It takes a village to produce a book and I have to thank many involved in the production and promotion of the book. Mark Baven and Diana Fitter did an outstanding job on the editing. Michele DeFilippo, Ronda Rawlins and the team at 1106 Design take credit for the book's aesthetics. My wife, Margaret Newman, contributed in many ways — most of all as conscience, so I stayed fair and balanced. There are many others — you know I am grateful even if I do not call you out here.

The Happiest Place on Earth

⋏→

Just as Orlando, Florida, starts to become uncomfortably warm around Memorial Day each year, thousands of executives fly in for the better part of a week. The lucky ones get to stay at the Peabody, where they do not have to wait for shuttle buses. Instead, they could watch the pampered house ducks march up a red carpet and waddle for hours in a fountain. Others stay a bit further away near Shamu, the killer whale at Sea World. Still others stay near the beautifully landscaped Epcot and other Disney parks.

They are not there, however, for the flora and fauna.

They have come to SAP's marquee event — Sapphire Now — which takes up much of the million-square-feet of the north and south halls at the Orange County Convention Center. Each year, these visitors witness event production details that make them go "Wow!" and which have won SAP kudos from meeting and event managers: A keynote theater with cantilevered doors and risers; giant, glass-front faux broadcast studios; live greenery; natural wood and leather seating; etc.

They come to listen to SAP executives, who look both tiny on the huge stage and yet larger than life on surrounding giant screens. Dr. Hasso Plattner, one of the founders, takes the stage every year for a part humorous and part deep-dive technical talk. On occasion, Dr. Plattner also breaks out a guitar, or tells sailing and Formula One racing stories. It is a far cry from the humble beginnings of the company which took a decade to reach 100 employees with headquarters in the *spargel* (white asparagus) fields of Walldorf, in the Baden-Württemberg region of Germany.

The visitors come to mingle with peers from the Fortune 500 and beyond. They walk by booths that represent the best and brightest from every technology category — infrastructure vendors like Cisco, EMC, HP and IBM, newer cloud players like Amazon and Microsoft, and accounting/advisory firms like Deloitte and PwC. Add to that global players like TCS, HCL and L&T Infotech from India, Stefanini from Brazil, Fujitsu and NTT Data from Japan, and Atos, Capgemini and T-Systems from Europe. The wide range of specialist offerings represented there includes benchmarking services from AnswerThink, fashion industry expertise from Attune, spatial data from Critigen and database services from Dobler.

This is the hub of corporate IT. At every turn, you are near someone who is responsible for technology that processes orders, invoices or payroll for well-known brands around the world. The power and influence is palpable. SAP advertises it as "the must-attend business outing of the year."

The entertainment is top notch. Bands from Bon Jovi to Van Halen have graced the event. Parties reflect flavors ranging from the Pub at Pointe Orlando to Fogo de Chão, the Brazilian churrascaria. There are hosted breakfasts, lunches, cappuccino stands, and cocktail hours.

The technology exhibitors gladly spend millions each year on the event. They rent booths as large as 2,000 square feet. The signage, up to 22 feet tall, is a burst of colors, shapes and sizes. Furnishing the booths is expensive, but chicken feed compared to the cost of flying and accommodating hundreds of their staff. SAP gives them 50 to 60 conference badges as part of their sponsorship, but many exhibitors share the badges to ensure more of their employees are available to host guests in the booths and hospitality suites, or to mingle with customers during the keynotes and breaks. They pay extra for shuttle buses, escalator clings, bottled water, hot coffee cup sleeves and other "swag" branded with their logos.

It is good return for their investment. SAP says "87 percent of exhibitors surveyed in 2013 reported that they were either extremely or very successful in reaching their objectives."

It's tough to not be happy here.

If you are a customer, you get to mingle with friends and associates at many peer companies. The U.S. user group, ASUG, hosts its annual event at Sapphire Now. In addition, a quarter of the attendees are from outside the U.S., giving the event the feel of a FIFA World Cup party. If you are a prospect, you get to evaluate the "intangibles" of meeting with SAP executives and other customers that you do not encounter in a typical software procurement process. If you are an exhibitor, you get lists of countless leads to chase. In recent years, SAP has focused on bringing more prospects to the event, even as existing customers return every year.

Sapphire Now is also a true media "happening," with tens of thousands watching livecasts of the proceedings. Others will read tweets and blogs from SAP's "social ambassadors" who cruise the event floor. Hundreds of analysts and media players that SAP invites submit their own columns. Customer and partner reps add their own blogs on the SAP Community Network. Over the course of the next few months, many more around the world will watch replays on SAP's YouTube channels. As Scott Schenker, former vice president of global events at SAP, put it: "Sapphire Now as a single destination for 72 hours is the old model. The new model is that Sapphire Now is always up."[1]

But like so much else in Orlando, Sapphire Now is kitsch, a pleasant escape from reality. When they return home, attendees realize their SAP environment is not "simple" or "minimalist," words SAP executives frequently use. They look back and wish technology works as well as it did at the event, which supports nearly 100,000 iPads, smartphones, laptops, and the walkie-talkies and pagers of the event attendees, security staff and "roadies." They wonder why SAP cannot extend its influence on its partners beyond the event. At the event, SAP has guidelines for exhibitors concerning every little detail: signage, dress codes, professional behavior, employment solicitation and "sensitive and/or non-complementary" materials.

As they share all the freebies they picked up at the event with their kids, it strikes the event attendees that nothing in the SAP economy is really free. They chuckle about the all-too-real joke they heard in Orlando: "SAP stands for 'send another payment.'"

Many customers have gone beyond chuckling.

---

[1]   http://www.bizbash.com/most-innovative-meetings-2012-1-saps-sapphire-now/new-york/story/23791/#.U6yoS41OU9g

And Still It Roars

CHAPTER 1

The Customer Pivot

∿➤

History credits February 23 with plenty of trivia — the Tootsie Roll was invented in 1896, The Rotary Club was formed in 1905 and the iconic photo of US Marines raising the American flag on Iwo Jima was taken on that date in 1945.

When the history of technology is written, it will, however, honor the 54th day in 2008 for a meeting which would change the trajectory of enterprise computing.

February 23, 2008, was a Saturday like so many others that Dave Duffield and Aneel Bhusri have spent together. Two-and-a-half decades separate them chronologically, but they have been finishing sentences for each other since they first met in the early 1990s. You can see how comfortable they are when they do joint keynotes at the annual Rising conference of the company they co-founded, Workday. They discuss cloud computing, tell corny jokes and throw snacks into the audience. It's mostly unrehearsed.

But, this Saturday afternoon was different, and the two executives had to be totally "on message." They were going to see Mike McNamara, the CEO of Flextronics. It sounded like an ambitious call. Flextronics was a global giant on a $20 billion revenue run rate that year. In the conservative enterprise software market, where companies wait for plenty of references and benchmarks, surely it was too big a customer for a three-year-old start-up. At that point, Workday could not show benchmarks that it could scale above 5,000 employees. Flextronics had over 160,000 employees at the end of 2008.

The meeting had been set up by David Smoley, then the CIO at Flextronics. I blurted out, "You did what?" when he first told me about the meeting, astonished at his audacity.

His IT council had given him the green light to proceed with a major global SAP project to consolidate 80 different HR systems around the world. His team had spent months evaluating options, systems integrators, budgets, and business cases.

Then came the "You did what?" moment. As I wrote in *The New Technology Elite* (2012), Smoley told me:

> "I thanked them for approving such a large project, and then I surprised them. I told them I may come back to them in the next month with a "better, faster, cheaper" option. But we have a "fail faster" culture here at Flextronics, so they were more intrigued with what I may come back with than surprised."

That's what the Saturday meeting with McNamara was about. It took McNamara all of 20 minutes to feel comfortable with Duffield and Bhusri. "Yes, they did not have size or scale at Workday, but these two had done this before a few times," he summed up.

Duffield and Bhusri committed to a partnership where Flextronics would provide a benchmark for process and priorities, and drive the development road map for Workday. In turn, Flextronics would draw upon the years of HR experience the Workday team had to shape and standardize Flextronic's processes. It was a breakthrough software development partnership.

You can understand what McNamara seeks in a supplier, because of what his customers seek in him. Flextronics is a contract manufacturer for a wide range of high-tech, medical device, appliance, and other rapidly evolving products. Its customers demand absolute security from competitive eyes, and their demand forecasts can change hourly. These customers expect extreme flexibility from McNamara, so you can see how he liked the flexible arrangement with Workday.

Yet, Flextronics is also an extremely complex operation. Differing from competitor, Foxconn, which manufactures mostly in China, Flextronics offers its customers plenty of regional choices. That way customers can produce closer to emerging market demand, as middle classes blossom around the world. Last year, Flextronics moved 25 percent of its manufacturing capacity across borders and regions. I queried, "Doesn't that need an astonishing level of logistical planning?" McNamara responded, "Actually, [it takes] rapid analysis on the logistics — we are pretty dynamic."

So, given that complexity, he took a huge risk on Workday. As McNamara explained:

> "But, Workday was fresh, not just peddling 20-year-old architecture. In Silicon Valley, we got comfortable with cloud computing much earlier than in other regions. And,

as you can see, cloud computing has given us plenty of flexibility including rapid transition to mobile and later waves of computing."

(By "later waves" he means new categories like data-as-a-service (DaaS). Flextronics is an investor in DaaS pioneer Elementum, which we describe later in the book.)

He told his skeptical executives there was no Plan B. They had to make Workday work. His push toward Workday was as forceful as his pull away from SAP:

> "With SAP, I was afraid we would get something average, same as that at every one of their customers. Or, maybe even something mediocre. At a very high cost with one of its large services partners. We used zero external consultants on the Workday implementation. It was just us and them working hand and hand."

Now, McNamara is not a typical CEO. Few CEOs personally underwrite sponsorship of an IT project. As he says, "I like my hands on the wheel." And, not every company has a "fail faster" culture.

The Flextronics decision in 2008 was a harbinger of change at many enterprises I describe in this book. A few years prior, it would have been considered suicidal for a global company like Flextronics to not go with safe choices like SAP and its partners.

Not any more.

Similar Story from Pet Country
Across the country in Pittsburgh, PA in a very different industry from Flextronics, Dave McLain has a fascinating job. He gets to

track swings in pork belly futures and also follow server and storage pricing trends. McLain is CIO and Chief Procurement Officer at Big Heart Pet Brands, one of the country's largest pet food and treat companies. And, he shares a similar story about betting on a new breed of cloud application vendor.

The company's acquisition of Natural Balance Pet Foods in 2013 and the sale of the company's consumer products business, which included the Del Monte brand, allowed McLain an opportunity to evaluate newer options in ERP marketplace. Natural Balance had a patchwork of applications ripe for renewal. His preference was a cloud solution to reduce time and investment in data centers, database architecture and other IT infrastructure.

In the consumer packaged goods industry, SAP has been a dominant vendor with its ability to process millions of order entry lines with unique pricing, promotion, campaign, assortment and other practices that define the sector. McLain evaluated SAP and other vendors and ended up selecting Kenandy, an ERP solution built on the Salesforce.com cloud platform.

Kenandy is the latest chapter in the story of Sandra Kurtzig, one of Silicon Valley's first female entrepreneurs. She had founded the ERP vendor, ASK in 1972 (when SAP was also founded) and was the first woman to take a Silicon Valley technology company public. Ray Lane, former President of Oracle, is another backer of Kenandy.

The software pedigree of the founders factored in McLain's decision. He was also pleased that Kenandy would be able to leverage Salesforce.com's on-going platform investments in mobile, social, analytical and other emerging areas. McLain spent several years earlier in his career at software vendors and has a deep understanding of how best to extract optimal value from technology vendors and manage risks with startups. He knew, however, he was magnifying the project risk of going with a greenfield vendor while digesting a major acquisition. Says McLain, "I took appropriate risk mitigation steps including spending time with Kenandy's directors, ensuring source code was placed in escrow and putting other protections in the contract."

The payback came in the personalized attention from the vendor and the ability to influence the product development road map. Kurtzig promised (and delivered) to Big Heart Pet Brands a commitment to go live with Kenandy at Natural Balance just 90 minutes after the acquisition was complete. When you consider the scope of the project covered not just back office areas, but also production, quality management, shipping, and receiving, that is quite an accomplishment. McLain says, "We had the unique experience of being able to work with Kenandy and influencing the product design, specifically around the trade management and industry-specific order to cash and financial accounting features."

As with Flextronics, Big Heart Pet Brands also leveraged professional services directly from the application vendor, rather than bringing in an outside systems integrator. Says McLain, "With such a young product, we did not expect our service partners to have the necessary experience, and we would have had to pay them to learn. Working with Kenandy consultants allowed us to learn faster together in an agile process and accelerate our results.

A decade ago, a large company like Big Heart Pet Brands would have likely gone with a safe choice like SAP or Oracle. It is a sign of changing times that companies are increasingly finding that the bigger risk is missing out on the opportunity to work smarter with younger, more responsive vendors.

Meanwhile in the Oil Patch

Over my last decade of writing about technology-enabled innovation, I have repeatedly marveled at how the small team led by Phiroz Darukhanavala, VP and CTO for IT at BP, better known as "Daru," is constantly pushing boundaries.

Ten years ago — yes, a decade ago — BP was implementing sensors and motes (sensor nodes) on tankers and in refineries, even before the term "Internet of Things" was commonly used. In 2006, it ran several advanced predictive analytics applications on rotating equipment. Back in 2010, Curt Smith in Daru's team, described to me how BP had evaluated unmanned aerial vehicles to supplement manned Cessna flights for monitoring remote pipelines. BP is now operating the first FAA-approved commercial drones to monitor remote fields and pipelines.

Like many other large oil companies, BP is a major SAP customer. So, I asked Daru how SAP fits into their vision of technology-enabled innovation. Before addressing my question, however, he delivered a brief tutorial on how advanced digitization is impacting the fossil fuel industries — how it will affect safety, efficiency and productivity when applied to what he termed the "coal face," the front office operations or industrial side of his business. He described the specific technologies that are remaking the industry, and then how SAP fits in:

> "We are looking at intelligent wells, smart drilling rigs, highly instrumented and networked plant equipment — various ways of augmenting human intelligence with machine smarts. With 3D visualization, sensory analytics and massive computing power, we can enable the geologist to perform sub-surface analysis of a formation *remotely* and empower the corrosion planner to virtually

create plans in hours versus walking around facilities or in the field for days.

We see potential payback in the multi-billions of dollars — and that does not even count the safety impact. We were cautious deploying these technologies given safety concerns in our industry, but now we realize that this interplay between the digital and physical worlds can actually improve safety. Digital automation technologies can be used to enforce safety standards, keep humans out of harm's way and reduce human error.

When you think about our operations at the North Slope in Alaska or on remote offshore rigs, you can also see benefits in reduced travel to distant and potentially hazardous sites. Plus, you get the ability to rapidly simulate a variety of scenarios that couldn't safely be tried in the physical world.

The enormous amount of sensory, imaging and operational data we are collecting puts more demands on the back office. As we automate the front end, and integrate it with back-end systems, we are actually increasing the importance of the back office — SAP ERP and other transaction systems.

In the past, we tended to look at the back-office systems as infrastructure — like a highway system. We expected robustness, reliability, integrity … and that justified massive investments. You noticed them mostly when certain portions were not properly paved — when the road felt bumpy.

Now they are not just transaction processors, but enablers of front-office automation — we should be able to unlock much more value from the investments.

Having said that, as we automate the front end to release top-line value, we also expect our SAP and other back-office systems to become much more efficient. They have to continue to run robustly, but at the lowest possible cost. That means leveraging new architectures like cloud computing which can bring massive efficiency of scale to those transactions; adopting industry standard data architectures to promote easy integration; simplifying back-office processes to minimize dead time and ruthlessly rationalizing the back-office applications portfolio to eliminate redundancy and complexity."

Around the time Daru was making these comments, Accenture, a major SAP partner, announced its Upstream Solution for Independent Oil and Gas Companies. The press release said:

"Leveraging the SAP HANA® Cloud Platform, the solution has been created to provide an organization with a single view of production operations, integrated financial accounting and robust reporting, thereby helping to drive front-office growth and stronger bottom-line results. Upstream Solution for Independents is also designed to help improve business decision-making by providing timely insights into costs and revenues, making revenue accounting more manageable for companies operating in the fast-growing unconventional shale oil and gas market."[2]

---

[2] http://www.marketwatch.com/story/accenture-plans-to-launch-upstream-solution-for-independent-oil-and-gas-companies-on-the-sap-hana-cloud-platform-2014-09-19

While Accenture's solution moves the ball forward, its focus on accounting and reporting is a contrast to what Daru described to me — wellhead sensors, 3D visualization, drones, and other technology innovation in the oil and gas sector.

Like BP, many other companies are finding payback in their "coal face" — and expecting much more efficiency from their SAP environments. Throughout this book, we will see other SAP "customer pivots." We will see Embraer, the aircraft manufacturer, take the risk of third-party maintenance of the SAP software in Brazil, one of the most complex regulatory environments in the world. We will see Delta Airlines go with Microsoft technology for its in-flight point-of-sale applications even as it continues with SAP at headquarters. We will see how AstraZeneca is starting to in-source its SAP talent.

The customers profiled in the book are the "canaries in the coal-mine." For every one of these risk-takers, many other customers continue with business as usual. When these customers finally get ready to optimize their environments, they will thank McNamara, Daru and other pioneers.

Yes, history will recognize February 23, 2008, as a pivotal day for technology.

CHAPTER 2

The SAP Pivot

〜→

"Our 12th man is a woman," said a fan about Chancellor Angela Merkel as the German soccer team ran away with the FIFA World Cup in Brazil in the summer of 2014. She took time to visit the team on several occasions during the month-long event, and at the awards ceremony hugged every one of her players. On German social media, a photoshopped image started circulating of Merkel as Christ the Redeemer, the statue which towers over Rio de Janeiro.

In the soccer-crazy country, Merkel got plenty of credit for the German victory at the World Cup. She is also credited with stewarding Germany through the deep recession. She will not get as much credit for something which deserves even more attention — she has sponsored a technological revolution in Germany which is locally being called Industrie 4.0.

I first heard about Industrie 4.0 from Dr. Henning Kagermann, former CEO of SAP, and now President of acatech, the German

Academy of Science and Engineering. The first three industrial revolutions came about as a result of mechanization, electricity, and IT. Now, the introduction of the Internet of Things into the manufacturing environment is ushering in a fourth industrial revolution.

I conducted many interviews with executives at German companies like Daimler and Deutsche Bahn for the book *The Digital Enterprise* by Karl-Heinz Streibich, CEO of Software AG. I repeatedly heard about Industrie 4.0. They were describing how next-gen agile robots, urban factories, augmented reality training, 3D printing, predictive maintenance, and sensor technologies are reshaping manufacturing and logistics.

You would think that SAP, as Germany's biggest technology vendor, would be spearheading Industrie 4.0 efforts at most of these companies. It has not been doing so, which is surprising given the extent of its reach in the German economy.

In contrast, Plex Systems, a much smaller vendor based in the U.S. industrial belt in Michigan, is introducing Industrie 4.0 concepts to its customers. According to Jason Prater, VP of Development at Plex:

> "PCs will be nonexistent on the manufacturing shop floors of the future. To some, that may sound foolish, but to the innovative manufacturers I work with every day, the notion isn't that improbable. The reason I can say this with confidence is a combination of three powerful elements: One, cloud-based data, which connects businesses around the globe as well as vertically through the supply chain; two, connectivity that feeds data into the cloud; and three, mobility, which today means tablets, smartphones, sensors and wearable technology."

Fumbling the CRM Ball

Jim Cramer of the CNBC show *Mad Money* often hosts McDermott of SAP. On a show on January 31, 2013, McDermott was particularly focused on customer-facing technology.[3] He talked about SAP technology at the new stadium of the San Francisco 49ers (which had played in the Super Bowl the weekend prior, in New Orleans) and its impact on the fan experience. He did not mention that the stadium would not open for another 18 months. He also spoke about how Budweiser, the beer brewer, would leverage sentiment analysis technology: "What demographic they're winning with ... what messages are working ... what messages aren't working — so they can precision retail." He chose not to mention that the social analytics technology would come from a partner, NetBase. SAP's own social technology, called Jam, is focused more on internal employee collaboration and work streams.

Cramer should have steered the customer-centric talk to probe the SAP leader about his company's lackluster performance in the customer relationship management (CRM) space — sales, customer service, and marketing activities.

Instead, Cramer brought Marc Benioff, CEO of Salesforce.com, on the show a month later.[4] Benioff made the CRM point: "Why have SAP's largest customers become our largest customers?" Benioff could have also mentioned that, in fact, it was his company's marketing cloud, including tools like Radian6, which instantly showed Budweiser that its young Clydesdale commercial made it the most mentioned brand during the 2013 Super Bowl.

---

[3] http://video.cnbc.com/gallery/?video=3000144930
[4] http://video.cnbc.com/gallery/?video=3000151022

Even worse, an SAP press release stated "the CRM experiment has failed." Paul Greenberg, a best-selling CRM author known as the "Godfather of CRM," challenged them with, "If they truly believed what they said, they'd jettison all their applications that are CRM-related — like sales, marketing, and customer service."[5]

John Wookey, now an EVP at Salesforce.com, landed there after stints at SAP and Oracle. He likes to distinguish between "systems of record" and what author Geoffrey Moore has coined "systems of engagement."

> "ERP systems were designed in a time when typically only a chosen few corporate types had access to computers. Today, everyone has access to multiple devices — smartphones, tablets, PCs — and Salesforce tools like Chatter were designed for collaboration in this new democratized reality.
>
> At SAP, I found the user conference was designed more to attract executives and prospects, not so much users. The Salesforce.com definition of user is much closer to that of the end user, and our technology is designed to engage this user, not just his or her boss. And, our Dreamforce conference tends to carry that focus, and as a result has that much more energy."

Missing Opportunities Galore

With the emergence of social, mobile, analytical, cloud technologies and the Internet of Things, every industry has been ripe for a new generation of applications. Banking customers are looking

---

[5]   http://www.zdnet.com/crm-has-failed-i-am-so-tired-of-hearing-that-7000033967/

for mobile banking functionality. Auto insurers are looking for telematics-driven apps to better analyze driver risks. Asset-intensive businesses have been looking for predictive maintenance functionality. Consumer-facing industries are looking for social marketing tools. Retailers have been looking for "omni-channel" functionality to drive consistent experiences across brick-and-mortar stores, the Web and mobile customer interactions.

SAP used to be a dominant player in several verticals — process industries, utilities and retail — but competitors have been catching up.

For Oracle, it started in 2005 with a bidding victory over SAP around Retek, a retail industry merchandising player. Oracle has proceeded to acquire other industry players such as i-flex (banking), Primavera (complex projects), SPL Worldgroup (utilities) and several others.

At Oracle's IndustryConnect event in February 2014, Co-CEO Mark Hurd presented some of its industry business unit metrics — 20,000 employees dedicated to specific industries, 10 percent of total R&D, 26 industry-specific acquisitions in the last five years. The payback: In the past three-and-a-half years, Oracle's industry-specific revenues have tripled. At Oracle OpenWorld in September, Oracle announced 47 industry-specific cloud applications — an extensive portfolio.

Infor, which is a much purer enterprise applications vendor, has pushed the vertical pedal even harder since Charles Phillips arrived as CEO from Oracle in 2010. It has been pursuing a "micro-verticals" strategy, finding niches in fashion, hospitality, healthcare, nonprofit and other sectors. Instead of going in with more generalized food and beverage positioning, Infor can now present shelf-life management features to bakeries and sublot traceability to breweries. Rather than just go with an all-purpose fashion offering, it can offer unique features for sportswear vendors as well as uniform makers.

Phillips likes to talk about "last mile" considerations in various industries. At his company's Inforum user conference this year, Phillips described a call from an executive of a commercial real estate company asking if he would be interested in developing functionality for its micro-vertical. At many vendors, they would be lucky to get a callback. But, Charles's response was: "We will be glad to analyze the market, and if we can find a group of charter customers, sure we will."

Phillips can draw on industry-specific assets Infor has acquired, newer ones it has developed, talent it has recruited, and partners like Cerner in healthcare and Ciber around nonprofits.

A Cloudy Application Strategy

"When Business ByDesign (ByD) is coming at them like a 99-miles-an-hour fastball, let's see how tough they are,"[6] McDermott said of NetSuite in April 2010.

Instead of a fastball, ByD has turned into a boomerang coming back to hurt SAP.

Dennis Howlett had a lengthy analysis, at the site Diginomica, of the twists and turns ByD has undergone:

> "Sometime in the 2003–4 timeframe, (Peter) Zencke proposed a new suite aimed at SMBs [small and mid-sized businesses] that could be run as a hosted solution. At the time, cloud as we now know it was very much in its infancy. … Unfortunately, by the time SAP was ready to hit the market sometime around 2007–8, and

---

[6]   http://in.reuters.com/article/2010/04/29/idINIndia-48077220100429

had spent many millions in developing ByDesign, the world had moved on.... At that stage, SAP withdrew it from the market and spent 18 months reengineering so that it could get better operational metrics and performance. ... Quarters came and went, SAP talked up the ByD numbers, eventually plateauing at something like 1,000 customers... But SAP's core development was firmly focused on HANA and within 20 months, SAP had pretty much canned ByD development."[7]

WirtschaftsWoche[8] claimed that ByD had cost SAP €3 billion and it had only attracted annual revenue of €23 million. Additionally, SAP spent $17 billion acquiring SuccessFactors in 2011, Ariba in 2012, and Fieldglass and Concur in 2014. Those products make up the bulk of SAP's "cloud revenues," but even with that new expertise, the ByD trajectory has not changed much.

In the meantime, while waiting for the McDermott fastball, NetSuite has tripled its revenues. It has done well with many retailers looking for consistent omni-channel customer experiences. It has also done well in "two-tier" ERP settings, as we discuss in Chapter A2. And, it is running full-page ads in the *Wall Street Journal* with the tag line "Maybe somebody *should* get fired for choosing SAP."

Shifting Focus to Platforms

In a fast-moving world, SAP's long application development cycles have frustrated many customers. Take the hyperactive

---

7   http://diginomica.com/2014/07/18/deconstructing-saps-smb-strategy-and-bydesign/

8   http://www.wiwo.de/unternehmen/it/wartung-der-software-sap-stoppt-milliardenprojekt-business-by-design/8953320.html

fashion industry where SAP has many high-profile customers. The industry has pioneered global contract manufacturing, personalized products, omni-channel distribution, and many other trends. In 2014, SAP finally rolled out its fashion management solution — a wholesale, manufacturing, and retail solution. Before this, SAP positioned two differently developed industry solutions for fashion customers — one for Apparel and Footwear Solution (AFS) and another for IS-Retail, with a large amount of document flow between them.

As SAP explains:

> "The two systems treat information differently and have distinct databases. However, these differences are not apparent to the end-users, and, from their point of view, SAP Retail and AFS databases mirror one another, thanks to the almost constant flow of information between the two systems."[9]

When SAP announced its long-anticipated Integrated Business Planning (IBP) solutions in 2014 to support customers in a changed world of demand networks, Intrigo Systems, in a white paper, pointed out that "SAP is stepping up its offering beyond the traditional static planning denizens that they have occupied over the last 18 years."

What's going on here? Why has the world's largest enterprise application vendor missed out on so many application market opportunities?

SAP itself has pivoted.

---

[9] http://help.sap.com/saphelp_46c/helpdata/en/f4/2dc884d56111d29e6700805 f8f496c/content.htm

This shift started with NetWeaver, which was introduced in 2003, and continued with its $7 billion BusinessObjects acquisition in 2007, followed by its $6 billion Sybase acquisition in 2010, and has accelerated with an intense focus on HANA over the last few years. Where SAP did make application investments, it invested heavily in the back office with acquisitions like SuccessFactors, Ariba, Fieldglass and Concur for financial, HR, and procurement functionality, and in control and compliance areas — as we discuss in Chapter 6.

This strategy reflected the belief that the business applications market had matured and it made more sense to enter even markets where much bigger players like IBM, Microsoft, and Oracle had dominant market shares.

There may have been some bright MBAs and maybe even some McKinsey consultants behind the pivot, but two young men — one an Israeli, the other an Indian — became its face. While much has been made of the fact that neither spoke German and both chose not to relocate to Walldorf, their deeper flaw may have been they did not speak "package applications."

Shai Agassi came to SAP through its acquisition of his enterprise portals company, TopTier, in 2001. He was 33 years old at that time. Service-oriented architectures (SOA) were the rage, and Agassi pitched SAP's flavor, NetWeaver, with biblical zeal. TechTarget wrote "When SAP executive board member Shai Agassi talks about NetWeaver, he speaks of miracles, Red Seas parting and a new belief system."[10]

It was also reflected in the SAP budgeting system. As one SAP development executive told me, "My application area should have been in the top five in funding one year, based on

---

[10] http://searchsap.techtarget.com/news/956297/Shai-Agassis-passion-NetWeaver

customer demand and revenues. It was not even in the top 25. NetWeaver projects got the most investment."

SOA projects turned out to be fiendishly complex. Only a few companies have had successful projects after years of trying, and SAP's vision was even more ambitious than theirs: Apply it across its large code base, and then roll it out to its large customer base.

Anne Thomas Manes of The Burton Group wrote an obituary for SOA:

> "SOA met its demise on January 1, 2009, when it was wiped out by the catastrophic impact of the economic recession. SOA is survived by its offspring: mashups, BPM, SaaS, Cloud Computing, and all other architectural approaches that depend on "services"."[11]

Agassi was long gone by then, having resigned from SAP in March 2007. Behind the scenes, SAP's partners like HP, IBM and Microsoft had warily watched SAP's growing ambitions with platforms. Some had even hinted they would in turn become more competitive with applications. SAP's customers, in turn, questioned how their Microsoft.Net and IBM WebSphere investments would be leveraged.

With Agassi leaving, the NetWeaver passion at SAP cooled down, but acquisitions of BusinessObjects in 2007, Sybase in 2010 and Syclo in 2012 continued the pivot. Customer confusion continued, with mixed messages from SAP about Java versus the proprietary ABAP/4 language, Sybase Unwired Platform versus Syclo for mobile development, BusinessObjects versus analytics from a partner, Birst, and other meandering.

---

[11] http://apsblog.burtongroup.com/2009/01/soa-is-dead-long-live-services.html

Soon after Agassi left, Vishal Sikka, then aged 40, was named CTO of SAP. While Agassi was charismatic, Sikka was widely considered brilliant. Just as Agassi rode corporate interest in SOA, Sikka rode interest in an exciting new industry focus, Big Data, by pushing hard on the HANA pedal.

Dr. Plattner had been evangelizing in-memory, columnar computing for years by then. The Hasso Plattner Institute (HPI), funded by his foundation, had been validating his passion in Potsdam, Germany. SAP R&D had, however, been slow to commercialize it. Sikka became the champion of the product named HANA, frequently referring to it as SAP's "baby."

The Platform is the Message

The story of HANA is still being written, but it has suffered from a number of missteps, as we discuss in Chapter 6. SAP has emphasized speed of processing versus business value from advanced analytics. Most of its use cases center around internal, structured data when there is a growing recognition that external — sensory, satellite, social — data is delivering much better payback. SAP is counting on a new ecosystem of HANA start-ups to deliver more of the external data focus. It has priced HANA expensively — in the quest to show what McDermott boasts is "the fastest-growing software product in the history of the world."[12] The hardware to run the memory-intense computing is also pricey, especially for higher-end machines that do not leverage commodity components. The connectivity to the HANA Cloud center via MPLS circuits is expensive. While not exactly comparable in usage, the economics

---

[12] http://allthingsd.com/20130114/seven-more-questions-for-saps-co-ceo-bill-mcdermott/

of open source tools like Apache Hadoop and MongoDB are far more compelling.

Sikka signaled the continuing pivot at SAP when he told *InformationWeek:*

> "It is not that the application is the future. The platform is the future. The applications are important for our future. But applications are now dwarfed by the platform."[13]

Sikka resigned from SAP in May 2014. He is now CEO at Infosys, which, interestingly, is all about applications — its services support a wide range of vertical applications. He has wasted little time building bridges with Oracle, which he had previously bad-mouthed. Sikka has traded his annual talk at Sapphire Now for a keynote at Oracle OpenWorld in San Francisco.

In May 2013, Apple announced 50 billion apps had been downloaded from its App Store. That's an astonishing number any way you cut it — made even more impressive by the fact that the store had been open only five years. Only a tiny fraction of those apps were developed by Apple itself. It built a platform and developers arrived in droves and so did customers. So what is wrong with SAP having chased a similar strategy?

Dave Kellogg, former SVP of marketing at BusinessObjects (which SAP acquired) and now CEO of cloud EPM vendor, Host Analytics, comments:

> "Application companies should do apps. They rarely build good platforms. Salesforce had numerous disasters

---

[13] http://www.informationweek.com/software/enterprise-applications/saps-extreme-makeover-4-key-changes/d/d-id/898875

with specialized database attempts and finally gave up and just stayed married to Oracle.

Besides, platforms are commoditizing and cloud-izing. Despite misleading marketing, HANA has virtually nothing to do with cloud. It is a column-oriented database system. So, if HANA is the answer to the cloud threat, it's not a good one. It's orthogonal.

I think HANA is quixotic and a desire to get out from atop Oracle infrastructure. However, just investing in improving PostgreSQL probably made more sense. If you want to help commoditize a market, use the commodity and prove it can work. Acquiring Sybase wasn't really about mobile, it was about databases. Again, I think they are irrational/obsessive in their desire to cut from Oracle, and there are more ways to cut them out than just having their own."

Anshu Sharma, former Vice President of Products and Strategy at Salesforce.com, now advises Silicon Valley cloud start-ups and venture capital firms. He talks about the allure and challenges of platforms:

"Ecosystem participants essentially resell your product at little to no distribution cost. Given that sales and marketing costs are usually between 30 percent to 50 percent for most software companies, a platform business can have much higher margins. In addition, once a platform becomes popular, it tends to have more value. Platforms tend to be natural monopolies (or duopolies), since ecosystem participants don't like to write products across multiple platforms. We see this not just at software tiers but also at hardware tiers, be it with Intel and now with Qualcomm.

In reverse, we have seen a customer aversion to monopolistic platforms. Companies have shown a tendency to deliberately back lower-functionality open-source platforms over proprietary products.

I would argue that the order of interests to consider when building a platform is — customers first, ecosystem second, and yourself last. Companies often want to build platforms for selfish reasons but don't understand the long-term sacrifice needed to earn that place — and therefore fail."

Of course, both Agassi and Sikka were protégés of Dr. Plattner, who never misses an opportunity or a Sapphire Now keynote to talk, professor-like, about some contemporary IT architectural topic. That's his passion. He has been heard to say Dr. Kagermann (his co-CEO for a long time) never appreciated SAP as a broad technology company and could not see past applications.

Talk to customers, however, and they are more aligned with Dr. Kagermann's position — he was much closer to operational details, understood customers were paying significant fees to SAP to maintain and enhance applications and did not want SAP to divert so much money into platforms.

After all these years of platform focus, the impact was pervasive throughout SAP. A friend at SAP sent me an exasperated email: "In all honesty, Vinnie, you didn't seem willing to give at all and start over."

He was saying HANA is the present and future, that applications are the company's past. To that I responded: "You (and others at SAP) may have moved on to newer stuff like HANA but your customers are 98 percent in the situation they were in three, four, and five years ago. …They may not be bitching to you as much, but they have in many ways given up on SAP and are back to custom development and buying from others. So, what they tell me forces me to not forget it is the past — because it is still the present."

Pivotal Consequences

There have been three major consequences from this SAP pivot:

- Customers became worried. After all, they were paying significant maintenance fees to SAP to maintain and enhance applications, not divert so much money into platforms. In an ASUG survey of 377 customer respondents, "30 percent believe that SAP will turn up the heat to get them to adopt SAP HANA during the next two to three years."[14]
- SAP's R&D became divided. Much has been written and spoken about the difficulty in bridging teams in Walldorf, Palo Alto, and elsewhere. Those are clearly sticky, cultural issues. An even wider chasm had developed between business, application-centric developers and those who wanted to work on platform areas. Deliverables from the 18,000-person development shop have been shockingly limited in the last few years.
- SAP's control over its ecosystem, never very rigorous, got even more diluted with the attitude that applications were passé. With the rise of HANA, it started focusing on an ecosystem of start-ups, claiming it had ramped

---

[14] "SAP HANA Adoption — What do customers say?" ASUG Research Report, 2014.

up the number to 1,500. Ask any venture capitalist how much care and feeding a portfolio of even ten start-ups takes and you have to wonder how much energy SAP is expending on this new community of entrepreneurs.

But Wait — There's More

Starting with its Ariba acquisition in 2013, SAP began to talk about the "network economy." As he announced the $8 billion Concur buy in September 2014, McDermott said:

> "Ariba's business network was the first step … with Fieldglass we expanded the network to contingent work-forces … [and] With Concur, we are expanding to the $1.2 trillion travel category.[15]
>
> The future business will run in the cloud, on the SAP HANA platform, and over the business network. SAP is the only company in the industry with the depth to help enterprises manage permanent employees, flexible workforces, goods, services, and now travel & expense on one cloud platform."[16]

While the description suggests a "new SAP economy," the reality is that SAP has acquired revenues of companies which were all over a decade old — Concur, for example, was two decades old. And SAP was back to its roots — cross-industry, back office applications — when customers in every industry are looking for a new generation of business applications.

---

[15] http://spendmatters.com/2014/09/18/analysis-sap-se-to-buy-concur-technologies-inc-by-the-numbers/

[16] http://spendmatters.com/2014/09/19/sap-buys-concur-for-8-3b-a-great-deal-but-out-of-weakness-not-strength/

CHAPTER 3

The SAP Economy —
The Un-pivot

～→

At least some customers are starting to pivot away from SAP, as we saw in Chapter 1. And, SAP itself has been pivoting away from an application focus, as we saw in Chapter 2, where it was dominant, and into platform markets where it has small market shares.

Aneel Bhusri, CEO of cloud application vendor, Workday, said this past summer: "Three or four years ago, I worried about one of the majors — like SAP — waking up. Right now, I see the innovation gap getting wider."

With those trends, I was convinced SAP customer spend must have peaked around 2008 and was in post-recession decline.

Anecdotally, however, I was getting feedback from several customers that their SAP spend had not fallen off, and in many cases it had actually gone up since 2009. Some of the customers' explanations:

- Pent up demand for projects/upgrades stopped during the recession.
- Wage/price inflation around consultants from countries like India.
- Investment in "instance" consolidation and other efficiency projects that cost more short term.
- Doubling down on SAP to not have multiple ERP solutions in their environments.
- Too exhausted to even think about optimizing SAP environments or moving away from them — just continuing to write operational checks on SAP.
- It's the "cost of doing business — our IT is only 2–3 percent of revenues."

Getting a Read on the Numbers

That got me thinking about ways to validate the size of the SAP economy. SAP marketing can come up with all kinds of trivia like "SAP customers produce 70 percent of the world's chocolate," "SAP customers distribute more than 71 percent of the world's food" and "SAP systems touch $12 trillion of consumer purchases around the world." As the accounting and analytical backbone for many of its customers, the data is certainly accessible to SAP and the fun facts make for good advertising fodder.

Surely it would be easy for SAP marketing to provide those numbers — head counts and dollars — for the economy around its own products? I thought I could rough-cut an estimate if I could get better customer demographics. I asked SAP to provide a breakdown of customer counts it posts on its website (and in KPMG-audited financials). They declined. For years, they have not broken out the acquired and organic customer counts.

I reached out to analysts who track SAP to see if they had estimates. I was surprised at how narrow their focus is. Many can tell you about SAP's metrics, but not much about its partners or its customers. Some cover implementation and managed application services, but not hosting. Few follow the SAP networking space. Those who analyze the SAP outsourcing space mostly focus on the top 25 players like IBM, Accenture, and TCS.

Gartner looks at SAP in many different "Magic Quadrants" — ERP, sales force automation, strategic sourcing, horizontal portals, master data management, mobile application development platform, implementation service providers, and data warehouses. However, it does not regularly publish a consolidated view — what used to be a strategic analysis report (SAR) — on SAP, as it did in the past.

I found other analysts defensive. One questioned why I was even trying to size the economy since I was not a "full-time SAP analyst." Another declined, saying "it's a sensitive topic."

I reached out to The Hackett Group, which has, over a couple of decades, gathered a vast database of business process and IT benchmarks. They said their data tends to not be platform specific (SAP, Oracle, etc). Still, SAP cites Hackett data in its marketing.[17] Hackett's AnswerThink unit is a SAP partner and reseller, so at an individual client level they presumably have more specific data, but have chosen to not generalize it. I tried the Sourcing Interests Group, which provides thought leadership and networking opportunities to executives in sourcing, procurement and outsourcing from Fortune 500 and Global

---

[17] http://www.sap.com/bin/sapcom/en_us/downloadasset.2013-09-sep-10-17
.Shared%20Services%20for%20Finance%20-%20Unlocking%20the%20Potential
%20for%20Greater%20Efficiency%20and%20Service%20Levels-pdf.html

1000 companies. Again, they have not conducted SAP-specific studies or research.

I reached out to other SAP watchers — journalists, user groups, academics, "Mentors" — described more in Chapter 11, and similarly drew other bits and pieces. I Googled "SAP economy," "SAP ecosystem," and other terms, and found few hits that would indicate the size of the economy.

Even more concerning, I found widespread skepticism among analysts about SAP customer numbers. I heard the same about membership counts in its community and its number of licensed users. An outsourcing analyst told me she routinely adjusts SAP partner headcount numbers downward by 20 percent.

I finally found Phil Fersht's estimate of 2013 worldwide customer expenditure around SAP at $156 billion.[18]

Fersht founded HfS Research, a leading global analyst firm covering IT and business services. He had previously worked at AMR Research (now part of Gartner), leading the firm's BPO and IT services practices and served as market leader for Deloitte Consulting's BPO advisory services. He knows how to analyze markets, so I reached out to understand his methodology.

He explained they had examined the application services revenues of leading outsourcers — and estimated the portion of SAP spend attributed to these providers. Then they added SAP's latest revenues. They estimated internal spend — and estimated the proportion of SAP delivered internally and externally based on survey work (12,000 quantitative interviews) based on effort/ work rather than dollar value. Then, they applied a dollar value to the internal effort based on standard IT department spend in Global 2000 companies.

---

[18] http://www.horsesforsources.com/lars-leaving-sap_052713

I was a bit unsure. If Fersht's higher numbers were correct, the amortization/write-off number would also be considerably higher at $50+ billion a year.

Dollars and Sense

In my mind, annual SAP revenues post-recession should have been $20 billion (mostly maintenance and services with shrinking new licenses), its ecosystem another $60 billion (with fewer new customers starting new projects, so mostly operations), and amortization and write-offs another $20 billion a year. (There is little consensus on the total amount of outstanding CapEx on SAP customer balance sheets, but Rachel Polson of the accounting firm Baker Tilly Virchow Krause, LLP estimates amortization over five years is common on ERP projects, and depending on customizations some push for seven years.) So, in my estimate, the SAP economy was running about $100 billion a year.

In that nebulous and even hostile environment, it is tough to play economist. Earlier this year, I had a chance to estimate the population of "SAP Nation." I came up with a rough cut of two million "citizens" around the world who either worked at SAP practices at outsourcers, or in SAP-related support jobs at customers.

Amazingly, armed with my new paper napkin-based headcount model, I began to think Fersht's estimate was actually conservative. My original estimate of $100 billion a year was certainly way off. So, I tweaked my model some more, and in Figure 1 is a summary that shows an SAP economy on a $204 billion annual run rate.

Please keep in mind the caveat that the model's numbers are raw estimates from polling multiple sources, none of whom has a feel for the entire economy. It is a broad estimate of the customer investment around SAP.

SAP Economy Model
Estimates of annual SAP customer spending

Labor	Customers	Avg Staff	Headcount	Annual Unit Cost US $	Total US $ billions	Notes
Outsourcers/ Staffing firms						
Top 25			225,000	170,000	38	a
Next 100			75,000	160,000	12	b
Next 1000			50,000	150,000	8	
Travel expenses					6	
Customer Staff						c
BusinessSuite	20,000	20	400,000	80,000	32	d
All-in-One	25,000	5	125,000	50,000	6	
BusinessOne	50,000	2	100,000	50,000	5	
Others	165,000	4	660,000	50,000	33	e
Software						
SAP (incl Sap Service, and HEC)			65,000		24	f
Other - database, testing, BPM, training, integration,					15	g
Infrastructure						
Hardware/hosting/ virtualization					15	h
Telecommunications					10	i
Totals	260,000		1,700,000		204	

a   Derived from multiple industry analyst estimates
b   From analysis of exhibitors at Sapphire Now with services offerings
c   SAP does not break out its customers by products. These are estimates from polling of various analysts
d   FTE of functional experts, Basis, ABAP/4, COE, program mgt, other SAP focused technical staff
e   Largely BusinessObjects, Ariba, SuccessFactors, Sybase customers. Does not include Concur customers.
f   Includes SAP Services and HANA Enterprise Cloud
g   spend on licenses, subscriptions, annual maintenance
h   includes data centers, disaster recovery sites
i   Telecom equipment/MPLS circuits/carrier charges

Figure 1   Credit: Deal Architect

SAP's Input

I asked SAP to validate the model and the assumptions. Its corporate strategy group working with various product groups (Business One, Ariba, etc.) confirmed that most of the numbers in the model looked reasonable. However, they thought the customer staffing cost section is too high. In the model above, it was originally $90 billion a year. Their calculations suggest $37 billion a year. (That conversation took place before SAP announced its $8.3 billion acquisition of Concur on September 18, 2014. Our model does not include Concur's estimated 23,000 customers or related costs.)

SAP would not, however, provide details of their calculations. SAP has traditionally not broken out its customer count by product — even the KPMG-audited annual report only shows the total customer count, so you can understand SAP's reluctance to change policy for this book.

After the SAP feedback, I reached out to Frank Scavo, President at Computer Economics. For 25 years, the company has been publishing research and metrics used by large and midsize companies as well as major consulting firms to benchmark IT spending and staffing levels. Its research includes typical staffing levels that are needed to support various ERP systems.

Scavo reviewed the model and, like me, speculated how SAP could come up with a much lower staffing cost number. It could be that they are only including staff who are included in IT budgets. Centers of Excellence and shared service units are often separately budgeted from IT. Scavo suggested I use a lower average staff count for the customers included in the "Others" category, given SAP's unwillingness to provide a breakdown. I lowered the average staffing from six to four for this category. Even with this reduction, the model shows staffing costs of $76 billion, still twice as much as what SAP suggests.

Conversely, I left out several components that could make the costs in the model balloon even more. I had validated the metrics in the model with executives who have worked with SAP and its partners for years. One laughed at my blended rate of $70 to $85 an hour for the outsourcers (as he has paid five times as much for consultants from SAP Services). Another thought my estimate of 20 customer staff for ECC was too low (as he has seen competency centers with hundreds of staff).

I did not add amortization/write-offs to my model, with the assumption that the expense from previous years would roughly be offset by current year capitalizations. In Chapter 7, we will see a spike in public stories about SAP failures in late 2013; if that indicates a trend of increased write-offs, my model also understates that expense. Additionally, the cost of nonhuman "users" such as smart meters in the utility industry, which SAP has suggested will soon account for a billion users, is not included in the model. Gartner has talked about "technical debt" — the backlog liability customers accrue when they do not keep up with latest vendor releases. We did not estimate that for the SAP economy even though, large number of customers lag behind the latest releases of its products. Similarly, Gartner estimates there are another 6,000 (smaller) consulting firms and channel partners who provide services beyond the 1,125 firms we have in the model above.

A Cloudy Network

In recent years, SAP has been emphasizing the HANA cloud and subscription- and fee-based business models of its acquisitions like Ariba. SAP is in transition to what it calls a "network economy" player, but none of the moves have much influence on the economics of Business Suite, Business One, BusinessObjects, and other legacy products. Those make up the bulk of the $204 billion annual run rate in the model above.

SAP has positioned most of the "network economy" to financial analysts to gain credibility as a large "cloud" player. Maybe some day it will bring the benefits of the new paradigm to its traditional customer base.

As Phil Wainewright at Diginomica pointed out:

> "Indeed, SAP actively discourages it, preferring to push a model in which each customer owns their own separate, dedicated instance. It seems like SAP is telling its customers to do one thing while it does something else entirely."[19]

What's striking is SAP's own charges to customers, while very high-margin, are only a tenth of the run rate. The rest is outsourcer/offshore firm fees, consultant travel expenses, customer staff, hosting/other infrastructure, MPLS/WAN charges, other software costs — many not very efficiently applied.

Wag the Dog

Now, consider further that only about 10 percent of what SAP is paid goes toward product research and development. And, consider how inefficiently that R&D has been invested, as we describe in Chapter 2. So, in effect, for $2 billion in annual development budget outlays, SAP customers are paying over $200 billion a year to its ecosystem. It's the proverbial tail wagging the dog. Actually, more accurately it is a really small tail wagging a very large bear.

---

[19] http://diginomica.com/2014/09/17/noah-built-hana-saps-cloud-strategy/#.VBxrOfldXdQ

In fairness, many of the hosting, telecom and outsourcing inefficiencies also apply to non-SAP IT markets. The SAP economy, however, has been a magnet for many of these inefficiencies.

$1 Trillion Is Likely the *Floor*

Fersht's numbers with amortization or ours of $204 billion a year suggests a $1 trillion run rate post-recession. If some of our outsourcing billing rates are low, if user staff head-count numbers are higher, and if write-offs are accelerating, the run rate may be significantly over $1 trillion over that time frame.

Even at $1 trillion, the run rate is terrifying. For perspective, for the first time in 2013, the entire Fortune 500 reported net income just barely above a trillion. That's a bucket load of money to be poured into a back-office infrastructure. If the SAP economy were a sovereign country, at $204 billion a year its GDP would put it in the top 50, as big as those of Ireland and Portugal.

The trillion-dollar run rate is disconcerting when you consider:

- SAP's sales and deliverables (at least around applications) had leveled off even prior to the recession.
- Consumer tech and IT economics — network, cloud storage and mobile apps — were following Moore's law of delivering more for less. Surely SAP's mature economy should be moving similarly.
- Most customers are investing more in front-office technology — product, customer-centric and digital transformations. Three of my books post-recession with hundreds of examples show that. Were SAP customers immune to this trend?

Trying to Make Sense of It All

Puzzled, I reached out to two senior Gartner analysts I had worked with in the 1990s to see if they could explain the SAP economy behavior. They are both big thinkers. One of them, Erik Keller, had coined the term ERP. He had earned my respect when he bravely called that the ERP market would slow down due to Y2K drivers in 1998, not 1999. We were hearing from many CIOs their "batten down the hatches" plans. Wall Street, other analysts, even Gartner Y2K analysts and the vendors disagreed with us, but Keller stuck to it and he turned out to be correct.

And, the other, Bruce J. Rogow, is a technology "historian." Prior to Gartner, he worked at IBM on training that today is packaged as ITIL. He spent ten years at Nolan Norton, consulting with a number of companies about technology strategy. Now, as part of his "IT Odyssey" initiative, he crisscrosses the U.S. talking to several CIOs each year, and keeping his finger on the pulse of the IT industry.

Erik Keller:

> "Perhaps one of the largest challenges that any corporation faces is how to easily and economically phase out existing technologies while incorporating new ones into their business processes. For example, over 20 years ago when the client-server and PC revolutions were redefining the computer platforms of the day, the workhorse mainframe computer did not disappear but was repurposed and used less for certain business processes as the new computing platforms (and associated software) took their place.
>
> Corporations were unable to cut their expenses much, as they needed to continue running their "legacy"

mainframe systems for other programs that were not being replaced. While they may have been able to potentially downsize the hardware footprint, the support and maintenance budgets would remain the same (or in some instances increase, because of the new need for integration between the old and new technologies). Unfortunately, corporations may well be repeating this scenario today when faced with supplementing technologies as sold by SAP for much of the same reasons."

Rogow compared the SAP era to previous waves of computing and provides guidance on his read of IT history, as we will explore in Chapter 13.

Big Picture Perspective

My questioning has led me to the following observations:

- SAP has made a habit of charging in different ways for "adjacencies" or repackaged functionality that customers have paid for previously.
- SAP's R&D has underdelivered for its annual budget approaching $3 billion.
- Consultants brag about having done thousands of SAP projects, then expect a premium for that experience, when they should be passing along economies of scale and repetition.
- Consultant travel continues at staggering levels even as telepresence has improved and many project phases should be done in "factories" — not at client sites.
- Some of the biggest IT project failures and write-offs in the last couple of decades happened in the SAP economy.

- Indian vendors who proudly delivered continuous improvements via their CMM Level 5 and Six Sigma programs on legacy and even arcane vertical applications, seem to have forgotten that for their SAP customers.
- Anyone with a credit card can buy cloud storage from Amazon at 3 cents/GB/month. SAP hosting partners charge ten, twenty, thirty times that.
- MPLS pricing for networks into centralized SAP sites continues to be shockingly high. They pay rates of $100 to $200 per mbps, when you and I as consumers pay $1–$5 per month for similar units. Of course the enterprise version is more reliable, but should it cost that much more?
- HANA hardware, being memory-intensive and only certified from a handful of vendors, is off the charts compared to other server pricing.

Before we get to the gory details of each of these realities, I want to close this chapter with two questions I kept asking and with some humor.

The Obamacare HealthCare.gov problem site cost taxpayers an estimated $1 billion and got all kinds of scrutiny with the delays it caused. The SAP economy is orders of magnitude bigger — *every single year for two decades now.* Why has it not seen much more scrutiny?

Why does SAP itself not size its economy to be able to manage it better? Here is a vendor that pitches itself as a "book of record." Its fans frequently call it "the single version of the truth." Yet it is striking for the lack of precision and consensus there is around its own economy.

I happened to mention to Howlett of Diginomica the multiple sources I had to mine for the model and how little hard information there is. I mentioned that such a large economy, as big as Ireland's, should have its own central bank, budget office, treasury, etc. The SAP economy is rudderless in comparison — there is no central management and few controls.

Without skipping a beat, he said, "It should also have a Department of Corrections." Touché!

Case Studies Group A: Un-adopters

∿→

Chapter A1: Customer Strategy – Flip It Off

In corporate parlance, "life events," such as a spin-off, give you a rare chance to revisit your IT landscape. In 2008, Delphi Corp, a major Tier 1 supplier to the auto industry, sold off its Interiors and Closures business unit as Inteva Products to a private investment company, The Renco Group.

Dennis Hodges, Inteva's CIO, is normally a confident Texan. He was, however, a bit nervous leaving the protection of a much larger parent within the 14 month transition phase. Besides, he was challenged by his CEO to cut IT spend as a percent of revenue in half.

In addition, his customers (demanding ones like Daimler, for which Inteva makes panoramic Mercedes sunroofs, among other products) expected him to spread manufacturing closer to their emerging consumer markets. As a result, Inteva has plants and operations in China, Brazil, Mexico, Czech Republic, India, Germany, U.S. and 11 other countries.

Inteva has to function in a demanding industry, as Hodges described in an interview:

> "The automobile is the most complex, mass-produced product there is. It's not as complex as planes, but there aren't many [planes] compared to cars. They [also] don't allow 16-year-olds or those who have bad eyesight to become a pilot."[20]

---
[20] http://profilemagazine.com/2013/inteva-products/

A safe decision, given the global footprint and industry complexity, would have been to stay with SAP implementation, as was the case at Delphi.

But, Ben Stewart, Enterprise Applications Director at Inteva, explains why the decision was not that simple:

> "Four years in, Delphi's SAP implementation had been heavily customized, with powerful divisions like Packard and Delco still to come. Each division had taken a year or two to roll out and the overall implementation was complex. We had a shared competency center with over 200 staff at one point.
>
> So, our version was already outdated by the time of the spin-off. We could have re-implemented SAP but the 14 month transition did not appear to be enough time.
>
> Besides, at Delphi, we had found the SAP manufacturing functionality lacking. We had separate sequencing, traceability, and other functionality with batch interfaces to SAP. Everything in the middle was a black hole. We determined what amount of product we needed to order about once a week. If there was a change in schedule, we could run out of parts or we could have too many.
>
> Even in the financials area that SAP was supporting, reporting was clunky. I supported the Business Warehouse area, and the adoption was not smooth. You needed a client component; the web version did not work well. We had a data quality issue, and extracts from the R/3 system were often

outdated and inaccurate. Today's BI tools are much more dynamic in terms of data currency.

The SAP partner support experience was even less appealing. We had offshored application management to TCS, hosting to HP and had a program manager in CSC. In a crisis situation, it took half-an-hour to figure out who everyone was and what they did before we could even get started.

Our TCS offshoring experience was rough as well, though not entirely their fault. We had a massive and abrupt layoff at the competency center, with the trendy decision to offshore the implementation. Four years of SAP and business knowledge walked out the door, and TCS was expected to fill that vacuum. Not only was the knowledge transfer to them choppy at best, but TCS ended up with more onsite resources than their typical business model recommends. So, neither the economics nor the user support was particularly impressive."

For all those reasons, Inteva opted to look for alternative ERP solutions. In 2008, the cloud application market was not mature, but Plex Systems looked attractive. It helped that Plex had a number of other customers who are Tier 1 suppliers in the auto and aerospace industries. Still, Hodges took a nervous plunge with Plex — as most peer CIOs would tell him, he was walking away from the safe choices: SAP, HP, etc.

Now, he wonders why he had not taken the plunge much earlier. At Inteva, he would have been small potatoes to SAP and its partners. Now, however, Inteva is big fish to Plex.

Continues Stewart:

> "Plex works with us to integrate localizations in a complex regulatory environment such as in Brazil, or develops the functionality along with the needs of other global customers like Invensys Controls [now Robert Shaw]."

And, as for the CEO's cost edict? Inteva has done even better.

Says Stewart:

> "At Delphi, IT was 2.5 percent of revenues. Here, we are under 1 percent, and Plex is not even our biggest budget line item — our outsourced network is."

That does not even include operational savings such as better scrap reporting, inventory controls and other Plex-supported functionality. In the next wave, Plex will move from the shop floor and core modules into enhanced quality management, business intelligence and other operational areas. Inteva will also work to maximize Plex's native supplier portal, which most other non-cloud ERPs don't offer.

Hodges, no longer nervous, is back to his colorful language and told *BusinessWeek*:

> "With SAP, you flip it on, and the costs make you want to flip them off — in more ways than one!"

Alabama County Opts to Ditch SAP

Jefferson County is the most populous in the southern U.S. state of Alabama. In September 2014, the county commission decided to move away from SAP, merely seven years after it implemented the software for financial functions. In fact, news stories as far back as 2010 show the county ready to move on even earlier.

County Commissioner George Bowman, who has been involved with the SAP project from its inception, describes his experience:

> "Partly in its design, partly how it was implemented here [several consulting firms including BearingPoint were involved in the implementation], but we found it to be cumbersome and not responsive to on-demand queries or broader reporting. That's not just my view — the rank and file, department heads ... all had similar complaints."

The county had fallen three years behind on its audits as a result of inadequate reporting from the SAP system. The CFO, George Tablack, has estimated that the lag cost the county another $1.3 million in audit fees.[21] That is in addition to the estimated $20 million the county is estimated to have spent on the SAP implementation and maintenance.

Part of that cost is explained by Commissioner Bowman as staff turnover-related: "We had a revolving door. SAP talent is constantly being targeted for recruiting."

---

[21] http://blog.al.com/spotnews/2014/03/after_10_years_and_nearly_20_ m.html

As a result of these problems, the county has decided to transition to the Munis system from Tyler Technologies. That will give the county an expanded functional footprint of fleet management, personnel and payroll management, public sector financial management and much more intuitive reporting and user interfaces.

The Tyler package is estimated to cost the county nearly $6 million with software upgrades and maintenance included for ten years.

Commissioner Bowman summarizes: "SAP may be fine for manufacturing companies, but we found it inadequate for our municipal needs." That justifies the Tyler decision even more. Tyler's website says, "Public sector software isn't just *what* we do, it's *all* we do."

U.K. Council ERP Transformation

From across the pond, with a very different accent in Northeast England, comes a similar story.

Steven Fletcher is an architect by training. Not an IT architect, a construction architect. But, he is comfortable in both physical and digital realms. He was Project Director for the Building Schools for the Future (BSF) at Middlesbrough Council. The BSF initiative, with a budget of £110 million, was the largest educational investment in council history, and has modernized the secondary-school landscape. Facilities reflect contemporary design, technology, and a focus on wellness.

He is now Corporate Program Manager for a massive IT and business process transformation project at the council. It is being similarly driven by contemporary design, technology, and wellness focus.

Middlesbrough, in Northeast England, is a reminder of the country's past industrial strength and maritime might. Captain James Cook, the famous explorer, was born there. It is also a reminder of how the blue-collar world of mining, steelmaking, and shipbuilding has moved on. Municipal wellness is defined today by the budgetary environment in which most government entities find themselves; Middlesbrough aims to reduce IT spend by £75 million over five years.

Says Fletcher, "There are consolidation and standardization opportunities across our eight service lines. We had three CRM systems across them. We saw insourcing opportunities in some areas. We are looking for more user and citizen self-service support. And, we were looking at attractive cloud economics for many IT infrastructure areas."

Over a decade ago, the council started a relationship with Mouchel, a public sector-focused services firm. Mouchel provided front-line customer services and administration services for the council, including tax and housing benefits administration, finance services, human resources, and IT services.

The economics of SAP — and the Mouchel costs related to supporting SAP — caught immediate attention as part of the streamlining.

Changing systems in the European government sector can be complex. There are open data transparency rules, as well as EU tendering and data privacy considerations. In the U.K., the CloudStore ("the G-cloud"), an initiative to encourage government adoption of cloud services, has its own guidelines.

Continues Fletcher:

"But, the ERP components were fragmented. Mouchel provided HR and payroll services using SAP and a variety of proprietary spreadsheets and financial functionality using a SAP system. Mouchel also runs shared services for other entities. So, many processes for calculating sickness and leave entitlement, or filing for mileage were complex or not customized for us. Probably unfair to SAP, but what Middlesbrough saw of it has led to a fairly intense dislike for the application.

We looked at alternative solutions, different systems and staffing combinations — best-of-breed finance and HR/payroll versus a single ERP solution, and we finally settled on UNIT4's Agresso cloud ERP platform (with its data center in Newport, Wales). Our internal staff will support finance and HR after they are trained, with Mouchel continuing with the payroll processing (as a shared service with other authorities, but using UNIT4 functionality). We expect to be live with UNIT4 by April 2015, and turn off the SAP system soon after we meet some data-archiving requirements."

It helped that UNIT4, with its Agresso ERP platform, has had plenty of traction with public sector organizations across the U.K. and Europe, particularly in local government. With over 110 U.K. local authorities using UNIT4 Agresso, there was already serious momentum with larger councils, such as Lincolnshire County's and neighboring council Redcar & Cleveland, moving away from other "big ERP" packages, largely due to their high costs and inflexibility.

Fletcher says, "This was a significant factor in validating our decision to move to UNIT4 Agresso." The Finance Director at the council was one of the few SAP fans having been part of the original implementation project. After talking to a few of his peers at other authorities who have previous experience with UNIT4 and its templated government solutions, he has become a champion for the Council's move to UNIT4 Agresso.

> "We also brought in senior managers from various service lines to attend various UNIT4 presentations and demos. Now, they are clamoring to have their teams trained earlier in the implementation cycle."

So there was little resistance to a move away from SAP.

Summarizes Fletcher:

> "We are looking at much lower operating costs as a result. And, the UNIT4 Agresso platform will be a lot more flexible and a lot more people-friendly. We should have control of our destiny around these processes as we staff up. Most importantly, senior managers should have far better cross-functional visibility and data. So, in many ways, it is a cornerstone of our transformation efforts."

The story is so familiar in SAP world. There is little doubt SAP's software could support an integrated ERP model for the council. But in its sprawl, it is difficult to find functionality and so easy to give up. In addition, the layers of partners that SAP has between itself and its customers prevent communication, as well as significantly damage its economics.

In the meantime, Fletcher reminisces about his BSF initiative from the physical architecture world: "It was a massive construction project. But, we moved from old to new buildings, and first day of term, the classes started without a hitch."

So, he can now apply a similarly demanding benchmark to a digital-world architecture, with the realization that an ERP transition requires significant change management and other organizational discipline.

Chapter A2: Customer Strategy – Freeze and Shrink

Just because you buy a Porsche does not mean you are required to buy service at their dealers. If anything, *Consumer Reports* surveys show independent garages often offer better value and service than many auto manufacturers' dealers.

That principle has long been known to IT shops. When a piece of packaged software matures, it is often better to freeze it in place and seek support from a cheaper source for bug fixes and regulatory updates. Some SAP shops are starting to reapply this principle in its updated incarnation.

Color Spot Nurseries is a Carson, CA-based horticultural company. It distributes bedding plants, vegetables, herbs, shrubs and other flora to more than 2,000 retail and commercial customers throughout the United States.

In 2010, faced with an expensive upgrade to SAP ECC 6.0 that had little attractive new functionality, Color Spot made a decision to stay with version 4.7C and to move support to a third-party maintenance (3PM) firm, Rimini Street. Not only did they save on that upgrade investment, they cut their annual maintenance costs in half and the level of support improved.

I had profiled Rimini Street and its founder and CEO, Seth Ravin, in *The New Polymath*. There I wrote:

"As we know, the 1990s were a chaotic time for Russia as the Soviet Union's centralized, defense-heavy infrastructure was gradually torn down and replaced by decentralized, commercial enterprises.

> Seth Ravin describes his work there blandly as "defense conversion" but it was dangerous work where he faced kidnapping and death threats. He is now into another type of conversion — going against what some would call today's "evil empires."

Eric Robinson, the CIO at Color Spot, was not unhappy with SAP. In fact, he calls it the lifeblood of the company. As he told *ASUG News*, "We're happy with [version] 4.7, and it meets our needs," and "It's rock solid."

He just could not justify the upgrade.

In the future, the company may consider acquiring other functionality from SAP around advanced planning and optimization. He also considered the risks, including the viability of 3PM in general and of Rimini Street as a going concern. (Oracle has outstanding litigation against Rimini Street.)

One area that gives pause for many companies is that 3PM providers often cannot deliver regulatory updates in time or cost-effectively. The Rimini Street Tax Engine for SAP Payroll delivers regular tax, legal, and regulatory updates and that keeps the organization in compliance with changes taking place at the local, state, and federal levels.

Besides the cost savings, Robinson likes the fact that he has the mobile phone number of his Rimini support engineer. Support is a phone call away, rather than having to work through the ticketing system layers at SAP.

Over in the U.K.

Across the Atlantic Ocean, United Biscuits, much larger and much more global than Color Spot, had already upgraded to ECC 6.0 — and has found a different set of value points from using Rimini Street. The snack manufacturer with popular brands such as McVitie's, Penguin, Delacre, Mini Cheddars and Twiglets had 2013 revenues of £1.1 billion. It uses a wider range of SAP functionality than does Color Spot. The company had come through the deep global recession, but dynamic raw material prices that influence their margins led the company to Rimini Street.

As with Color Spot, the United Biscuits maintenance budget dropped by using 3PM, but it got an added bonus. While SAP just supports the vanilla application, Rimini also supports its customizations for the price. That may sound trivial, till you realize SAP support staff is not required to understand unique nuances of a customer's business. The Rimini support engineer, however, does — with fast response, clear SLAs and regular reviews. Rimini Street also delivers, for the lower price, U.K. SAP payroll tax, legal and regulatory updates.

And in Brazil...

The Brazilian conglomerate Embraer, the world's third-largest aircraft manufacturer after Boeing and EADS (Airbus), is much bigger, with 2013 revenues of $6.2 billion, than either Color Spot or United Biscuits, and much more complex in its demands of Rimini Street. Like Color Spot, it wanted to stay on 4.7 and avoid the expensive 6.0 upgrade.

Embraer's SAP system is highly customized to accommodate many specific aerospace and defense requirements, as well as Brazilian tax specifics and the country's Public Digital Bookkeeping System (SPED). As a major exporter (with its planes operating in over 80 countries), it faces additional regulatory scrutiny. This complexity has challenged Rimini to work on over 70 localization projects.

CIO Alexandre Baulé (who has been recognized by *Information Week* as 2013 IT Executive of the Year — Financial Performance) comments on what the move to Rimini Street has allowed his company to achieve:

> "Our ratio of IT maintenance costs to innovative projects, which formerly was 70/30, is 50/50. And we envision opportunities to go even further than that, putting even more money into innovation, reversing the original ratio to 30/70."

Freeze the SAP application in place at its current stable level and reduce your maintenance budget while improving service levels. That's a triple dip, which over a hundred SAP customers are now enjoying. This comes with the assurance that Rimini Street will support their SAP version for at least a decade.

Actually, "freeze" may be too strong a term. Rimini encourages customers to download the latest release before they turn off SAP maintenance. That way they can, at some future point, benefit from the new features at their own pace.

A Brief History of the SAP Economy

CHAPTER 4

The Roaring 1990s

∿→

I remember my first trip in the mid-1990s to SAP headquarters in Walldorf, Germany. Two things stuck out. The place was rural — *spargel* fields all around us. White asparagus is a German delicacy — best eaten locally and fresh because it does not travel well. The area honors the "royal vegetable" with an annual event complete with mayoral speeches and bands.

In contrast, the SAP lobby had this massive, revolving "ball fountain." It was an architectural marvel designed by Kusser Granitwerke. The granite sphere appeared to float on water.

The five-foot-diameter orb and the fields provided a nice contrast. There was the perishable vegetable, and there was the symbolism of global ambition. Two decades later, SAP's ad agency, Ogilvy & Mather, launched its campaign "Run Like Never Before" with footage from China, Hong Kong, India, South Africa and the United Kingdom, and said it "supports the company's goal of reaching 1 billion people using SAP software by 2015."[22]

How did this small, rural company far from Silicon Valley and other technology hot spots grow so fast and break so many rules of physics to dominate global technology discussions? It took IBM many decades to become a "safe choice" for IT. How SAP, with under $100 million in revenues in 1987, became a "safe" bet for so many customers in a couple of decades is a remarkable story.

Even though SAP grew slowly in its first decade (after being founded in 1972), it was "global" from birth. ICI, the U.K. chemical company, was its first customer. As Dr. Plattner said in an interview, "The first presentation I gave at ICI was in English because any serious manager in ICI was English, or not German at least."

And, IBM's problems in the early 1990s, (pre-Lou Gerstner as CEO) provided a vacuum for SAP to become a new "safe haven." Fortuitously, IBM's problems led SAP to de-emphasize the mainframe and move to UNIX platforms as it developed R/3 in the late 1980s. A decade later, a services-focused IBM cemented the safe image for SAP with its own acquisition of PwC Consulting with its sizable SAP practice.

Year 2000 urgency, the move to client/sever computing, and growing buy versus build reasoning in IT shops provided a "perfect storm" for SAP to exploit. Partners like Andersen Consulting (later Accenture), Ernst & Young, Deloitte, PwC, and other Big Eight firms (back then; now down to the Big Four) provided even more comfort.

---

[22] http://www.ogilvy.com/News/Press-Releases/April-2012-SAP-Highlights-Business-Transformation-in-New-Global-Campaign.aspx

A Front-Row Perspective

I invited Brian Sommer, former partner at Andersen Consulting, to describe SAP's explosive growth. Sommer said:

> "During the 1980s and 1990s, I had possibly one of the best, front-row seats anyone outside of SAP had in watching their growth. During that timeframe, I began to work with Andersen Consulting's Worldwide Software Intelligence unit, and I got to help hundreds of clients select their ERP software.
>
> At that time, one cluster of application software vendors was peaking, while another was about to take off. In the former group of software vendors were names such as MSA, McCormack & Dodge, Cullinet, and many others. The new entrants or upstarts included vendors that would come to be known euphemistically as the JBLOPS (i.e., J.D. Edwards, Baan, Lawson, Oracle, PeopleSoft and SAP). A shift was about to occur, and SAP would be one of its beneficiaries.
>
> In the 1980s, application software vendors wrote huge software programs in low-level programming languages as computer memory, computer hard disk storage, and throughput of computer systems was so constrained. Complicating matters, vendors had to write products for one narrow technical platform at a time as systems were so diverse, between the mainframe, minicomputer, and other platforms. For example, applications written to support a mainframe environment involving CICS/VSAM would not work with an IMS DB/DC environment on the same mainframe computer. You also had to forget about building applications across multiple

countries, multiple platforms, and multiple languages. That just was a bridge too far for much of that decade.

SAP's timing was serendipitous. Because of its German roots, the company built a product line that was designed for Western European firms. As a result, the software could do things that many North American-based products were missing. More specifically, the software product could handle multiple languages and multiple currencies — key functionality that would be needed as this second generation of applications rose to prominence."

Ironically, the international features had been developed for a U.S. company — John Deere, which was an early customer. Dr. Plattner explained:

"And [John Deere] came up with the idea that our software should run on one computer and serve several countries — legal entities with different legislation, with different languages."[23]

Sommer continues:

"By the early '80s, SAP's expansion across Germany and Western Europe had begun to attract the attention of my firm [Andersen Consulting]. By the middle of the 1980s, the partnership saw an opportunity to create a closer relationship with SAP.

---

[23] http://www.cwhonors.org/search/oral_history_archive/hasso_plattner/oral_history.pdf

Recently, I had a conversation with Dr. Hasso Plattner, one of the original SAP founders. He recalled his reaction when he was "summoned" to Andersen Consulting's world headquarters in Chicago in the mid-1980s. He told me he was puzzled that his little firm at the time (total revenues were only approximately $50 million), which had virtually no business in North America, would generate this sort of request from a major consulting and systems integration firm. Andersen Consulting's leaders wanted to meet with him, as they saw several changes occurring in the software space (e.g., improving computing capabilities, a need for more multinational solutions, etc.), and SAP might fill some of that market need.

Dr. Plattner did go to that meeting, and the relationship between those two firms began to rapidly take off. Andersen Consulting quickly built custom, computer-based training materials for use by its field consultants, and before long, thousands of its employees were trained on SAP's products.

In the 1990s, for the first time ever, global firms could create regional- or worldwide-shared service centers. These service centers would need a global-enabled, software solution to manage all aspects of their far-flung empires. Frankly, SAP was one of the few vendors that offered such a solution. Global telecommunications had improved and were faster and more reliable than previously available. This further connected global business units to one another. Computer hardware costs went down just as more commodity-based technologies were becoming available. And the Internet was starting to become the ubiquitous technology we know today.

And, the growth further exploded in the mid-1990s as companies grappled with their year 2000 (Y2K) liability. The Y2K phenomena engulfed business IT decisions and drove massive, outsized software replacements. Firms that had mountains of old custom-built or early package software found themselves needing to patch or replace their soon-to-be-obsolete software. Rather than rework or replace much of the older software, many businesses chose to license new application software that already met the Y2K data standards. SAP was a major beneficiary of this trend."

If Sommer had a front-row seat, Paul Melchiorre was on the playing field. He was one of the most successful "elephant hunters" — big transaction salespersons — at SAP and later at Ariba. He is now president of an insurance-focused, SaaS-based CRM company, iPipeline. He describes the SAP rocket ship in the 1990s:

"It was a truly transformational time for the technology industry. We replaced thousands of departmental and mainframe systems. We put MSA, M&D, and many others out of business. We didn't really have much competition. In deals it would be SAP v. SAP v. SAP — that is, SAP/Accenture v. SAP/KPMG v. SAP/PwC.

We were literally sitting on boxes in the old Scott Paper building by the Philadelphia Airport (where SAP US was headquartered), we were hiring so fast. It was musical chairs; you knew the music would eventually stop, but in the meantime, you ran really hard. If you had revenues less than $1 billion, we would not call you back — we were not interested in mid-sized customers back then. It was an exclusive, invitation-only group.

People were clamoring to put SAP on their resumé. We even had an informal CIO placement service."

Dr. Plattner said in an interview:

"We had the right product — a UNIX-based product — when all of the world was about to downsize. Downsizing was the number one buzzword in 1992/early 1993, and we had a product. It wasn't perfect — by far not as good as [the] R/2 system. But, everybody could see what SAP can deliver as far as functionality is concerned. They trusted us."

The Consultant and Integrator Channel

Sommer continues:

"All of those industry changes helped SAP's growth explode during that timeframe. But, I would also argue that SAP's growth was materially facilitated by its relationships with consultants and integrators. In the '80s and '90s, it was this integrator and consulting channel that decided which application software vendors would be included in their clients' software selection projects. Back then, clients didn't have access to the Internet-powered information resources businesses have today. Information about software products was the domain of consultants and IT research firms then. Smart vendors knew this, and cultivated relationships with consultants.

The smartest ones also granted consultants access to their products and product training.

SAP cultivated channel partner relationships with most every large systems integrator on the planet — and they did this well, too. While the company sometimes had conflicts with its partners, the business savvy of the individuals involved on both sides generally worked together to mitigate these as quickly as possible. The result was often a mutually beneficial ecosystem where both parties saw their revenues increase dramatically.

SAP's strongest channel partners often included Big Eight consulting firms. These companies often possessed thousands of trained SAP implementers as well as economically motivated executives who were tasked with making the relationship successful."

SAP's affinity with the accounting firms, in particular, came easily. Dr. Plattner has been quoted as saying in the first couple of decades of SAP: "You couldn't standardize in those days the sales and distribution system of a company. And, we concentrated on financials and the purchasing part." SAP's R/2 (and later R/3) system was multilingual and multicurrency from its roots, and it was designed to be real time, so the book closing was a real time, not just a month-end batch, process.

It would not be an exaggeration to say many of the Big Eight accountants and consultants thought the product was the greatest thing since sliced bread. I was a certified accountant at Price Waterhouse and I was myself pretty impressed. I say that even though my first exposure to SAP was in 1989 on an unappealing, green-screen user interface and when the English documentation was basic.

Extrapolating from my Price Waterhouse experience, I suspect few of these accounting firms had more than a handful of consultants who had spent time on the shop floor, or in a supply chain node, or any blue-collar setting. Sure enough, in many of their SAP projects they convinced their clients to implement "white collar" processes — financials, procurement, etc. — first.

Their sales pitch often was, "You can close your books in one day instead of 30!" If these customers had tried out the "edge" functionality first — on the shop floor, warehouse, etc. — they may have found out SAP's weaknesses earlier. And, their payback would likely have been better, through inventory optimization, plant consolidation, and other operational efficiencies.

Instead, many ended up with what a customer called a "glorified general ledger" (admittedly with the benefit of being year 2000-ready). With the project overruns that were so common in SAP shops, many ran out of budgets to take SAP to the "edge" of the enterprise.

They also ended up with a new breed of staff — highly specialized and highly compensated. The "Basis Administrator" sat at the junction of operating systems (like UNIX), the database (like Oracle), and the SAP application. It is a critical IT role at most SAP customers. Functional specialists, often called "super users," were adept at SAP tables, transaction codes and navigation in specific areas — FI/CO for accounting, SD for order entry, etc.

These roles were heavily recruited, and many an SAP customer lost these resources to contracting and consulting firms. Indeed, competitors have started to highlight the problem as "the tyranny of the super user," pointing out the dependence of enterprises on such individuals.

If you read SAP job boards, you see comments like the following:

- "If you can cope with boredom and extract pleasure and satisfaction from money only, then SAP is your choice."
- "Staying too long with ABAP can make you virtually skill-less and unemployable as a developer outside the SAP domain. This is mainly due to the intellectual stagnation one undergoes working with ABAP."

Sommer explains how even other consulting partners became more aligned with SAP:

> "Consultants and integrators were becoming less interested in 'providing independent advice and counsel' to clients regarding software selections and instead were becoming more focused on 'providing solutions' to customers. This difference is more than just semantics as the solution focus pushed more integrators to round out a vendor's product suite with more vertical knowledge and complementary bolt-on solutions. The effect of this caused an even greater tie between the vendors and integrators. It also benefitted the vendors, as their partners were doing some of their sales and R&D work for them. Over the years, SAP integration partners developed scores of vertical solution extensions that they take to market for SAP.
>
> I've seen software firms prematurely enter the market, and others come in years too late. Timing is wonderful when you get it just right. SAP benefitted from some

great relationships and tectonic shifts in technology in the 1980–1990 timeframe that served it well."

Paul Wahl, CEO of SAP Americas, left for a start-up in September 1998. Within a few months, he had joined Siebel Systems as COO. He contrasts consulting partners at both SAP and Siebel:

"When I left SAP we had finished the first wave of large R/3 implementations. We had seen the consulting firms were spending a lot of time documenting as-is versus to-be processes. It was not uncommon to see an astronomical ratio of SAP licenses to implementation services, often 10 to 15X. In fairness, these were complex, multinational customers, and many wanted customizations, and separate instances for various countries and business units."

Virtually any firm could become an implementation partner. Back then, SAP did not have global standards, so we developed our own in the Americas. We had started to put quality measures in place and methodologies like ASAP [the AcceleratedSAP methodology] to guide partner projects, but honestly the genie was already out of the bottle.

When I got to Siebel, I could see a much tighter focus. We used function-point analysis to estimate task-level effort. We assigned technical account managers to customer projects, and we set boundaries for the services-to-license ratios, and watched for early warnings of project problems. At the highest level, we would have quarterly meetings with partners and do fairly detailed project performance reviews. I remember conversations with IBM, before they acquired PwC Consulting, and our feedback on how their projects tended to be technically sound, but lacking in CRM functional depth."

Adds Michael Krigsman, founder of CXO-Talk, about ASAP:

"With ASAP, the company put its full weight behind efforts to improve implementation success for customers. The program was a reaction to system integrators and skyrocketing implementation costs that had started to give SAP a poor reputation in the market. My company at the time, Cambridge Publications (CPI), developed the ASAP tools and related software such as the Q&Adb, Roadmap Composer, ValueSAP, and others."

My experience running a software intelligence group at PwC Consulting, was similar to Sommer's. When I moved to Gartner in 1995, I was expected to provide more independent analysis of SAP, and I started to worry that the company was growing too fast and its partners were self-serving in creating the "SAP is safe" illusion.

Gartner does not permit excerpts of research that far back, but various trade publications provide an archive on some of those warnings.

From *Integration Management*:

"A hard hitting, two-part report titled, "Application Implementation Consultants — Overpriced, Overhyped, Overworked" and "The Mirage of Choice" to be released this week raises the question, "Are systems integrators strategic partners in the ERP implementation market or merely opportunists?" It also offers candid, sometimes scathing reviews of integrators performance by their own clients."[24]

In *Manufacturing Systems*:

"It's easy to beat up on integrators, but part of the blame goes back to how little scrutiny enterprises put into services analysis," Mirchandani says. "The same enterprise that spends six months torturing two or three application vendors before making an ERP software choice may spend only a few days choosing a systems integrator."[25]

From *Human Resource Executive*:

"Gartner predicts that within the next five years, software licensing costs will be as little as 5% of the total cost of implementing application software."[26]

In spite of Gartner's warnings and ASAP, the first wave of spectacular project failures started to show up. And, they have continued unabated, as we show in Chapter 7.

Melchiorre summarizes:

"Customers and SAP grossly underestimated the impact of the business process change — departments which

[24] Stacy Collett, SIs under Fire, Integration Management, May 18, 1998
[25] Roberto Michel, IT Services Take Center Stage, Manufacturing Systems, September 1998
[26] Tom Starner, Integral Circuits, Human Resource Executive, November 1998

never talked to each other, were now on a common platform. And, that's where the big SIs came in to help with
the change management. For a while it was a symbiotic
relationship, as their executive reach would complement
our selling. But, soon, their time and materials charges,
the project overruns, and the failures started to show up
on the front page of *The Wall Street Journal*."

CHAPTER 5

The Tumultuous 2000s

∿→

Bill Wohl was a communications executive with SAP for 11 years, beginning in 1999. He was known as the company's primary spokesperson to the press and analysts, and the mouthpiece of SAP's competitive battle with Oracle. In his last role, he supported McDermott as co-CEO of the company, and left in 2011 to become chief communications officer of HP, working for Apotheker. Today he runs a global consultancy, advising companies on public relations, reputation, and crisis communications. He reminisces about his decade at SAP:

> "It was quite a roller-coaster. In May 2000, at Sapphire in Berlin, we were being painted as existentially threatened because SAP was perceived to be inwardly focused and did not understand the new web economy. Our branding around an initiative called mySAP.com had not been well received. Dr. Plattner had a painful experience at the SAP press conference debating SAP's market position with

reporters. Bruce Richardson, analyst at AMR Research, was overhead leaving the press conference saying, "This is like the Titanic. The only thing missing is the band." The press — in particular, the German business and trade press — widely criticized the company and Plattner.

Just two short weeks later, working closely with new CMO Marty Homlish, we completely changed Dr. Plattner's keynote for Sapphire in Las Vegas. We were able to announce a major win at Nestle, the largest SAP customer sale at that point, and celebrate our Commerce One acquisition. The media reviews said "SAP gets the Net." The turnaround was stunning in just a few short business days. It was a proud moment for the Sapphire team, a combination effort between the communications and marketing teams."

In the late 1990s, SAP's weaknesses in emerging areas like customer-relationship management and supply-chain management started to be magnified. Best-of-breed players like Siebel, i2 and Commerce One got more analyst and customer focus. As web commerce and dot.com start-ups took off, *The Wall Street Journal* wrote "Trouble is, electronic commerce has reinvented the way SAP's corporate customers do business, and the company was painfully slow to see how fundamental the change would be."[27]
Continues Wohl:

"We started the decade threatened by a new set of best-of-breed players, particularly in the customer-facing and

---

[27] http://www.wiley.com/college/man/schermerhorn371939/site/reading/sap.htm

supply-chain areas — companies like Salesforce and Siebel. Our ecosystem — customers and partners — were still focused on implementing ERP functionality we had sold in the 1990s. By 2005, we had richer functionality in those areas and we had successfully communicated the cost of integrating best-of-breed solutions. Best-of-suite had trumped best-of-breed."

SAP also benefitted from its acquisition of Business One, which started life as TopManage in Israel. That gave it a lighter ERP product much better suited for smaller customers. SAP continued expanding globally. The R/3 product was increasingly being positioned as ERP for nonmanufacturing verticals, even where it was a stretch.

Adds Paul Melchiorre:

"SAP was what I would call "MRP III" — [it] worked well for bill-of-materials-driven environments, and we had adapted it well to process industries: chemicals, pharma, oil and gas. [The U.K. chemical company, ICI, was SAP's first customer in 1972.] But, we could not adapt that bill of materials paradigm to insurance, telecoms, financial services. Even today, two decades later, [in] the financial services sector where I sell to … today the middle and back office is run by legacy products from CSC, IBM and Accenture, not SAP. Newer back office players have emerged like Guidewire to replace the legacy administration systems of record. SAP is mostly HR, payroll, GL coverage and now procurement, thanks to the Ariba acquisition."

A Columbia Business School case study described the many changes Homlish made to SAP's previously inconsistent branding.[28] SAP's field started to sell based on "value engineering" studies that highlighted specific payback areas — something which had been elusive in the earlier wave.

The momentum continued.

The Global March

SAP globalized its operations in a big way. As Dr. Kagermann told *The New York Times* in 2007:

> "A decade or so ago, we did nearly 100% [engineering] in Germany. Now, it's two-thirds in Germany and one-third outside. Palo Alto was the first, and we now have about 1,400 engineers in Silicon Valley. Today, we have about 3,000 engineers in India, about 1,000 in China and 900 in Israel. There are other engineering centers around the world, but those are the big four."[29]

In the meantime, the SAP diaspora continued to grow. Plenty of German SAP employees and consultants moved to the U.S., Brazil, and elsewhere. At the same time, several U.S. customer executives traveled to India, Eastern Europe and South America, looking for SAP talent. Plenty of Indian, South African, and Filipino outsourcing talent traveled around the globe implementing and supporting SAP products.

---

[28] http://www4.gsb.columbia.edu/filemgr?file_id=10149
[29] http://www.nytimes.com/2007/06/09/technology/09interview.html?_r=0

Wohl continues:

"The pace of industry innovation was accelerating. Cost of memory was shrinking. Virtualization had gone mainstream. Mobile technologies took off. With all the changes in IT infrastructure taxing their focus, many of our customers were telling us they were having a tough time consuming our growing functionality. The competitive market was telling us to speed up, but our customers were not keeping up.

The Larry Ellison $50 billion acquisition spree starting in 2003 sent all kinds of waves through the software industry. Customer anxiety about their software assets increased, and they became more acutely focused on value from maintenance. Executives in the acquired companies left to start new companies. It was a period of massive change. It helped SAP in some ways — we were able to position ourselves to customers of Oracle's acquisitions as a safe harbor. It hurt us in other ways."

The decade also saw the emergence of the SAP Developer Network (SDN) [which later morphed into SAP Community Network (SCN)], social media, and more global coordination of user groups. SAP became one of the first technology vendors to converse with bloggers and invite them to its events.

Jeff Nolan, then with SAP, described the rather unconventional thinking about bloggers in 2006 in a post aptly titled *"When everyone has a suitcase nuclear weapon."*[30] The group

---

[30] http://jeffnolan.com/wp/2006/05/15/when-everyone-has-a-suitcase-nuclear-weapon/

of bloggers Nolan invited ended up being christened "the Enterprise Irregulars" as a tribute to the Baker Street urchins of Sherlock Holmes fame. The group has since grown into a community of 75 enterprise bloggers, many of them quoted in this book.

Jon Reed, one of the Irregulars, called it "the emergence of a more informed and networked SAP customer. Not all seized that opportunity, but the point is the resources were there. In the 1990s, the best you had was an 800-page book. Now you can get a gut check 24/7, and not just from SCN, but from all kinds of sites, forums, blogs and events."

Dennis Moore, now SVP/GM of data quality and data-as-a-service for Informatica, describes his stint at SAP from 2001–2007:

> "SAP accomplished two very important (and related) outcomes in the early part of this millennium — a time shaped for us all by recession, global terrorism, war, and a weak economy.
>
> The first accomplishment achieved by SAP is its transformation into a "global German company" rather than a "German company." The official language was established as English, making it possible for many individuals to be successful and influential even if they were from India, China, the U.S. and other countries where English was a "second language" GBUs [global business units] were run from outside of Walldorf. SAP hired Americans and non-Europeans in senior, leadership and executive board positions. SAP opened up to a vast pool of executive talent, well beyond what would have been available in German-speaking populations only.

The second significant accomplishment is that SAP went from poor results in the U.S., the world's largest IT market by far, to outstanding, market-leading results.

There were many other successes — the growth of the ecosystem, the establishment of SDN (and later SCN), the growth to number one market share in virtually every geography and industry vertical, the explosive growth in the brand recognition, the influence on government policies, the transition from essentially a single product company to a multiproduct company and the transition from founder management to professional management (with fits and starts).

SAP matured into an industry, political, and global icon during the first decade of the 2000s. Those of us who were privileged to be a part of this transformation gained at least as much as we gave, got to work with some of the best people in the industry and experienced a real high point of our professional lives."

Adds Wohl:

"I look back at the 11 years of work at SAP with an enormous sense of pride and accomplishment. As was promised when I was recruited to join SAP, I got to work with some very talented and smart people, and expand my horizons globally. But, even more so, most of us felt we individually had the opportunity to really contribute to the success of SAP and of its customers — to make a difference, and we did!

It is easy, in my view, to jump on the criticism bandwagon and suggest the overall investment in enterprise software had a poor ROI. It's foolish, and I strongly disagree. With the benefit of hindsight, we can look back on how companies were managed in the 1960s through 1980s: many had no handle on their assets and operations; I knew of companies still tracking physical assets by hand! The implementation of ERP solutions in the 1980s and 1990s, including the adoption of standardized business processes in key areas like human resources, manufacturing, supply chain and financial reporting, changed business operational management for the better and enabled companies to operate globally in a shift analogous to how the industrial revolution changed business in the 1800s. And, that successful transformation set the stage for how distributed computing and mobile computing would again change business in the early 2000s."

The expression spread in even more markets — "Nobody ever got fired for buying ~~IBM~~ SAP."

The Ecosystem Grows Rapidly

While SAP matured into a global powerhouse, its focus on the economy around it became more diluted.

As I blogged a few years later:

> "The problem is back in 1996 we did not anticipate that the systems integration cost, bad as it already was, was just the tip of the iceberg. As SAP customers went into production, they outsourced their hosting. They had massive upgrades every few years. As they consolidated and put shared services around SAP, their network needs grew significantly. They outsourced their application

management to the Deloittes, and then to offshore vendors like TCS. The ecosystem around SAP grew and grew
and grew, and every Sapphire we would dance around
the topic and SAP would keep talking about certification
of SIs — which only focused on the implementation cost,
and not much on the other layers I describe above."[31]

The landscape of accounting firm partners that had dominated SAP attention in the 1990s underwent lots of churn.
PwC Consulting was acquired by IBM in 2002. Five years
later, when its noncompete with IBM expired, the accounting firm started ramping up its consulting practice again.
KPMG's consulting arm was spun off as BearingPoint, and
its U.S. operations ended up bankrupt by the end of decade.
The Enron scandal led to Arthur Andersen's demise, and its
alumni showed up at firms like Huron Consulting, Hitachi
Consulting, Navigant, and others.

The Sarbanes-Oxley legislation in 2002 put independence
requirements on accounting firms to restrict their consulting
reach. It opened up, instead, a vast new source of compliance
revenues, many utilizing SAP's governance, risk, and compliance products. In many ways, SAP's relationships with
accounting firms grew even more complex. As an example,
Deloitte auditors opined on internal controls around SAP
systems, their consultants helped implement SAP software,
and their advisors helped clients evaluate competitive BPO
and offshore services around SAP. So, the conflicts of interest
grew even more thorny.

---

[31] http://dealarchitect.typepad.com/deal_architect/2011/05/those-who-ignore-
history.html

In that unsettled consulting market, offshore firms, especially the Indian ones fresh from their Year 2000 projects, had some impact, especially with post-implementation, SAP-application-managed services. Companies like GE had helped these firms optimize global delivery models where 70 percent to 80 percent of application management services could be done at cheaper offshore locations. The knowledge transition, the geographic coordination, and the continuous improvements across years (lowered bug rates, ticket volumes) were well-honed and appeared transportable to the SAP world.

Their actual move into the SAP market was rougher. Business process skills and functional SAP knowledge (to configure specific financial and other processes in the software) took a while for Indian firms to develop. Longer transitions of customer-specific knowledge broke the 20/80 onshore/offshore economic model; few were able to show the continuous improvements at SAP projects they had built their reputation around. Worse, the heated labor market in India, and related wage inflation and staff turnover diluted the impact many of the Indian (and later other offshore) firms had on the market. In addition, Indian firms acquired relatively pricier Western SAP talent via acquisitions. Infosys acquired Swiss firm Lodestone, and HCL acquired Axon, diluting their economic impact even more.

By 2005, I had started to warn of the "offshoring bubble" into which many SAP customers had started to move:

> "Physical infrastructure continues to be a major turnoff for a number of prospects and existing clients. I have been to several major Indian cities in the last year or so — same everywhere. Staff turnover is rampant. Getting

named resources is increasingly chancy. There are still not sufficient local U.S. staff (or Americanized Indians) to manage client relations or program management."

Many SAP hosting partners supported their customers from outdated, inefficient data centers. Mark Thiele is EVP of data center technology at Switch SUPERNAPs, which boasts ultra-efficient and extremely power-dense Tier IV (Elite) data centers like its 525,000-square-foot facility in Las Vegas. His view on the state of the hosting market:

"Many of the traditional, large, managed service providers (HP, IBM, etc.) have a significant legacy footprint of data center capacity. This older footprint is comprised of millions of square feet of data center capacity that is built with legacy design characteristics like raised floor and single-method cooling solutions like the old CRAC cooling on the floor.

Each of the big MSPs has a few data centers they've built in recent years that demonstrate innovation in design, but overall these "showcase" data centers comprise only a fraction of their total footprint. Unfortunately, the vast majority of the data centers that have been a part of organizations like Perot Systems, EDS, IBM, HP, and Dell are designed to the same standards as data centers built in 2000 or earlier. The end result is that, even within these large organizations whose business it is to make money off of data center capacity, there is still a tremendous amount of opportunity for improvement in energy and space use efficiency."

Upgrades turned out to be significant implementation projects in their own right, as I described:

> "Because the software is now in production, little downtime can be tolerated. Thus, our analogy to refueling a plane in midair — it cannot be landed, just slowed down. Similar to that deceptively simple procedure, the upgrade cutover process must be frequently rehearsed and flawlessly executed. Upgrades carry an additional risk — typically, few vendor or systems integrator resources are really up to speed with the new release."[32]

Amit Bendov, now CEO of SiSense, describes his experience at Panaya Ltd, a company that was focused on upgrade tools for SAP environments:

> "The challenge was what SAP developed in Walldorf versus what customers had added. Vanilla SAP upgrades were relatively easy, though a survey we did in 2009 showed SAP customers would find as many as 23 BAPIs [Business Application Programming Interfaces] removed after upgrading to SAP ERP 6.0 from version 4.7, and as many as 39 different BAPIs changed when upgrading from SAP ERP 5.0. Still, SAP managed the changes to its code pretty well.
>
> The problem was in SAP world, customers have hundreds of custom objects. Our tools could show which custom programs would break as a result of an

---

[32] http://dealarchitect.typepad.com/deal_architect/2009/08/dont-upgrade-escape.html

upgrade, explain how to fix them and derive the most efficient test plan. But, that still involved a lot of effort to upgrade.

By the way, the challenge continues even in SaaS world with any customizations. SaaS vendors do have the advantage of being able to upgrade their core at thousands of customers at one go. In the SAP world, the upgrade was one customer at a time.

The other challenge was most SAP customers considered upgrades a necessary evil. So it was an IT-driven, technical project, and bid as a commodity project to be awarded to the lowest SI. Most SIs who chased after upgrade business viewed it as a loss leader, a stepping stone to other business at the client or a way to preclude other firms from getting in the door."

While SAP was getting plenty of praise for its SDN (then SCN) community, the actual economic benefit to customers was less visible.

As I wrote in 2006:

"SAP awards points for posts in SDN — 10 points for code samples, six for forum posts, etc. It then tallies them by contributor. So, I ran a query on the top 10 firms which contributed to SDN from Jan. 1, 2006 to today — eight of the 10 are outsourcers and systems integrators. Wipro leads with a whopping 126,000 points.

I realize it is for the common good, but certain SAP customers are likely bearing the brunt of the contributions. A fair way would be for SAP and outsourcers to kick back to client sites where the contributing consultant is currently placed, an amount in line with the post point (or provide future billing hour credit)."[33]

Since first-level queries were getting resolved in the community, should not SAP have shaved its maintenance 2–3 percent a year? And, could not application management services providers have shown a reduction in SAP tickets?

Customer Revolt

Instead of a reduction in maintenance rates, the decade ended in tumult again as SAP tried to *increase* them in the deep recession, leading to a customer revolt. I wrote, in 2009, after a call with SAP:

> "Dennis (Howlett) and I kept pushing for a more analytical justification of the increase with support metrics (which every software vendor has in spades), breakdown of support economics and performance ratings of SAP partners which supposedly are increasing its support costs. In my book, maintenance costs should have been declining not increasing over the last decade given SAP's growth in cheaper non-German staffing, the SDN community which is increasingly handling routine queries and the support automation which reduces labor costs."[34]

---

[33] http://dealarchitect.typepad.com/deal_architect/2007/02/who_owns_sdn_co.html

[34] http://dealarchitect.typepad.com/deal_architect/2008/08/how-do-you-measure-empty-calories.html

Wohl describes the maintenance increase crisis from the SAP PR angle:

"Toward the end of the decade, we had the crisis around the maintenance rate increase. We had positioned Enterprise Support at 22 percent a year (from the previous standard support at 17 percent) as years of catching up — we had not raised maintenance rates in a while. It came, however, in the middle of the deep, global recession, with customers already sensitive to the value from their maintenance dollars that the Oracle acquisition spree had magnified.

The optics of the rate increase announcement in Germany and Austria were particularly bad. Due to local laws, customer contracts had to be re-signed for SAP to charge the new rates, and that was perceived as high-handed. The German user group, DSAG, rebelled; some analysts took advantage and piled on; and soon the firestorm of customer protests spread worldwide. We eventually worked through the issues, but the reputational damage was considerable. It was one of the factors which contributed to Apotheker's exit as CEO.

Looking back, the way that Apotheker exited SAP and HP will forever brand him as unsuccessful as an IT industry CEO, and likely that is accurate. However, his track record of leading sales at SAP was remarkable — dozens of consecutive quarters of no-miss performance and strong relationships with the world's leading companies are the proof point of his legacy of accomplishment in helping SAP grow and sustain its market leadership, and he is due appropriate credit for that."

As we saw in Chapter 4, SAP started off poorly in the 1990s when it came to managing its economy. Amazingly, in the 2000s things actually got worse. It would get another chance with its intense focus on HANA and cloud computing to change things in the 2010s.

CHAPTER 6

The HANA and Cloud 2010s

⌁⤳

At the 2009 Sapphire Now in Orlando, I heard a brilliant talk by Dr. Plattner about columnar databases, storage compression and in-memory computing. I later saw him admiring a McLaren Formula One race car on the Expo floor. He was mildly irritated when I interrupted him to ask where I could learn more about the technologies he had talked about. He gave me the name of one of his staff at the Hasso Plattner Institute (HPI) in Potsdam, Germany.

I thought it was curious he had referred me to HPI, not to his R&D staff in Walldorf. Dr. Plattner initially found more excitement for his vision with the institute's students than among SAP staff. That led Ellison of Oracle to mock Plattner's in-memory vision as "his five guys in a garage."

Fast-forward five years, and SAP and Sapphire Now are all about HANA. As an ASUG research report described:

"In the last year, SAP has spared no effort to package SAP HANA in a more cost-friendly manner, offering cloud options and various SAP HANA permutations. SAP executives have announced scores of new products to that end. And, since 2011, SAP HANA has matured from a fledgling database that the vendor pledged would upend the entrenched marketplace into a robust platform with even more room to grow."[35]

The twitter stream at the 2014 Sapphire Now reflected it:

@paulhamerman: #SAPPHIRENOW #SAP Simple Suite will be a natural evolution of Suite on HANA, says Bernd Leukert. HANA only, cloud only

@pjtec: #SAPPHIRENOW @SAP drinking its own champagne by running all of its mission-critical systems on HANA. #EnSW

@rhirsch: HANA Cloud Integration can now be used standalone (without other SAP products) http://t.co/AvadmNer4U #sapphirenow >> impt change

@bradsawchuk: @Porsche manages 80+ customer touch points. Real time and predictive marketing with @SAP HANA #SAPPHIRENOW http://t.co/NWicFS9CIc

---

[35] http://www.asugnews.com/article/asug-member-survey-reveals-successes-challenges-of-sap-hana-adoption

Somehow, though, SAP's customers have not been that excited about the product. As the same ASUG report pointed out:

"While SAP says that more than 3,600 customers have purchased SAP HANA in some form, that leaves hundreds of thousands more that, of course, have not."

The reality is that in the past five years all kinds of alternative solutions had emerged as "Big Data" became the hot industry buzzword.

There are lighter analytics tools — like SiSense, whose CEO Amit Bendov says:

"We are third generation, business intelligence tools. Gen 1 was the BusinessObjects, Cognos type tools. Very scalable across many users, but IT-dependent, and not analyst-friendly in that sense. Generation Two was vendors like Tableau and QlikView. They are analyst-friendly, but constrained on data set size because they were RAM-dependent, so [they] tend to be focused on departmental data or spreadsheet replacements.

Our technology is developed as a columnar database which slices and stores information as columns rather than as rows as relational databases do. This capability pulls a column on the disk without pulling the entire table, which is extremely efficient for analytics as most people run queries using only a few columns of data, no matter how big the data set.

Our technology also takes advantage of cache memory on modern processors — that's why we call it in-chip technology. Since memory found in the CPU is faster than when in RAM, SiSense is able to move data 50–100 times faster than in-memory solutions. And, we can handle larger data sets with the extra memory we can access so [we] are encouraging customers to analyze cross-functional data and external social, sensory, and other data.

We don't see ourselves competing with SAP HANA. By focus and pricing, they are a Fortune 500 solution. We are going after the Fortune 5 million. They have a data-base tool, and go after the IT buyer. We have the whole stack — apps, visualization, ETL — and are going after the operational, financial, sales analyst. HANA needs systems integration resources. Ours you can download from the Web and be productive in 20 minutes. At the high end, HANA requires expensive, purpose-built boxes. We are going after commodity hardware. We call ourselves the 'world's smallest Big Data solution.'"

Data-as-a-Service Start-ups

There are growing "data-as-a-service" offerings. Readers likely have not heard of a company called Elementum. Or Bluekai. Or Identified. They are next-gen analytics companies focused on specific business process areas.

Talk to Elementum's CEO, Nader Mikhail, and you hear terms like "exposure by supply chain node." His customers get all kinds of metrics on their global transportation network, so they can anticipate delays and fix them before they impact customers. They get visibility to their exposure — risks across component suppliers across their supply chain. They monitor KPIs on new product launches and can benchmark against other customers in the growing Elementum family. They can be up and running in a couple of weeks without the CapEx of software licenses and data centers.

Bluekai CEO Omar Tawakol is just as passionate as Mikail about "separating signal from noise." He is into marketing data — mining consumer intent from billions of profiles from its own database and many third-party sources.

Identified focuses on mining HR candidate data in social networks like LinkedIn. Co-founder Adeyemi Ajao is as animated as Mikhail and Tawakol about algorithms and machine learning.

All three are about selling intelligence and "data-as-a-service," not licenses or hardware. Indeed, the Elementum website promises that "we are going to free companies from the clutter and frustration of traditional enterprise software." BlueKai and Identified, acquired by Oracle and Workday, respectively, must coexist with their parents' business models, but its leaders are still certain the technology consumption model is evolving.

In comparison, HANA is just a tool, and customers have to buy expensive gear from its hardware partners and load terabytes of data, then crunch that load.

There is little context that comes with HANA — it's not process- or industry-specific as you would expect from an enterprise application vendor. HANA customers are far removed from insights and even further from the kind of comparative benchmarks and actionable intelligence that start-ups like Bluekai can deliver.

Other Big Data Solutions

At the high end, Cloudera can show growing use cases of its implementation of the open source Hadoop platform. In an interview, [36] Charles Zedlewski, VP-Products, described some of the customer examples:

- A number of customers are handling hundreds of billions of IT events where they're looking for patterns that might represent a threat as compared to "normal" behaviors.
- Monsanto is taking geo-spatial and other data to figure out the seed-sowing patterns that will deliver better yields for its customers. Early results are encouraging. That data is being sold as an additional service to farmers.
- Skybox uses satellite images to tell traders how busy specific ports are for different types of commodities. It can also tell retailers how busy their shopping areas are by counting the numbers of vehicles in their own and competitors' parking lots.
- A large bank combines marketing and risk data, resulting in a continual analytic process. This optimizes marketing efforts while minimizing risk.

Godfrey Sullivan, CEO of Splunk, says that over a third of use cases at his customers are ones they did not anticipate:

> "...a Japanese company's indexing and analysis of elevator data, which disclosed that foot traffic was a leading economic indicator of lease renewals. Another customer, in Europe, was using Splunk to index data from electric

---

[36] http://florence20.typepad.com/renaissance/2014/03/cloudera-big-data-use-cases.html

car charging stations, but also discovered it was massively exceeding its mobile phone bills.[37]

Swiss Army Knife

As SAP ports more of its legacy functionality to run on HANA (what it has termed sERP), Dr. Plattner has dared comparisons to transactional databases like Oracle and IBM DB2. He has goaded his customers with comments like, "That's because we [SAP customers] were wimps and thought we'd go the easy way and do the read-only [analytical] applications first. My radical approach, if I may say so, scares people, but they're starting to see that they don't have to be scared."[38]

And, in a blog post, he asked:

"So, an increase of a factor two in OLTP and a factor 10 to 100 in OLAP shouldn't be more than welcome?!? Speed is the number one reason for business processes to be supported by information technology."[39]

That's easier said than done. As Thorsten Franz, an SAP Mentor, has written:

"In order to achieve the amazing performance HANA is capable of — executing queries and calculations hundreds or even thousands of times faster than other databases — one has to change the applications so that they let the

---

[37] http://www.computerweekly.com/news/2240182913/Splunk-CEO-unintended-use-cases-important-to-machine-data-business
[38] http://www.informationweek.com/cloud/software-as-a-service/sap-chairman-hasso-plattner-exclusive-qanda/d/d-id/1269486
[39] http://www.saphana.com/community/blogs/blog/2014/08/29/the-benefits-of-the-business-suite-on-hana

database do the things it can perform much faster than the ABAP application server. This means that a portion of the application code must bypass the abstraction layer and be written natively and specifically for HANA."[40]

In a blog comment, Dr. Plattner explains further:

"That r/3 didn't use stored procedures is true. The sERP version of the suite on hana not only dropped the transactionally maintained aggregates and all redundant materialized views, but heavily uses stored procedures and other libraries of the HANA platform. The application code is being simplified dramatically. The transactional performance increases accordingly."[41]

SAP has positioned HANA as a Swiss army knife. In a press release, it describes the tool as:

"The platform provides libraries for predictive, planning, text processing, spatial and business analytics. By providing advanced capabilities, such as predictive text analytics, spatial processing and data virtualization on the same architecture, it further simplifies application development and processing across big-data sources and structures."[42]

---

[40] http://scn.sap.com/community/hana-in-memory/blog/2013/01/13/and-push-down-for-all-news-about-abaps-adventurous-relationship-with-the-database
[41] http://www.saphana.com/community/blogs/blog/2014/08/29/the-benefits-of-the-business-suite-on-hana
[42] http://www.marketwatch.com/story/enterra-solutions-partners-with-sap-to-deliver-cognitive-computing-big-data-analytics-and-insights-to-iconic-brands-2014-09-04?reflink=MW_news_stmp

Stan Swete, CTO of Workday, has a more pragmatic point of view:

> "SaaS enables companies with the right architectures to continuously enhance the technology used to deliver their services without disrupting their customers. Customers don't want to be bothered with the details of the infrastructure used to support their operations, but they do want the assurance that their vendor will be able to evolve and not get stuck on outdated technologies. When Workday was founded nine years ago, we used MySQL for all storage. Over time, as business requirements changed and new technologies became available, we moved to MySQL for transactional data, Basho Riak for storage of unstructured data, and Hadoop for storage of third-party data for our Big Data analytics offering — all without disruption to our customers. Storage technologies continue to change quickly, and we would not be surprised to see other technologies make their way into our stack in the future."

To its credit, SAP is approaching the HANA ecosystem a bit differently than in the past when it relied on bigger partners like IBM and Accenture. For example, it is experimenting with a massive online open course (MOOC) about Business Suite on HANA.

SAP has also played "small ball" — differently from its previous focus on larger systems integrators, it has encouraged an ecosystem of start-ups to build apps using the HANA platform. It claims over 1,500 start-ups spread across the world. In many ways, that's going to the other extreme.

As I blogged earlier this year:

> "Personally, instead of start-ups in 55 countries, I would
> have loved to see just 55 start-ups with several million
> [dollars] of revenue and capital by now. A 1,000+ start-
> ups (already) must be taxing SAP's resources, not to
> mention the scrum for capital which you need plenty of
> for enterprise-class (compared to iOS) apps."[43]

HANA Execution Issues

SAP has made other mistakes. Memory-intensive hardware
is not cheap. Nothing beyond 4TB of memory is available on
commodity hardware at this stage — larger memory sizes
incur a steep price. As data continues to explode in volume,
will customers need to look at IBM's custom-made 128TB Blue
Gene/Q supercomputer?

As a customer told me:

> "HANA is the new "UNIX." Big iron, expensive, and
> niche. H/w vendors have to make their margin some-
> where. They certainly can't run a business selling two-
> socket servers. Some time ago, SAP did have suggested
> hardware pricing on their website, but it caused a revolt
> with their "partners," and they took it down. Attached
> is a copy of the cached version."

---

[43] http://dealarchitect.typepad.com/deal_architect/2014/02/the-sap-hana-
ecosystem-the-excitement-and-the-caution.html

Another customer's perspective:

"SAP could end up becoming the Sony Betamax — elegant but niche, with its memory intensity compared to the VHS solutions that its disk-focused Big Data competitors are pushing."

Dr. Plattner disagrees. In a blog comment, he pointed out:

"The data explosion is taking place with mostly read-only data (text, video, sensor output, etc.) which can easily be organized in a scale-out fashion on cheap hardware. Actually, HANA is happy to calculate the indexing and keep data only as indices in (memory) for processing."

John Appleby, a consultant at Bluefin Solutions Ltd, describes a typical use case he sees:

"At Bluefin, we regularly work with 2–10TB of memory in a single HANA DB, and this is where we find most business cases make sense. Remember that a 10TB HANA appliance can store a vast amount of data (as much as 50–100TB from a traditional RDBMS due to HANA's data compression capabilities); this could represent all the credit card transactions for a top 10 bank for 10 years or more."[44]

---

[44] http://www.saphana.com/community/blogs/blog/2014/09/09/the-sap-hana-faq

Dr. Plattner has also discussed the broader HANA hardware issue:

> "The certification process for HANA (has) made people think that HANA requires special hardware. That is not true. SAP only wanted to make sure that the configuration recommendations were followed. One reason was: HANA needs DRAM. I believe vendors can now self-test their configurations. But how much (memory)? Let's take SAP's ERP system: the hot data will require less than 500 gigabytes (I predict less than 300); the cold data will then be around 500–700 gigabytes. The data requirements are in fact really small. For the hot data I recommend that all data is always in memory. For a hot standby, which will be used for read only applications, I recommend a HANA maintained identical replica. Any of the two terabyte single image systems is good enough. For the cold data, you can use similar hardware or a cheaper scale-out approach with smaller blades. Not all cold data will stay loaded in RAM. A purging algorithm will remove data without access requests. SAP itself is in the top 5% (my guess) of (SAP customer volumes). The largest SMP system available for HANA has currently 32 CPUs with 480 cores and 24 terabytes. I don't see any hardware capacity problem. The pricing varies from vendor to vendor, but the fact that there are several vendors will take care of it. So where is the problem? The hot/cold split hasn't yet shipped and the purge algorithm is only in the later releases of HANA. It will be soon available like the HANA managed replication. I urge every suite on

HANA customer on-premise to contact SAP for sizing and configuration assistance."[45]

Dr. Plattner's comment, "The pricing varies from vendor to vendor, but the fact that there are several vendors will take care of it. So where is the problem?" reflects an optimism in free market forces and impact on pricing that have historically been absent in many elements of the SAP economy, as we saw in Chapters 4 and 5.

With HANA, SAP has tried to bring the economies of shared infrastructure via its HANA Enterprise Cloud (HEC) with a data center in Sankt Leon-Rot, Germany, not far from its Walldorf headquarters.

HEC economics are still evolving. Marks and Spencer's CIO Darrell Stein has been quoted as saying:

> "We are doing it ourselves; we couldn't get the money to stack up on the enterprise cloud. Which is a bit disappointing actually; I would rather have done it that way. We just couldn't get the financials to work."[46]

Part of the economics is about connecting to the cloud. Amazon Web Services, with its Direct Connect, and Microsoft Azure, with AT&T's NetBond, have tried to combat the MPLS and WAN costs that carriers charge individual customers. SAP may need to offer something similar.

But wait — there's more.

---

[45] http://www.saphana.com/community/blogs/blog/2014/08/29/the-benefits-of-the-business-suite-on-hana

[46] http://www.computerworlduk.com/news/applications/3493602/ms-testing-operational-resilience-of-sap-on-hana/

SAP has also introduced the HANA Cloud Platform (HCP) — its version of platform-as-a-service. As Holger Mueller at Constellation Research points out, partners are involved in the HANA data center game:

> "And while SAP started out doing everything themselves, they have signed up partners on the data center side; [it] will be good to check in at another opportunity to see how these partners are supported and how successful they are at this early point of product life for HCP."[47]

GE's Data Vision

When you hear what GE is doing with its data management strategy, you will get a sobering view of how SAP could have thought about its economy with a HANA lens.

"We knew we had to dramatically lower the cost of managing a terabyte of data," says Bill Ruh, GE's Vice President and Global Technology Director. He is describing what they had to do to prepare for an avalanche of data triggered by what GE calls the "Industrial Internet."

It is an exciting concept around how data generated by "smart" aircraft engines, wind turbines, locomotives, healthcare scanners, oil and gas drilling and other equipment can be mined to deliver massive operational economies. GE calls it "the power of 1 percent" and it promises large savings: 1 percent of aviation fuel savings is $30 billion over 15 years; 1 percent in better optimization of healthcare facilities adds $63 billion over 15 years; 1 percent reduction in oil and gas CapEx adds another $90 billion.

---

[47] http://enswmu.blogspot.com/2014/09/hana-cloud-platform-revisited.html

The data generated by its equipment is considerable. A GEnx jet engine can process up to 5,000 data samples per second. GE turbines generate half a terabyte a day. In the oil and gas sector, sensors continuously measure downhole pressure and temperature data. Ditto for its locomotives, MRI scanners and other equipment.

Ruh continues:

"We were spending as much as $27,000 a year to manage a terabyte of data. Worse, it was taking us nearly a month to ingest the data. And, that was even after significant automation of data extract, massage, cleanse, etc., and plenty of labor. We had to rethink the three "truisms" behind the last couple of decades of data warehousing — rigorous master data and data structure definitions, upfront formatting and cleansing of data, and the storing of the data in relational format.

We looked around to see who was doing it differently and much more efficiently. It was the Internet consumer giants — Google was a pioneer with its file system, Yahoo with large investments in Apache Hadoop, others with NoSQL.

So, we challenged those three previous truisms of data warehousing. We created a lake, and started filling it with data. There is some structure to the data, but nowhere near what we had in the past. We removed much of the upfront extract and cleansing infrastructure. And, our analytical model, semantics, etc. are more defined by the point of use, rather than the point of data population.

We have seen an order of magnitude reduction in [the] cost of managing data. And, instead of weeks, our ingestion time is down to minutes."

The result is GE's industrial data lakes. As ZDNet reported:

"Created in partnership with platform-as-a-service (PaaS) provider Pivotal, GE says the data lake approach has a "2,000x" performance improvement on analysis time, which will allow industry players to spend less time and money managing intensive processes and focus more on turning the data into action — improving supply chains, customer service and operations."[48]

Ruh continues:

"Not just data architecture… we have also had to revisit computing and networking architectures — which data is best processed locally versus in the cloud. Does it make sense to transmit terabytes of data from an engine mid-flight, or only transmit key data and wait for the rest as soon as the plane lands? What about massive data streams from remote oil fields or turbines from around the world?

We are at a cusp of a data management revolution. It's the beginning of a Moore's Law for Data and we should

---

[48] http://www.zdnet.com/general-electric-launches-data-lake-service-to-streamline-industry-big-data-7000032489/

see incredible waves of efficiency even as data volumes continue to explode around us."

SAP's new management team needs a pivot to be better positioned for this new world of Moore's Law for Data.

Jon Reed, a long-time SAP watcher, summarizes:

"SAP should have been thinking much more about "HANA-as-a-service" in consumable apps. Many of the HANA startups are thinking this way, but the customer license costs still present an obstacle to adoption — especially in high-volume-use cases. New HANA cloud options improve the situation but the Big Data market is moving fast.

[The] biggest problem, in my opinion, was trying to swing for the fences with a new big-ticket sales product instead of radically redefining sales/cost of ownership/ delivery/pricing along with the new product."

To the Cloud

This decade has also seen a more intense SAP focus on cloud computing. We saw in Chapter 2 how SAP's internal efforts around ByD have been disappointing. An acquisition spree estimated at an investment of $20 billion since 2012 signaled SAP's seriousness to become a cloud player as competitors like Salesforce.com and Workday grew and got increasing customer and Wall Street attention. See Figure 1 for a longer timeline of acquisitions.

SAP Acquisitions

Companies or Assets Acquired	Calixa Khimetrics TIM Triversity Lighthammer iLytix systems DCS Quantum Tomorrow Now	Factory Logic Praxis Frictionless Virsa	Silk Europe Yasu Busines Objects Wincom MaXware Outlooksoft Pilot Software	Visiprise	SOALogix SAF Highdeal Clear Standards SkyData Coghead	Div of Cundus Sybase Technidata	Success Factors Right Hemisphere Crossgate SECUDE	Ariba Purisma Datango Syclo	KXEN GK Software hybris Camilion SmartOps Ticket-Web	Concur SeeWhy Fieldglass
Year	2005	2006	2007	2008	2009	2010	2011	2012	2013	to 3Q 2014
Estimated Investment $ billions	0.5	0.5	7.5	0.1	0.5	6.0	4.0	5.0	1.0	9.5

Figure 1   Credit: Deal Architect

While the acquisitions have allowed SAP to compete more in HR and procurement software markets, they highlight the thorny integration challenges SAP has amassed. As a customer commented:

> "SAP used to publish A0-sized wall posters with the R/3 data model (entity relationship diagrams). How about similar for the existing SAP portfolio? Integrating even among 100 percent SAP assets must increasingly be a nightmare."

Bill Kutik, a long-time watcher of the HR software market, described some of the challenges around SuccessFactors:

> "SAP Group Vice President David Ludlow and SF's Krakovsky have broken the deployment options and integration challenges into three models:
> "Hybrid HCM" has SF SaaS talent-management apps, workforce planning and analytics being integrated into an on-premise SAP Core HR.

"Two Tier HCM" has the full SF suite, called Cloud HR, including Employee Central, perhaps at several locations integrated into one on-premise SAP Core HR. In most cases, EC acts as a "slave" system, but there is a sub-option of it sharing the responsibilities of the "system of record" with Core HR.

Finally there is "Full Cloud HCM," where SAP Core HR has been completely replaced, but now it must integrate with SAP ERP!"[49]

Pierre Mitchell at Spend Matters explains the challenge with the Ariba Network Economy:

"In fact, just within SAP's existing procurement line of business applications, there is a shocking level of fragmentation under the hood not only in terms of fragile process integration, but also master data fragmentation (e.g., having to transfer data from different lookup tables between different supplier master files).

Now, add in the complexity of the Ariba Network (which is slowly morphing to become the true Borg in terms of adding business trading partner business logic and external content driven logic) and the announced acquisition of Fieldglass, and perhaps even a supply chain acquisition down the road, and suddenly, things are looking a little dicey. The great battleship starts looking like a flotilla of ships trying to avoid crashing into each other."[50]

---

[49] http://www.hreonline.com/HRE/view/story.jhtml?id=534356170&ss=kutik+handicap&sp=AND&date=
[50] http://spendmatters.com/2014/04/15/dont-fall-for-the-myth-of-integrated-erp-procurement/

Further, Mitchell says:

> "I'm hopeful that SAP will honor its stated direction of connecting to multiple marketplaces (e.g., by having HANA-powered connectivity partners) and include networks like Basware, Hubwoo, IBX/Capgemini, Tungsten, Tradeshift, and others who don't charge suppliers a percentage of the transaction. Buyers like choice and I'd also venture to guess that most like their technology suppliers to be technology suppliers who automate rather than intermediate."[51]

Jason Busch, also at Spend Matters, adds:

> "Concur has grown up with intimate knowledge of end users and their needs, partners, and their capabilities. SAP on the other hand has long operated far removed from end users, with a large cloud of systems integrators and consulting firms protecting them from the cold winds of end user preferences."[52]

David Barrett, CEO of the mobile expense company Expensify, sent an offer to Concur users playing on some of the fears above:

> "Create your next report using Expensify as normal — including our cutting-edge mobile app and revolutionary SmartScan technology — and when you submit, we'll connect via the Concur API, upload the receipts and

---

[51] http://spendmatters.com/2014/06/13/on-sap-ariba-networks-and-more-eternal-vigilance-is-the-price-of-interpreting-analyst-research/#sthash.BpihzcSV.dpuf
[52] http://spendmatters.com/2014/09/18/analysis-sap-se-to-buy-concur-technologies-inc-by-the-numbers/#sthash.clHGYOan.dpuf

create the report for you. So, whether you're in charge or not, there's no reason to suffer through to the bitter end: you can make the switch to Expensify by yourself, today, without waiting for the rest of your company."

Franken-soft and Executive Attrition

Brian Sommer, writing in *ZDNet*, raised the specter of what he called "Franken-soft":

> "A vendor with a history of stitching together acquired or new technologies to existing products will see new tools like analytics, cloud, mobile, etc. as merely something else to append to the Franken-soft creation. That's a mistake. Some things, like a new application, can be bolted to the existing suite and may, in fact, deliver value to customers. Other items require platform changes, data model changes and more."[53]

The lack of access to the newer/acquired products is also leading to resentment from older customers who have been paying maintenance for years.

As one told me:

> "We pay maintenance for HR, but don't have entitlement for SuccessFactors. We pay maintenance for BW, but don't have entitlement for BOBJ/HANA. We pay maintenance for R/3 MM and SRM but don't have entitlement for Ariba, etc. We paid maintenance for SAP Mobile Asset Management (from 2005) but got no entitlement to SAP Mobile (from 2014)."

---

[53] http://www.zdnet.com/erps-franken-soft-and-how-workday-avoids-it-7000007200/

While HANA and cloud computing has dominated SAP attention for the last five years, the company has also had a revolving door. While the technology industry is dynamic, the exit of executives over the last decade is striking in emerging cloud, mobile, and analytics areas, and at the SAP acquisitions.

For a vendor described as a "safe choice" by many of its customers, SAP executives have been in an awful hurry to move on, as we show in Figure 2. Those are senior executives; there has been significant turnover at other staff levels, and the exodus has benefitted companies like GE, Infosys and Schneider Electric.

The big honking issue in most IT budgets has long been that 70 percent to 80 percent is spent to "keep the lights on." SAP and packaged software, in general, were supposed to lower that ratio and free up more for innovation. SAP has replaced the old systems but not improved the ratio. Today, with all kinds of innovation opportunities with sensors, robots, drones, satellites, etc., the SAP budget is crowding out many of those investments. As the CIO of Embraer says in Chapter A2 about the improvement he has seen since moving to third party maintenance, "Our ratio of IT maintenance costs to innovative projects, which formerly was 70/30, is 50/50."

Everywhere you poke in SAP shops you see premium pricing. Of course, you get the usual validation — oh, it comes with better SLAs, responsiveness, QoS etc.

You can see why many customers are pivoting away from SAP and its partners. Many have concluded they bought a shiny car, but did not realize it would also need premium fuel, deliver low mileage, need $100 oil changes and $1,000 tires and more and more.

SAP Executive Departures

Date	Name	Title
Nov-09	Zia Yusuf	EVP Ecosystem
Feb-10	Geraldine McBride	Regional President AsiaPac
Feb-10	Leo Apotheker	CEO
Feb-10	John Schwarz	CEO BusinessObjects
Mar-10	Pascal Brosset	Chief Strategy
Dec-10	Bernd-Michael Rumpf	Head Global Field Services
Dec-10	Bob Stutz	VP Mobile
Dec-10	Doug Merritt	Exec VP
Dec-10	Singh Mecker	SVP Global Sales Partners
Apr-11	Marty Homlish	Chief Marketing Officer
Apr-11	John Wookey	Head On-Demand
Jul-11	Angelika Dammann	HRO
Oct-11	Ike Nassi	Chief Scientst
Mar-12	Peter Lorenz	Head ByD
Apr-12	Robert Courteau	President North America
May-12	Jose Duarte	President Global Services
Oct-12	John Chen	CEO Sybase
Oct-12	Paul Melchiorre	VP Ariba
Apr-13	Oliver Bussmann	CIO
May-13	Lars Dalgaard	CEO SuccessFactors
Jul-13	Sanjay Poonen	EVP Mobile
Jan-14	Bob Calderoni	CEO Ariba
May-14	Vishal Sikka	Head Development
May-14	Jim Hagemann Snabe	Co-CEO
May-14	Shawn Price	Head Cloud BU
Jun-14	Peter Graf	Chief Sustainability Officer
Aug-14	Michael Reh	EVP Business Information & Tech
Oct-14	Navin Budhiraja	Chief Architect SuccessFactors

Figure 2   Credit: Deal Architect

Even worse, in many cases the car just plain broke down. In Section III we will look at the shocking run of SAP project failures and other opportunities SAP customers have missed.

Case Studies Group B: Diversifiers

∿➤

Chapter B1: Customer Strategy –
"Ring Fence" with Clouds

Even on a normal day, running a $120 billion company with over 300,000 employees in 170 countries is a daunting task. Add to that the distractions from the well-publicized issues at the company, and you would understand if HP persisted with the "safe choice" — its SAP investment. HP is also a significant SAP partner, with plenty of hardware, software, hosting, and consulting offerings. Its ConvergedSystem 900 is one of the most powerful HANA servers certified by SAP, with a 12TB/16s scale-up system and an 80TB+ scale-out system.

Yet, as part of the company's operational transformation, CEO Meg Whitman has focused on making it easier to buy technology and services from HP and over 150,000 of its distribution partners. The systems to support that transformation will make HP the largest Salesforce.com implementation in the world. It also boasts some of the largest Workday (for HR functions), Fieldglass (for contract labor procurement), and DocuSign (for electronic contracts) implementations. The Workday implementation at HP covers almost twice as many employees as the Flextronics project discussed in Chapter 1 and was accomplished in just 14 months.

These new systems largely replace Oracle-owned products, Siebel and PeopleSoft, and HP continues with many SAP modules. It is representative, however, of many companies that are choosing to adopt cloud products as a "ring fence" around the core of SAP.

The HP project is breaking down silos — so contracts, contacts, and commissions are in one place, facilitating better integration of sales with legal, HR, contingent labor procurement, and with countless channel partners. Daryl Ganas, Director of Sales Operations at HP, described the business angles of the transformation project in a webinar:

- Homogenization of the customer experience across products — as he put it, customers keep asking, "Please come to us as one HP,"
- Standardization of processes across divisions and geographies.
- Leveraging HP's massive economies of scale to the benefit of its partner ecosystem.
- Automating the (complex) product configuration, pricing and customer quote process.
- Integrating the customer quote and sales compensation process.[54]

Salesforce.com is facilitating consolidation of customer profiles, and directly generating sales quotes rather than handing them to another system for processing. Workday is replacing PeopleSoft software, as well as over 150 customizations. Fieldglass (which was acquired by SAP after the HP project started) is replacing home-grown services contracting capabilities and related payments to

---

[54] https://www.salesforce.com/form/conf/webinar-futureofsales.jsp?d= 70130000000t6iF

subcontractors. DocuSign, with its electronic signature capabilities, is streamlining many contracting processes.

John Hinshaw, the new CIO Meg Whitman recruited, has commented :

> "(Sales) efficiency has gone up. Their satisfaction with their own work has gone up significantly. It was 7 percent. It's now 70 percent. The second thing is the speed at which we can implement new functionality. We've done four releases so far, and we have a fifth one coming up. We can implement them much faster in Salesforce than we could before."

And:

> "When we would sign up a new reseller, it used to take five weeks in the whole transaction process. Now it's five days. HP Financial Services would take two or three days of paperwork back and forth. Now it's 10 minutes."[55]

HP's growing cloud experience as a customer is being packaged into its service offerings. Specific to Workday, HP says on its website, "Whether you have already licensed Workday HCM or are in the process, HP Enterprise Applications Services for Workday helps you get the most value from your investment. Our Workday services encompass functional configuration, technology integration, change management, testing, and program management,

---

[55] http://allthingsd.com/20130319/seven-questions-for-the-man-shaking-up-hps-operations-john-hinshaw/

ensuring Workday data connects to the right endpoints. Our understanding of cloud solutions can help you maximize the business value of this revolutionary technology."[56]

The AstraZeneca Cloud

AstraZeneca is a London-based pharmaceutical company with annual revenues in excess of $25 billion. It is integrated across the "value chain of a medicine from discovery, early- and late-stage development, to manufacturing and distribution."

With declining revenues attributed to healthcare budget reductions in many world markets and with several of its patents expiring on blockbuster drugs, it reorganized its executive team in early 2013. Joining the team as CIO was Dave Smoley, whom we first met in Chapter 1 when he was CIO at Flextronics.

Smoley is widely considered a cloud pioneer, having worked with Workday at Flextronics and with Salesforce. com and Service-now.com in other roles. In the regulated industry that AstraZeneca is part of, he knows it will continue to depend on validated processes that SAP supports, but he is looking for cloud applications at various parts in the enterprise.

He also knows cloud computing needs a different mindset:

> "The old world software economy thrives on complexity and multiple ecosystem partners and slow

[56] http://www8.hp.com/us/en/business-services/it-services.html?comp URI=1700717#.U9l3wvldXdQ

pace of product uptake. Cloud solutions are much easier to consume; they require much less training and customization. But, the rate of change is faster — so you have to anticipate new releases and capability, and to provide input into what you would like to see. You have to rapidly test it and decide which capabilities you are going to deploy and which you will not."

To reflect this "whole different world", he recruited Shobie Ramakrishnan as CTO. Ramakrishnan had previously implemented several cloud applications, including a large Google Apps deployment at Genentech, the pioneering genomics company, and now a Roche subsidiary. She also ran portions of technology operations at Salesforce.com.

She talks about cloud computing at AstraZeneca:

"We are judiciously deploying cloud applications. We evaluated both Microsoft and Google clouds for our calendaring, and went with Office 365. We are a Veeva user — a pharma-focused CRM SaaS product. We first deployed Salesforce.com for sales force automation in China and other emerging markets and then more to our bigger markets.

Salesforce and Workday are centerpieces of our CRM and HR architecture, and we will keep adding other functionality around them. We collaborate extensively using Box.com functionality and that will evolve with our use of Office 365. We

are looking at applications in many other functional niches like R&D and to expand our use of
infrastructure-as-a-service."

What has this growing cloud footprint meant for integration with the SAP backbone?

"In some ways, we have yet to tackle some of the
harder parts, like point-to-point interfaces. With
Workday, we took a service-oriented-architecture
approach to abstracting as much as possible. But,
clearly, we have many end points we need to address.

Cloud platforms have connectors which make
it far easier to integrate with other web services, but
not so much with on-premise and legacy applications. On the other hand, the legacy applications
don't look like they are going to offer open APIs
any time soon. Fortunately, lots of smart people are
looking at solving integration problems.

IT has always had to deal with integration issues;
it's just that the flavors have become more much
hybrid and nuanced. So, in my view, the acronym
CIO is becoming more Chief Integration Officer."

Contrast that with the view many SAP customers have
that they bought the ERP suite to get out of the integration
role. AstraZeneca has a much more pragmatic view on
the integration challenge as they "ring fence" SAP and its
ecosystem with a series of cloud applications.

Chapter B2: Customer Strategy –
Change the Talent Model

The city of Madras in South India has long been associated with hot curries and plaid shirts. Renamed Chennai in 1996, it has emerged as a leading global hub for high-tech talent, and will be a major node in AstraZeneca's bold move to reverse a decade of outsourcing.

Chris Day, AstraZeneca's VP of IT Transformation, says:

"We tried a single-source outsourcing model with IBM, and then a multisource arrangement with an ecosystem of eight providers. Neither model has worked out very well. Benchmarking ourselves even against pharma industry peers, our IT costs are very high. And pharma is not the most efficient industry to start with.

We also found it painful to get work done with multiple layers of supplier management and multiple handoffs. Overall, the worst impact of these rounds of outsourcing was that they resulted in a loss of knowledge and skills, both in AZ and in suppliers. Outsourcing leads to a culture of generalist service and contract managers on both sides who don't understand the technologies they are accountable for — so everything is "we'll get back to you" as they seek out those that do understand, which is especially painful when issues cross supplier boundaries. The end result is service is put at risk with costly, non-agile project delivery and no improvement in user satisfaction scores.

Any idea that outsourcing partners are able to drive down ticket volumes and raise user satisfaction scores without considerable involvement and expertise from AZ is now long gone. In a regulated business, the support and delivery processes need active involvement and leadership from in-house staff so that compliance is delivered with productivity — this is very difficult for suppliers to do.

We are looking to invert the 70 percent outsourced model in our SAP, infrastructure operations (network monitoring), application development and maintenance, and cloud and mobile IT areas. We expect to bring over 4,000 outsourced jobs back in-house in a network in Chennai, Silicon Valley and Eastern Europe over the next three years.

The Chennai center will be up to 300 employees by the end of 2014. Not only are internal labor rates going to be dramatically lower, we expect to have more productivity as handoffs drop off."

CIO Dave Smoley talks about how he expects to compete for talent in a city where outsourcers have been the biggest recruiters in the last couple of decades:

"We have been in India since 1979 and have a good recruiting brand here. As a global organization, and with the competency centers we are setting up, there is plenty of opportunity for motivated tech professionals to grow, travel internationally and work on challenging areas.

Besides SAP jobs, we are doing exciting Big Data work with genomic sequencing, building a variety of mobile apps for our 25,000-strong sales force and addressing thorny middleware issues as we grow our cloud application footprint.

Our center in Chennai is state-of-the-art — we have invested $10 million in the infrastructure. Its location is also attractive for a number of recruits."

Smoley expects the transition from the outsourcing partners to be smooth:

"We will still be outsourcing 30 percent of our needs — it's a smaller pie, but still a significant one for partners to compete for. They realize this is an integral step in halving our global IT budget of $1.3 billion."

In Chapter 7 we will see the sobering track record of SAP project failures, and in Chapter 10 we will see the poor economic performance of SAP's systems integration, hosting, and application management partners. Given that track record, it would not be surprising to see other SAP customers follow AstraZeneca's in-sourcing path. They may not be able to do it on the same scale, but the 70/30 internal/external staff mix is definitely worth emulating across the SAP project and support lifecycle.

Chapter B3: Customer Strategy – Tiers of Joy

In the 1980s, as AS/400s and LANs matured, many multinationals adopted two- or three-tier application strategies — a mainframe-based application for corporate and domestic subsidiaries and regional hubs, with decentralized versions for international subsidiaries. J.D. Edwards (now part of Oracle), Platinum (now Epicor), Sage, and other vendors were beneficiaries of such tiering.

Things have evolved quite a bit since — now companies can go with SaaS systems for smaller subsidiaries, and as a result not even need local IT support. Also, integration across subsidiaries has become easier with tools like Informatica, IBM Cast Iron, and Dell Boomi.

SAP did well with small and midsized enterprises with its Business One solution (technology which it had acquired in 2002), and as a two-tier option for subsidiaries of multinationals. The VAR channel around Business One has done well to follow a "configure to needs" method as opposed to the "make to order" approach SAP's larger partners have typically taken. That has reduced cost of ownership with respect to upgrades and new features.

SAP did not do as well with its All-in-One solutions — industry-templated versions of its Business Suite. It has had even less success with its cloud Business ByDesign solution, as we saw in Chapter 2.

The SAP hiccup has opened the door for several newer competitors in two-tier scenarios.

NetSuite Two-Tier Solutions

Procter & Gamble, a major SAP shop, rolled out NetSuite to its major distributors in the Philippines. Conversely, ABS-CBN Global, a Filipino company, kept SAP at its headquarters, but adopted NetSuite for global operations.

ABS-CBN caters to the Filipino diaspora — estimated at nearly two million immigrants in the U.S. It also serves several million migrant workers in the Middle East and other global markets. Its products include TFC.tv (streaming content), StarKargo (shipping services), Easy Remit (banking services), and Sarimanok One (calling card services).

ABS-CBN uses NetSuite to support CRM, sales management, inventory, and accounting for its international operations.

Brad Peters, Chairman of the analytics vendor, Birst which partners with both SAP and NetSuite explains the co-existence strategy "NetSuite talks about being in organizations departmentally, SAP corporately. What (Birst) does is make that more seamless."[57]

A FinancialForce Example

Lexmark International, based in Lexington, KY is a leading provider of printers and global managed print services. In *The New Technology Elite* I had written about the innovative design principles and social marketing launch around their Genesis printer. Lexmark is a major SAP customer using BusinessObjects, HANA and many other SAP products.

---

[57] http://diginomica.com/2014/10/09/sap-birst-steal-salesforce-coms-cloud-analytics-thunder-dreamforce-eve/#.VDkGXvldXdQ

It is also an SAP partner helping its customers with print solutions.

In 2010, it acquired Perceptive Software, a leading provider of Enterprise Content Management solutions. Perceptive was using, and has continued to use Professional Services Automation functionality from FinancialForce.

Says Patrick Loetel, Senior Financial Analyst:

> "FinancialForce is our ERP to manage the operation of our consulting and project services business. It provides us the ability to track the flow from bid to bill on implementation projects. Built on the Salesforce platform, it enables us to integrate Salesforce CRM and Force.com in one consolidated services management application.
>
> When opportunities roll from the CRM account, if there is a professional services component, a record is setup via a project object in FinancialForce. That then becomes the vehicle by which the Project Manager monitors bookings, what revenue has been recognized, resource planning, and many other project milestone and resource specific metrics. As a company it drives cross-project visibility and benchmarking against various KPIs.
>
> Project financials post in the back end to SAP since that is the corporate book of record, and SAP also generates the customer invoices, but we have been pleased with FinancialForce, and have not been required to transition the services functionality to SAP."

FinancialForce being built on the Salesforce.com cloud platform has allowed Perceptive to also leverage its social and mobile functionality. Explains Loetel:

> "Salesforce's Chatter functionality drives collabora- tion between groups across geographical distances as well as functional roles. Because it is embedded within the tool, these conversations can be easily categorized by the same data points as the project objects themselves. Similarly, the Salesforce1 mobile app provides a base for the same cloud-based proj- ect dashboards to be accessed via a mobile device."

Microsoft Scenarios

The use cases with Microsoft technology in two-tier set- tings at SAP customers are even more diverse.

Last year, I ordered a sandwich on a Delta flight, and courtesy of the in-flight GoGo WiFi I had a receipt in my inbox a few minutes later. Curious, I asked the flight atten- dant how it worked and she showed me the point-of-sale functionality on her new Nokia Lumia. Later, I asked some Microsoft employees about it on a visit to their headquarters. What they told me was even more impressive: The company had woven together Avanade's Mobile Airline platform utilizing Microsoft Dynamics for Retail and customized the Nokia Lumia 820 device for Delta. It is an example of the complex packaging of multiple features the vendor is doing as part of its "One Microsoft" strategy.

A few weeks later, I met a Delta executive who told me the payback from the system was immediate — the airline is able to validate transactions in real-time. Previous POS systems were asynchronous, leading to losses from expired or invalid credit cards. It is also looking forward to being able to offer upgrades in-flight on international flights — a potentially significant revenue source — with the new POS technology.

Microsoft is itself an SAP shop and uses its finance, controlling, material management, demand planning, sales, human capital management, and global trade functionality. It also has more than 20,000 (with plans to grow to 60,000) users on its own Dynamics AX product in areas like manufacturing, retail, professional services, expense, time and project management. It provides a showpiece of integration between the two platforms.

An example of this integration is the implementation of Microsoft Dynamics AX in all of its retail stores. The retail group needed both a more cost-effective and agile solution than the central SAP solution supported. It rolled out Dynamics AX and integrated that solution back into the financial and human resources management functions of the SAP system. In addition, the stores use Microsoft Dynamics CRM to support effective, informed customer service. The stores have also integrated Dynamics AX with many other innovative tools used onsite, including capabilities for service management, contract tracking, cell phone activation, technical support, and the tablet computers that store associates use.

The Würth Group, a German distributor of a variety of furniture and construction fittings, has more than three million customers across 400 subsidiaries in over

80 countries with global revenues of over €10 billion. The Würth Phoenix Group, the company's IT sub, developed Trade+, a template based on Microsoft Dynamics AX with customized inventory functionality and reporting.

The template has been deployed in 65 of those subsidiaries so far (55 running AX, ten running CRM). The distributed architecture allows efficient local handling of low-value, high-volume customer orders with centralized finance and materials management on the SAP system in Germany. The CIO has asserted that they now can "integrate new businesses into the group practically at the touch of a button." Würth has gained the ability to standardize its diverse environment, providing the needed flexibility at the subsidiary level while still maintaining the enterprise-wide visibility into the corporate SAP solution. This has meant leaner processes — for example, replenishment has been able to reduce workloads on orders by up to 50 percent.

According to Ricky Klint Gangsted-Rasmussen, Director of Worldwide Product Marketing for Microsoft Dynamics AX, "This is a hot area for Microsoft, as an increasing number of SAP customers are shifting gears toward growth, and delivering great experiences to their own customers. To do so, they are finding that their SAP solution is struggling to expand to cover this change in focus from a time-to-solution, cost, and user adoption perspective."

Chapter B4: Customer Strategy – Agility Through Best-of-Breed

"The big change in our IT thinking in the last few years has been that speed and responsiveness to customer needs get far more priority over detailed specifications or feature rich technologies," says Francois Martin-Festa, Vice President of Supply Chain Planning & SIOP at Schneider Electric, the global specialist in energy management. "We have become big believers in proof of concept and pilot projects and then rapid deployment." Martin-Festa added, "This is very different from the long specification cycles we used to have."

"Our approach has also led us to more "off-the-shelf cloud solutions," as we leverage our traditional SAP and Oracle tools," says Christophe Gallet, VP, Supply Chain IT Transformation, Schneider Electric.

The two supply chain executives, Martin-Festa and Gallet, speak the same language as the company has a "two in a box" philosophy where IT and business executives are tightly coupled across various axes of their transformation journey. Schneider Electric, with 2013 "pro-forma" revenues of €25 billion, started in the iron, steel, and heavy machinery industry, and has since become a global player in electricity and automation management over the course of its 170-year history. It services four major end markets: residential and nonresidential buildings, utilities and infrastructure, industrial and machines, and data centers and networks.

Global electricity consumption is expected to double in the next two decades, and demographics, industrialization and urbanization in emerging markets will be even faster. Schneider Electric's customer base, accordingly, has expanded geographically. The company has also been evolving from selling products to solutions and diversifying its product portfolio to include charging solutions for electric vehicles to software and IT services. Schneider Electric has added to its product offerings through a wide range of acquisitions — 15 transactions since 2010, including the U.K. engineering company, Invensys.

From an IT perspective, the end result is Schneider Electric has ended up with a sprawl of over 100 ERP systems. Spearheading the drive to simplify and consolidate systems and invest in the tools to build a best-in-class planning process has been Annette Clayton, the company's Chief Supply Chain Officer. She joined the company from Dell in 2012 and has led a massive supply chain transformation across the dimensions shown in Figure 1.

Our Global Supply Chain figures at a glance

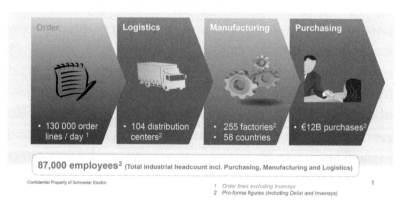

Order	Logistics	Manufacturing	Purchasing
• 130 000 order lines / day [1]	• 104 distribution centers [2]	• 255 factories [2] • 58 countries	• €12B purchases [2]

87,000 employees [2] (Total industrial headcount incl. Purchasing, Manufacturing and Logistics)

Confidential Property of Schneider Electric

1 Order lines excluding Invensys
2 Pro-forma figures (including Delixi and Invensys)

Figure 1   Credit: Schneider Electric

According to Martin-Festa, while the consolidation of ERP systems continues in parallel — Schneider Electric is consolidating into a "federation" of 11 ERP instances, most of them SAP-based — the real value is from the sales, inventory, operations, and planning (SIOP) tools on top of these ERP transaction feeders.

'We get an end-to-end view with Kinaxis, the planning vendor we have partnered with," says Martin-Festa. "That allows collaboration and connectivity all the way from key customers to critical suppliers." Kinaxis is an Ottawa-based vendor that reported $50 million in revenues in 2011 when Schneider Electric evaluated it.

Figure 2 shows the four planning areas that the tool helps with. Martin-Festa emphasizes the "end-to-end" aspect because Schneider Electric was fully prepared to implement best-of-breed tools in each area. Decisions were being made in silos, and they did not expect a single vendor to be able to provide end-to-end planning across the globe.

Overall progress status at program mid term

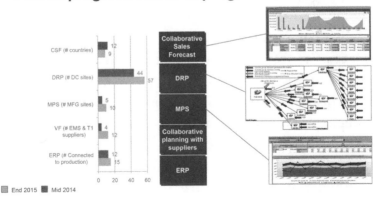

Figure 2   Credit: Schneider Electric

Even SAP with its Advanced Planning and Optimization (APO) functionality has individual modules that include Demand Planning, Supply Network Planning, Product Planning and Detailed Scheduling. Schneider Electric was focused more on the best collaboration/orchestration on the end-to-end supply chain than on optimizing its network. SAP is much stronger for network optimization than for collaboration.

The planning areas look deceptively simple from their descriptions. But global companies like Schneider Electric have multi-tier distribution networks with inventory outside factories, which feed regional distribution centers (DCs) (e.g. Hub Singapore), which in turn feed local DCs (e.g. Thailand, Vietnam) and other regional hubs (e.g. U.S., Europe). They do this because the customer order lead time is far shorter than the supply lead time so they have to have finished product relatively close to the customers. With as broad a portfolio as Schneider Electric has and with 60 percent to 70 percent of the cost of goods sold attributable to suppliers, there is a need to share the short-term and medium-term material supply forecast with suppliers and get their commitment for delivery. This can sometimes be as far out as six months in advance given the lead time of the end-to-end supply chain.

"The other thing we liked about Kinaxis was the speed of deployment and the lower cost," says Gallet. "We also liked the user interface — APO had an engineer's not a planner's feel to it. And, we liked the what-if scenario planning as it allowed us to easily perform, as well as the ability to propagate assumptions — what's included, what's not — as we were rolling out the tools across the supply chain." Indeed, Kinaxis can unify multiple dimensions of functional, cross-functional and scenario planning, which is one of its selling points.

Martin-Festa continues, "In 2012, we did an initial proof-of-concept with Kinaxis involving 30 professionals from various countries and supply chain nodes. In our rollout, we did not have a rigid implementation model. Critical needs drive the implementation at each factory and every distribution center. Eighteen months into the rollout we leveraged the large centers we have in Cavite City in the Philippines and in Barcelona, Spain, to set up a Kinaxis competency center. A small number of employees in these centers acted as our integration glue — they coordinated the flat-file traffic across the sites." Gallet added, "Instead of waiting for a few months to find the perfect "middleware," we went with a set of connectors for the ERP systems feeds. Speed and criticality drove many of our deployment decisions."

By all accounts, the rollout has progressed well.

By the middle of 2014, as Figure 2 shows, collaborative sales forecasts were available for nine countries, distribution planning across 57 distribution centers, and manufacturing planning across five plants. Clayton has shared, at industry events, some of the early returns on investment, including €778,000 of excess inventory in Russia that has been turned into extra revenue and a significant reduction of inventory levels in Saudi Arabia. Internally, the company is benchmarking routinely against a Gartner supply chain "maturity model." And, there is a regular conversation within the Kinaxis executive team to continue the alignment and mitigate risks.

More and more companies are realizing the responsiveness and flexibility of a focused specialist vendor. That often outweighs the traditional viability and integration risks IT focuses on as they try to play safe and stick with a major vendor like SAP. In that sense, they sound exactly like McNamara, CEO of Flextronics, taking the risk with Workday in Chapter 1 and what Dennis Hodges of Inteva did with Plex Systems in Chapter A1.

The Casualties of the SAP Economy

CHAPTER 7

Still Trying After
All These Years

⌁➔

Most technology news in November and December focuses on Cyber Monday, new electronics for the holidays and other B2C news. The business-focused technology media typically enjoys a lull. The phrase in media circles is "everyone's gone dark."

The year 2013 was no exception, but there was also an unusual spike in SAP-related news starting on November 18, when *The Nashville Post* reported:

> "In the end, Bridgestone paid IBM in excess of $78 million for this rebuild that took more than two years. And after that 24-month wait, what did Bridgestone say was delivered? A "defective system [that] lost or deleted scheduled customer orders, would not process orders, duplicated, or partially processed orders and, for those

limited orders that were processed, did not complete critical corresponding business applications."[58]

November 21 in the *Los Angeles Times*:

"The battle over California's failed effort to upgrade its payroll system for public employees is heading to court. Controller John Chiang on Thursday sued SAP Public Services, the contractor he fired in February after deep problems with the project were revealed."[59]

December 6 in *Business Insider*:

"In 2007, IBM won a contract to build a new payroll application for the Queensland's Department of Health using SAP software. At first it said the project would cost AUS$6 million and then told Queensland it would really cost $27 million. Things went awry from there, with the system taking years to build, never working properly, a parade of people assigned to it (over 1,000 worked on it) and spiraling costs."[60]

December 11 in *The Wall Street Journal*:

"Avon Products Inc. is pulling the plug on a $125 million software overhaul that has been in the works for

---

[58] http://nashvillepost.com/news/2013/11/18/bridgestone_files_massive_fraud_and_deception_suit_against_ibm

[59] http://articles.latimes.com/2013/nov/21/local/la-me-pc-california-sues-sap-20131121

[60] http://www.businessinsider.com/queensland-sues-ibm-over-1b-project-2013-12#ixzz36PtFZXfX

four years after a test of the system in Canada drove away many of the salespeople who fuel the door-to-door cosmetics company's revenue. Avon began using the new order management software system in Canada in the second quarter. While the new system based on software supplied by SAP AG worked as planned, it was so burdensome and disruptive to Avon representatives' daily routine that they left in meaningful numbers."[61]

December 12 in *Computer Weekly*:

"Npower [a U.K. energy company] today admitted its customer accounts are in disarray after it moved to a new SAP IT system. The news comes just two weeks after the company announced large job cuts and contracts to outsource its backend systems."[62]

December 19 in *PC World*:

"In its fourth quarter Quanex recognized roughly US$15 million in depreciation related to the (SAP) implementation that started 3 years ago."[63]

Two decades of SAP implementation experiences would suggest that problematic projects such as those above should be slowing down, not spiking.

---

[61] http://online.wsj.com/news/articles/SB1000142405270230393250457925194161 9018078?mg=id-wsj
[62] http://www.computerweekly.com/news/2240210923/SAP-system-leaves-npower-customer-accounts-in-disarray
[63] http://www.pcworld.com/article/2082160/building-products-company-halts-sap-project-citing-strategy-shift.html

In reality, they continue a drumbeat of failures from the previous two decades:

1997

> "In January 1997, Dell Computer quietly canceled most of a two-year-old R/3 project after its budget swelled to $150 million from $115 million and tests showed that the software couldn't handle the sales volume Dell was expecting."[64]

1998

> "In 1998, the bankruptcy trustee of FoxMeyer launched two separate, US$500m each, lawsuits against SAP and Andersen Consulting. FoxMeyer charged SAP with fraud, negligence and breach of contract for persuading them to invest in a system that failed to deliver, leading to the demise of FoxMeyer.
>
> Andersen Consulting was charged with negligence and breach of contract for failing to properly manage the implementation."[65]

And:

> "SAP Installation scuttled: Unisource cites internal problems for $168 M write-off."[66]

---

[64] *The Wall Street Journal*, March 14, 1997.
[65] http://higheredbcs.wiley.com/legacy/college/turban/0471229679/add_text/ch08/fowmeyer.pdf
[66] *InformationWeek*, January 26, 1998.

1999

"Massive distribution problems following a flawed implementation of SAP's R/3 ERP system, which affected ship-
ments to stores in the peak Halloween and pre-Christmas
sales periods. In a booming stock market, Hershey
shares ended the year down 27% from its year's high.
And Hershey wasn't alone in its misery. In November
1999, domestic appliance manufacturer Whirlpool of
Benton Harbor, Mich., blamed shipping delays on dif-
ficulties associated with its SAP R/3 implementation.
Like Hershey, Whirlpool's share price dove south on the
news, falling from well over $70 to below $60."[67]

2000

"Volkswagen AG is having trouble delivering spare
parts to some car dealers there after turning on SAP
AG's R/3 software in its central parts warehouse. An
SAP spokesman in Germany confirmed that the enterprise resource planning (ERP) vendor has assigned 13
employees to help Volkswagen fix the problems, which
are forcing some owners of VW and Audi cars to wait
up to several weeks for needed repairs."[68]

2001

"Back in 2000 and 2001, Nike spent $400 million dol-
lars updating their supply chain system and ERP

[67] http://www.cio.com/article/2437803/enterprise-resource-planning/erp-training-
stinks.html
[68] http://www.computerworld.com/s/article/40471/ERP_Problems_Put_Brakes_
On_Volkswagen_Parts_Shipments

implementation. They were surprised to find that what it got them was a ghastly 20 percent dip in their stock, $100 million dollars in lost revenues and a myriad of class action lawsuits."[69]

And:

"High street newsagent WH Smith is scaling down its Connect2U Internet trading platform, despite spending millions on its implementation. Connect2U, which runs on SAP software, provides newsagents with account data and delivery information from WH Smith's news distribution division."[70]

2002

"The German Federal Armed Forces has delayed using a new set of bookkeeping applications from SAP due to problems installing the software, according to an article published Thursday in the German business magazine Handelsblatt. The delays are costing the German government 350,000 euros ($350,664) a day in unplanned fees for outside consulting on the project, the article says.

The SAP applications are the centerpiece of a 10-year, 6.5 billion euro ($6.5 billion) computer modernization

[69] http://blog.360cloudsolutions.com/blog/bid/94028/Top-Six-ERP-Implementation-Failures

[70] http://www.computerweekly.com/news/2240042856/WH-Smith-freezes-trading-platform

effort under way at the military agency, the magazine said."[71]

2003

"The heavy cost of failures in software projects hit home last week when ICI lost 39% of its share value — about £400m — after warnings that its pre-tax profits were expected to drop to about £50m from £66m last year. The desperately poor figures — which saw ICI shares hit a 28-year low — were in large part brought about by failures in the implementation of a SAP-based supply chain management system at the company's Holland-based fragrance-making subsidiary Quest."[72]

2004

"Federation of Health Services (AOK) budget estimate grown from initial €360 million to €540 million ($675M, 50% overrun), and delayed from 2006 to 2009."[73]

And:

"An HP spokeswoman confirmed this afternoon that the problematic migration was based around SAP software, but she was unable to immediately provide additional details. In a conference call with reporters earlier in the

---

[71] http://news.cnet.com/SAP-project-with-German-military-stalls/2100-1001_3-966780.html

[72] http://www.computerweekly.com/feature/ICI-pays-price-for-side-effects-of-IT-project

[73] http://www.computerwoche.de/a/sap-projekt-der-aok-kriselt,1053629

day, Fiorina said the problems cost the ESS group about $400 million in revenue and $275 million in operating profit."[74]

And:

"PwC complained that NASA couldn't adequately document more than $565 billion — billion — in year-end adjustments to the financial-statement accounts, which NASA delivered to the auditors two months late.... NASA says blame for the financial mayhem falls squarely on the so-called Integrated Financial Management Program (IFMP), an ambitious enterprise-software implementation. In June 2003, the agency finished rolling out the core financial module of the program's SAP R/3 system. NASA's CFO, Gwendolyn Brown, says the conversion to the new system caused the problems with the audit."[75]

And:

"Dozens of British Airways' planes have had to sit, idling in repair hangars since July waiting for the right nuts and bolts to turn up, it emerged yesterday. The troubled airline has been hit by "teething problems" with a new supply chain management system, designed by software firm SAP. It has meant component and fluid shortages at

---

[74] http://www.computerworld.com/s/article/95223/SAP_implementation_contributed_to_HP_shortfall
[75] http://ww2.cfo.com/accounting-tax/2004/05/nasa-we-have-a-problem/

repair hangars when planes from BA's 300-strong fleet have come in for their regular service."[76]

And:

"Furniture retailer MFI has ditched two board members after serious problems with its SAP inventory system forced it to make a profit warning. The £50m system was supposed to turn things round for the troubled retailer but it is now facing an additional £30m bill to sort out problems with customer orders and fix the system. MFI became aware of the problem in July but said it was dealing with the symptoms rather than the causes. A review of August Bank Holiday sales revealed the true scale of the problem."[77]

2005

"The halting of two controversial SAP AG ERP system rollouts — valued at more than $380 million — this month has ignited a political firestorm in Ireland.

The Irish Health Service Executive (HSE), an oversight committee for the national health department, suspended work on the Personnel, Payroll and Related Systems (PPARS) project, which was started 10 years ago to handle payroll functions for the unit's 120,000 employees."[78]

---

[76] http://www.telegraph.co.uk/finance/2894107/BA-planes-sit-waiting-for-right-spare-parts.html
[77] http://www.theregister.co.uk/2004/09/14/mfi_sap_problems/
[78] http://www.computerworld.com/s/article/105468/Irish_agency_halts_work_on_two_SAP_application_projects

And:

"The US Navy has wasted \$1bn (£588m) since 1998 on four flawed enterprise resource planning pilot projects based on SAP software, according to a report from the US Government Accountability Office (GAO)... IBM, Deloitte & Touche LLP, and EDS had been involved in these pilots."[79]

And:

"MASIS — or Materiel Acquisition Support Information System — started in 1997 as a \$147-million undertaking. What began as a focused effort to cover a single equipment category in each of the navy, army and air force soon mushroomed. By 2001, MASIS had morphed into a nine-year affair to include all assets — from spare parts to boots — in all three forces. Two years later, Defence officials estimated MASIS would be in place by 2006 at a cost of \$325 million, more than twice its forecast budget. To date, \$182.3 million has been approved — not including the expense of replacing staff who take part in related workshops and testing. A full introduction of the complex software has now been extended until 2011, but Defence officials would not confirm a new forecast of total costs."[80]

---

[79] http://www.computerweekly.com/news/2240075819/US-Navy-wastes-1bn-on-SAP-ERP
[80] *The Canadian Press*, Oct 23, 2005.

2006

"Hipple said she believes Rowe's implementation of an enterprise resource planning system in 2005 "created a spiral of events that brought us to this point." While Rowe deliveries now are back on track, bugs in the system had created some four-month lead times for Storehouse. Half of the chain's customer orders included product from Rowe, she said. Hipple said Storehouse posted same-store sales increases for 30 consecutive months until early 2005, when the ERP system went online."[81]

2007

"Payday has left hundreds of employees of the Los Angeles Unified School District in the lurch, as the mammoth district's new payroll system has been roiled by glitches. After 18 months of preparations to roll out the $95-million computer system, clerical errors and outdated employment data led to about 1,000 teachers and other staffers either not being paid or being paid too little, district officials said."[82]

2008

"The trash-disposal giant Waste Management is suing SAP, saying top SAP executives participated in a fraudulent sales scheme that resulted in a failed ERP (enterprise resource planning) implementation. Waste Management said it is seeking recovery of more than US$100 million

---

[81] http://www.furnituretoday.com/article/481864-storehouse-liquidating
[82] http://articles.latimes.com/2007/feb/07/local/me-payroll7

in project expenses, as well as "the savings and benefits that the SAP software was promised to deliver to Waste Management.""[83]

And:

"The weak economy has companies of all sizes and types moving to cut costs, and for U.S. bedding manufacturer Select Comfort, those choices have included a decision to halt all work associated with a wide-ranging SAP ERP (enterprise resource planning) project. And documents on file with a government regulator indicate that shareholder pressure may have contributed to the move."[84]

2009

"Shane Co., the family-owned jewelry retailer that sought bankruptcy yesterday, told a U.S. judge the company's decline was triggered partly by delays and cost overruns for a $36 million SAP AG inventory-management system."[85]

2010

"Marin County on Friday filed a lawsuit against Deloitte Consulting alleging fraud related to an SAP ERP software

---

[83] http://www.itworld.com/waste-management-sues-sap-080327
[84] http://www.cio.com/article/2431619/strategy/sap-project-halted-after-shareholder-pressure.html
[85] http://www.bloomberg.com/apps/news?pid=newsarchive&sid=awweg53wmmJw

implementation the county said is still not working four years after it initially went live."[86]

2011

"Operating and net income, however, did not meet our [Ingram Micro's] expectations largely due to complications with our ERP system implementation in Australia. We're diligently addressing these issues to drive improved profitability and performance as soon as possible. We are confident the future benefits of the new system outweigh some of the hurdles we are facing today."[87]

And:

"A major SAP ERP (enterprise resource planning) software project being conducted by the New South Wales Department of Education and Communities has hit a rocky patch, with projected costs for the first phase ballooning from A$153 million (US$157 million) to A$210 million (US$215 million), according to a new report by the Australian state's auditor."[88]

2012

"Avantor's complaint was filed on November 8, 2012, in the U.S. District Court for the District of New Jersey. It

---

[86] http://www.zdnet.com/blog/projectfailures/marin-county-sues-deloitte-alleges-fraud-on-sap-project/9774

[87] http://phx.corporate-ir.net/phoenix.zhtml?c=98566&p=irol-newsArticle&ID=1556620&highlight=

[88] http://www.pcworld.com/article/245625/auditor_big_aussie_sap_project_behind_schedule_over_budget.html

alleges that IBM, retained by Avantor to upgrade the company's global computer systems to an SAP platform, fraudulently misrepresented the capabilities of its proprietary software solution and engaged in other misconduct leading to a failed implementation in Avantor's U.S. locations. The complaint includes claims for fraud and breach of contract."[89]

Death by a Thousand Cuts

Most of these disputes, and many others which do not get reported in the media, get resolved in private. Of course, countless other implementations run over budget and over time, and are declared reasonably successful.

Less publicly reported are the many outages and downtimes in the SAP hosting world. In contrast, just about every Amazon or Workday outage gets reported (even though Workday has delivered 99.95 percent uptime, far better than most hosting companies deliver to SAP customers). Similarly, the backlog of ticket volumes in SAP world remains stubbornly high even when the outsourcers have contracted to deliver continuous improvements. The same applies to upgrades which most customers take months to plan and execute. Those are the "death by a thousand cuts" that do not get anywhere near the public exposure.

Is the glass half full or half empty? ERP projects are notoriously prone to overruns and failures. So, with SAP's more successful record of sales, a proportionately higher ratio of failures is defensible. Or you could argue after tens of thousands of SAP projects, the performance should be continually improving.

---

[89] http://www.prnewswire.com/news-releases/avantor-performance-materials-files-suit-against-ibm-over-failed-sap-software-implementation-177970931.html

Michael Krigsman, who has written often at ZDNet about what he calls the "IT Devil's Triangle," says:

> "Three parties participate in virtually every major software deployment: the customer, system integrator or consultant and the software vendor. Since each of these groups has its own definition of success, conflicts of interest rather than efficient and coordinated effort afflict many projects. The Devil's Triangle explains how economic pressures can drive software vendors and system integrators to act in ways that do not serve customer interests. It also offers insight into the ways some enterprise software customers damage their own projects.
>
> Devil's Triangle relationships are a short-sighted and self-interested way of life for too many participants in the enterprise technology landscape."[90]

Shaun Snapp is more direct:

> "After reading a number of articles on SAP project failure, I have noticed a consistent theme in much of the coverage. This is another example of how every time an SAP implementation goes sour, it seems as if the official publications put more of the blame with the clients. SAP gets to make a statement, which is positive and boilerplate and has something to do with the idea that SAP always does the right thing and its software works great,

---

[90] http://www.zdnet.com/blog/projectfailures/exploring-the-devils-triangle/5676

so they don't know what the problem could have been. The next entity they go to is the consulting company which often issues a similar boilerplate statement, which typically involves a back door brag, and then finally an IT analyst. The IT analyst is supposedly an unbiased source of information — however the analyst almost always says something convoluted, which seems very carefully crafted to emphasize the process rather than the performance of either SAP or the implementation partner. This may have something to do with the fact that SAP and the implementation partner advertises in these publications."[91]

Between what Krigsman and Snapp say, a root cause analysis of SAP failures has to look at four contributors — SAP, SAP partners, SAP customers and yes, even SAP market watchers. In Section IV, we have chapters which explore how each of the four constituencies contributes to the situation.

The failure causes vary from customer to customer, but it is shocking such major failures happen even after two decades of trying. It's almost like software which continues in an unstable, early "beta" stage. Except that in most cases, it was not the software, more the unrealistic SAP promises and the poor partner implementations which are to blame.

And yet, remarkably, SAP's reputation as a "safe choice" has stayed untarnished.

---

[91] https://www.linkedin.com/today/post/article/20140714232858-8617925-the-art-to-blaming-the-client-when-and-sap-project-goes-south

CHAPTER 8

The Slumber Party

⁀⇢

SAP has conducted many "Value Engineering" studies for prospects. The slides are well done — the work of ex-strategy-firm consultants SAP has hired, and embellished by support teams in India (which mirrors a knowledge center model McKinsey established in India earlier).

These studies often become the content for business cases that are presented for SAP project approval. The presentations discuss a variety of benchmarks and tools like "Collaborative Value Assessment." They promise millions of dollars in "one-time raw material inventory reduction," "annual savings from head count or overtime reduction" and "increased Web commerce revenue." The most promising value areas were typically in operational areas — shop floor, supply chain, etc.

In many ways, these studies were paid proposals for SAP. An ex-SAP salesman told me they often offered contingent pricing to customers tied to value promises, in addition to the option of regular licensing prices. He said such proposals were difficult to get internal approvals for — in software accounting, contingent pricing complicates revenue recognition.

Most customers, however, would opt for the nonvalue-based pricing. You can understand why — most customers realize results are rarely driven by any single contributor so why pay more for the software or the consulting when the economic environment or other external factors influence performance just as much? Additionally, the baseline changes often across a two or three year project.

Think about that for a minute. Few customers called SAP's bluff and tied payments to results. Also, the value results were most promising in operational areas when only a fraction of SAP customers have successfully implemented modules in those areas.

The other truism in the corporate world is that business cases are needed to get projects approved. They typically do not get audited after the fact. I asked SAP if it could share any postmortem analysis it has done at customers where it did Value Engineering. It declined — it either has not done such analysis or preferred not to divulge the results.

I scanned academic research for payback analysis. I found a few studies which measured impact on stock prices upon announcement of SAP and other ERP projects. I did not find much on actual payback.

Whether customers got tangible payback from their SAP projects or not, one thing is more certain: SAP customers have mostly missed out on four waves of IT transformation — industrialization, consumerization, externalization, and boardrooming. Like Rip Van Winkle, many SAP customers have snoozed through two decades of tectonic changes in enterprise computing, lulled by the idea they were "safe" with SAP.

The Industrialization of IT

The Ruhr Valley is famous as the heart of Germany's industrial belt with its mining and steel industries. Not surprisingly, cities there like Dortmund even today proudly maintain that blue-collar history with museums like the Zollern Colliery with its well-preserved engine house.

Three big German SAP customers decided in the mid-1990s to combine their efforts at a "factory" in Dortmund to provide shared IT services. The data center soon started offering hosting and other services to more SAP customers — midsized ones which make up Germany's renowned "Mittelstand."

In 2004, an outsourcer acquired this operation and planned to open it to even more SAP and other customers using a utility "ERP factory" model. A customer executive went to the center on a due diligence visit when the center was said to support 150 customers.

This executive was unimpressed:

> "I would grade it as a Tier 1 data center (Tier 4 being most robust). The disaster recovery site was only about ten miles away — not exactly comforting from a redundancy perspective. For a multitenant setting, there appeared to be too much glass to feel comfortable. Several portions of the center did not have a raised floor. And, it appeared very quiet for the suggested customer count or related support staff."

Even more striking in this city of giant factories and industrial might, this was such a puny facility compared to cloud data centers — the "pyramids of the twenty-first century" that Microsoft, Google, and Amazon were building.

In my book, *The New Polymath,* Mike Manos, then with Microsoft, told me the company had pioneered the use of containers filled with as many as 2,500 servers that could be easily shipped in and out of its data centers. One of those containers had more servers than the entire Dortmund facility described above (which had less than 500 of them) and the Microsoft data centers could hold 60 to 80 of these containers.

The new data center thinking located these centers — some of which cost $500 million each — in previously-unheard-of places like Quincy, WA, based on a complex matrix of considerations including energy proximity and costs, telecommunications, and taxes.

Another major hosting provider opened a data center in Colorado in the late 1990s. A visitor there a decade later remarked how much it reminded him of a "cold war bunker" with its thick, reinforced walls, graying operation manuals and proud talk of mainframes. In the meantime, Facebook was pushing data center thinking much further with its Prineville, Oregon, data center.

Amir Michael of Facebook described eye-popping, world-beating performance in a case study I wrote in *The New Technology Elite,* including:

- PUE (power usage effectiveness) of 1.07 at full load.
- WUE (water use effectiveness) of 0.31 liters/kWH.
- Savings of over 120 tons of packaging and other materials by ordering "vanity free" HP and Dell servers.

The data center has undergone a renaissance but few SAP customers benefited, because SAP hosting partners were too busy trying to recover their investments in older facilities. Of course, there were exceptions — the Capgemini "Merlin" data center in Swindon, U.K., opened in 2010, and "private clouds" SAP partners have recently been offering and partner virtualization efforts with VMware. SAP also gradually certified and introduced Amazon Web Services and Microsoft Azure offerings to its customers. (SAP had internally used AWS for years before it introduced it to its customer base.)

Inefficiently run data centers have been called some of the world's worst polluters. SAP has emphasized sustainability and published an online annual report of its environmental and other investments with factoids such as reducing its "carbon footprint by 9 percent since the beginning of 2008." It would be interesting to see a similar metric for its hosting partners.

If the U.S. CIA with its unique security requirements can pick Amazon over IBM for its infrastructure, and even offer to pay more for the Amazon bid,[92] it shows we have moved to a new world of IT industrialization that SAP customers could have leveraged.

SAP has since opened a data center in Sankt Leon-Rot, Germany, not far from its Walldorf headquarters, as part of its HANA Enterprise Cloud (HEC). The good news is this data center should put more pressure on its hosting partners. Imagine if SAP had done it much earlier around its Business Suite transaction processing areas. Instead, many of its customers are still stuck in multiyear hosting contracts in outdated data centers.

They have missed out on a wave of industrialization.

---

[92] http://www.informationweek.com/cloud/infrastructure-as-a-service/amazon-wins-best-cloud-in-cia-bake-off/d/d-id/1110504?itc=edit_in_body_cross

Consumerization of IT

I first heard Malcolm Frank, EVP of Strategy and Marketing at Cognizant describe the "Sunday night, Monday morning disconnect." We spend the weekend with HDTV, Microsoft Kinects, Bose audio gear, and Apple retina displays, and then head off to work on outdated and unfriendly technology.

Frank was describing the trend called the "consumerization of technology" and how IT has had to respond with initiatives like "bring your own device" and introduce mobile, telepresence and other technologies to their employees.

The major disruption in IT is consumers now spend as much on technology as do enterprises. Consumers are now generating twice as much data as enterprises. According to *CIO Insight*, consumers generated 2.9 zettabytes (10^{21} bytes) in 2013 compared to 1.5 zettabytes by enterprises.[93]

That is a stunning reversal from just a few years ago, when governments and corporations spent the majority of technology budgets. As a result, passengers often have better flight status and weather data than do airline employees. Retail employees have less competitor data than do their customers. Sports fans have better (and cheaper) seats at home than those at stadiums.

The "Sunday night, Monday morning disconnect" was on vivid display at a SAP-hosted meeting in February 2009 in New York when it launched Business Suite 7. I asked a panel of SAP and customer executives how come with talk of innovation there had not been a single mention of iPhones. Apple is an SAP customer, and I was hoping SAP executives would share

---

[93] http://www.cioinsight.com/it-strategy/storage/slideshows/digital-universe-expands-at-an-alarming-rate.html

insights into the amazing supply chain and logistics of that hugely successful launch. (By that point, Apple had already sold over 13 million iPhones since its introduction in June 2007. Since that meeting, it is estimated another 400 million units have been sold.)

Most of the responses from the panel were dismissive. Several CIOs said Blackberries were their standard. (This was 2009 after all.) Apotheker, then co-CEO of SAP, said, "I'm totally unable to complete a sentence on the iPhone. Perhaps I'm clumsy." Another said, "Our job is to translate buzzwords into products." There was a "we worry about more complex stuff in the enterprise" tone to the answers.

In many ways, the iconic images of consumer tech — Apple's elegant products, Amazon's no-training-required website, Google's minimalist home page — are the opposite of what the world thinks of SAP and its consultant-intensive implementations.

Indeed, I was in a session with Dave Girouard, then of Google, when I asked him about a statement he had made that "Enterprise software is entirely bereft of soul." Without batting an eyelid, he asked me "Are you from SAP?"

SAP engineers can confirm they have seen users in tears as they learn to use the software.

Here is an (extreme) example from *Information Week*:

> The result is that more than a third of the 300 independent sales reps who reported to Edwards quit, and she estimates Avon lost as many as 16,000 reps across Canada. Avon uses a multilevel marketing approach (also used by Amway and Tupperware) that relies on many part-time people who sell to friends through in-home networking

events. "With all the trouble they had using this system, the people making $50 or $100 per month figured it just wasn't worth their time and effort" Edwards says.[94]

The promise for SAP to improve its customer experience has long been present. SAP works with some of the most innovative companies in the world like Apple, BMW, and Nike. Its previous Chief Marketing Officer, Homlish, had come from an innovative global brand, Sony. Dr. Plattner made a significant donation to fund the respected Institute of Design at Stanford University, and often taught classes there. SAP has an Imagineering Group that has been rethinking UX for years, and in 2011 launched AppHaus, a start-up concept in Silicon Valley. John Hagel III and John Seely Brown, respected business authors, wrote a flattering section on SAP's ecosystem and ability to nurture innovation in their book, *The Only Sustainable Edge*.[95]

Other industry players have been raising the bar. Infor has a dedicated design agency, Hook & Loop, which has helped it redesign its software look-and-feel. Infor unabashedly calls its product "beautiful," a term not heard much in enterprise software circles. The agency has also helped with the décor of its New York headquarters, its user conferences and the aesthetics of its advertising. Hook & Loop has over a hundred "creative" staff with credentials such as Pulitzer Prize-winner for infographics, Digital Effects Editor of the movie *The Avenger*,

---

[94] http://www.informationweek.com/software/information-management/inside-avons-failed-order-management-project/d/d-id/1113100
[95] http://www.amazon.com/The-Only-Sustainable-Edge-Specialization/dp/1591397200/ref=sr_1_1?ie=UTF8&qid=1413132512&sr=8-1&keywords=the+only+sustainable+edge

fashion designer for Kenneth Cole and creator of Rise, a successful iOS application

Many vendors including Workday have taken advantage of retina displays Apple and others have delivered in their tablets and mobile devices. Apple and others have declared war on "skeuomorphism" — the use of icons which retain historic ornamental elements. They have been simplifying their software to keep up with mobile hardware, which has become sleeker. Amazon says, "We want the devices we design and engineer to disappear as you read ...." Microsoft says in a product announcement: "With Kinect, technology evaporates, letting the natural magic in all of us shine."

Customers have long pressured SAP to improve the user experience. Several SAP customers have invested their own funds in what some call "lipstick on a pig" projects to improve the user experience. They got tired of waiting. SAP's partners have thousands of employees who are millennials and have grown up with consumer tech and added their own discontent.

ASUG CEO Geoff Scott put it well in a blog:

> "As an experiment, take a millennial fresh out of college, sit her at a desk with a computer and happily show her the job duties accomplished via SAP's UI. She will look at you like you are from another planet, and she simply won't get it — and why should she when she's been immersed in Facebook, Twitter and simplified mobile applications for years?"[96]

---

[96] http://www.asugnews.com/article/time-for-a-ux-revolution-not-evolution

Cristian Gheorghe ended up at SAP after OutlookSoft was acquired in 2007. As he walked the halls of the company before he launched another startup, Tidemark, in 2010, he says he had his "heretical moment." It bothered him that less than 5 percent of employees at SAP's customers were using its analytics tools. His mission now is to increase that penetration dramatically. He is convinced a better, richer UX in the form of infographs via Storylines, one of Tidemark's features, is the path.

One of his early customers is US Sugar. The company previously shared performance data with field managers every two weeks in a 600-page document. Now that data is shared via Tidemark's apps on iPads. He has other examples where boring, old reporting is being replaced with interactive storytelling.

Of course, not everyone is leaving SAP to create newer UX. When Sam Yen became the global head of design and user experience at SAP, blogger Reed wrote, "I half-joked that he now had 'the hardest job at SAP.' With more than 300,000 screens and 20+ UI technologies to contend with, Sam's team inherited a big bowl of UI spaghetti at the exact time customer UX expectations are peaking and devices are proliferating."[97]

Progress is being made. SAP has been rolling out its Fiori UX and Screen Personas. Brian Sommer wrote:

> "SAP (has) focused on the high use transaction input screens. SAP gets the most bang for the buck quickly but there still are a lot of other screens and other product lines that need reworking."[98]

---

[97] http://diginomica.com/2013/08/30/sap-ui-overhaul-sam-yen/
[98] http://www.enterpriseirregulars.com/65397/saps-ui-makeover-taking-a-measured-approach-to-300000-screens/?utm_source=feedburner&utm_medium=feed&utm_campaign=Feed%3A+EIblogs+(Enterprise+Irregulars)

While progress on 300,000 screens is bound to take time, many would argue with the comment that SAP is moving "quickly." Gartner first used the term "consumerization" back in 2005. Others would react even more strongly to the comment "bang for the buck." SAP had a user revolt when it announced plans to charge extra for Fiori. It backed down, but left a poor taste given the years of disappointment customers have had with SAP's user experience.

And, while SAP has progressed slowly, it is still miles behind UX innovations happening at many of its customers.

In its auto customers, for example, radar is helping drivers with assistive cruise control; sonar with parking; cameras with rear view and blind spot vision; sensors with low tire pressure; lasers and proximity sensors with gestures to raise rear tailgates; eye-tracking with reduction of knobs and buttons in the cabin; and Bluetooth and other audio technology to answer calls and play music.

Meanwhile, its retail customers are experimenting with soft POS and self-checkout technologies. They are using facial recognition and unique audio signals to mobile phones to identify frequent and VIP customers. They are using depth sensors to analyze shoppers' reactions toward various products and full-body scanners to take measurements of customers.

And its healthcare customers are using bracelets to monitor various vital signs, subskin sensors to communicate with embedded devices, and brain/machine interfaces. Bar codes and audible, escalating alarms are the staple interfaces of most devices in hospitals.

At home, the UX innovation SAP users see is even more dramatic. De Dietrich offers "smart" induction hobs (burners). Should the user move the pan anywhere in the cooking zone, the hob's automatic pan detectors ensure that the temperature of the pan remains constant. The user no longer has to guess where the hot spots are. The Nest thermostat glows orange when it's heating and blue when it's cooling. In addition, it turns on when you approach it, and it discreetly goes dark when nobody is nearby. It also "learns" from the user's manual adjustments.

Tony Fadell, founder of Nest (now part of Google), has been quoted as saying:

> "Whether it's Tesla, or SpaceX taking Ethernet cables and running them inside of rocket ships, you are talking about combining the old-world science of manufacturing with low-cost, consumer-grade technology. You put these things together, and they morph into something we have never seen."[99]

Another facet of consumerization is the emergence of the "sharing economy" — the ethos of "in each other we trust." *Wired* has written:

> "Over the past few years, the sharing economy has matured from a fringe movement into a legitimate economic force, with companies like Airbnb and Uber the constant subject of IPO rumors."[100]

Dave Duffield, co-CEO of Workday, likes to talk about "the power of one." He says in all the companies he has started he has never felt as much customer unanimity as he does at Workday.

---

[99] http://www.businessweek.com/articles/2014-09-04/as-software-hardware-advance-together-next-innovation-wave-rises
[100] http://www.wired.com/2014/04/trust-in-the-share-economy/#slide-id-772351

The customers are on the same release, and thus have plenty to talk about at customer events. In contrast, on-premise software in his past companies and those of many present competitors are on multiple releases, different database platforms, with different customizations, and sunset schedules.

Twice a year, Workday customers get migrated to a much richer version. They have painlessly been upgraded through 23 releases over the last decade. This happens like clockwork — the entire customer base is on the new release in a matter of hours. Compare this to the SAP customer base upgrade experience — risky and expensive, so many customers wait and wait before they finally attempt it (and some customers use it as a jumping off point as we see in Chapter A2 to move to third party maintenance rather than upgrade).

Jason Prater, Vice President, Development, at Plex Systems, adds:

> "From a development standpoint, one of the key benefits of cloud versus on-premise solutions is the ability to combat "code bloat" — in other words, trimming obsolete code in order to maintain a leaner, more highly functional piece of software.
>
> In Plex's cloud model, if we see that there are pieces of functionality that no longer serve a purpose to our customers, we can easily prevent code bloat by removing those lines of code from the entire solution. In the last year alone, Plex's developers have removed what amounts to approximately one-third of the code within The Manufacturing Cloud, resulting in a cleaner and more nimble solution that is much more cost-effective to maintain."

In contrast, SAP has only a high-level understanding of which specific features its customers are using because it is far removed from operating its software at their sites.

Workday and Plex are describing the payback from multi-tenancy and shared services that their SaaS offerings allow their customers.

In the SAP world, many of the Indian outsourcing firms cordon off application management staff by customer. They may be in the same building in Bangalore or Mumbai, or even on the same floor, but there is little sharing of BASIS or functional staff.

The challenge is SAP's ambiguity about the "sharing" concept.

At Sapphire Now in 2013, Dr. Plattner said:

> "We introduced multi-tenancy in 1976 for German wine-makers and farmers. But large companies do not want to share [computing space] with competitors, they want to be within a firewall. Ask any of the large SaaS suppliers — when they get a huge customer, they get a private system."[101]

Albert Pang blogged after Sapphire Now in 2014:

> "During a Q&A session, SAP chairman Hasso Plattner dismissed the benefits of multi-tenant delivery of its enterprise applications, primarily those that deal with mission-critical functions like supply chain and financials. Plattner recalled a heated debate over the merits

---

[101] http://www.computerweekly.com/news/2240184309/Sapphire-2013-Plattner-Sikka-hail-HANA-growth-beyond-SAP

of multi-tenancy with Lars Dalgaard of SuccessFactors after it was bought by SAP in 2012. To this date, Plattner's position, though not unique, remains that SAP's biggest customers — fearing unnecessary business disruption — would still prefer deploying their applications either in a private cloud setting or as managed services, all without the intrusion of continuous updates commonly found in other Cloud applications"[102]

It is said that SAP mostly cares about 300–400 of its biggest customers which generate a sizable percentage of its revenues. It would be interesting to find out which of these customers still resist the sharing for back-office applications, because most have been trying out multitenancy in a variety of SaaS applications around SAP. My first paper as a Gartner analyst in 1995 was about the shared service centers that many global companies were utilizing for various financial and HR processes. They wanted to leverage economies of scale in the back office. Next, many had looked at BPO providers hoping to leverage even more scale across multiple customers.

Even more interesting would be to find out why the interests of these few are stopping SAP's partners from sharing efficiencies for thousands of other customers.

The irony is customers bought into SAP with the promise of shared economies of software development. This may have been true during the initial licensing, but they have been left to fend for themselves during the implementation, upgrade, and

---

[102] http://www.appsruntheworld.com/opinions/index/143#sthash.mLvlWBt0 .dpuf

lifecycle management. Wave after wave of SAP partners have charged premium rates in a variety of categories.

Another lesson from consumerization is to "deliver good enough" to start, then continue with rapid improvements.

Wired wrote in 2009:

> "We get our breaking news from blogs, we make spotty long-distance calls on Skype, we watch video on small computer screens rather than TVs, and more and more of us are carrying around dinky, low-power netbook computers that are just good enough to meet our surfing and emailing needs."[103]

Things rapidly improve afterwards.

Take Apple iTunes. In spite of billions of MP3 downloads, Apple found audiophiles still preferred buying CDs and ripping music from them to downloading from the iTunes store. So, in 2007 it announced with EMI Music a 256 kbps AAC codec, resulting in audio quality indistinguishable from the original recording. Over the next few years, Apple convinced other labels to offer similar higher-quality, DRM-free, iTunes Plus tunes.

It has since introduced a Match (cloud storage) feature, and now streaming versions.

Samsung's Galaxy S, introduced in 2010, had a five megapixel camera and 400 × 800 resolution screen. Every year since it has delivered a next generation version, and the S5 has a 16 megapixel camera and 1080 × 1920 pixels.

Good enough to start, then things keep improving.

---

[103] http://archive.wired.com/gadgets/miscellaneous/magazine/17-09/ff_good enough?currentPage=all

Compare consumer technology economics and continuous improvements with what's happening in the SAP economy.

Anyone can sign up for Amazon Web Services and get storage at three cents a gigabyte a month. SAP customers pay much more at hosting sites supposedly for much better SLAs.

SAP's website www.sapdatacenter.com is meant to showcase to its customers the changing state of the data center. There is a section on "How a Data Center Works" with plenty of focus on privacy, security, and data protection. Contrast this with Google's website, https://www.google.com/about/datacenters/, and the focus there is much more on the innovations since 2001 — efficient servers, container design, and carbon neutrality, among other initiatives at its data centers. The contrast between the two sites highlights how SAP is just beginning to apply principles that the consumer tech world has been pioneering, then rapidly improving, for over a decade.

Another example comes from the networking world. Eastman Kodak was one of the earliest SAP customers to migrate to a single instance environment. While that helped reduce IT costs and improved business intelligence, the project challenged its global network.

John Parsons, who managed global telecommunications at Kodak, told *NetworkWorld* in 2004:

> "We had to make sure people had good performance from Rochester to the inner cities in China. Increasing data bandwidth [for SAP] was one of the drivers to put out bids for an (Multiprotocol Label Switching) MPLS network."[104]

---

[104] http://www.networkworld.com/article/2324827/lan-wan/full-exposure--how-kodak-converged-its-net.html

I caught up with him — he is now retired.

> "SAP was actually not the biggest data traffic on the network — email, file transfers, other applications were more traffic. But response times for SAP users influenced the service levels we needed for the MPLS network. And we did pretty well negotiating network costs down year on year."

The Kodak MPLS model was replicated by a number of SAP customers, especially as they tried to consolidate instances and set up shared services. Not all of them were as cost-conscious as Parsons at Kodak.

Fast forward a few years. From another article in NetworkWorld:

> "MPLS is typically priced at $300 — $600 per Mbps per month for the copper connectivity typically deployed at all but the very largest enterprise locations, while the monthly price of (consumer) broadband connectivity is now $1.50 — $15 per Mbps per month."[105]

Other benefits of consumerization — attractive economics and continuous improvement — have also eluded many SAP customers.

---

[105] http://www.networkworld.com/article/2222196/cisco-subnet/why-does-mpls-cost-so-much-more-than-internet-connectivity-.html

Externalization of IT

Living in Florida for 25 years, I have a lot of respect for the analytical prowess at the National Hurricane Center. Their track forecast error in the 1980s, 48 hours out, was 225 nautical miles. Today, that comparable error is down to less than 100 nautical miles. The track forecast is used by the NHC to declare hurricane warnings depending on likely time and location of landfall.

After the global recession of 2008–2009 where most companies missed their estimates and forecasts in spectacular fashion, I was even more curious how the NHC keeps continually improving its forecasts. I interviewed the organization for *The New Polymath* and profiled its satellites, ocean-buoy-based sensors, Hurricane Hunters, dropsondes, and other data capture technology in a case study.

As I wrote:

> "To deliver those forecasts, the NHC team takes an invasive approach to collecting a wide variety of external, real-time data. Too much business forecasting today is based on internal and historical data or looks at Google or external sources, such as Bloomberg and Gartner for its primary data."

Since that book came out in 2010, I have been pleased to see companies start to leverage all kinds of external data.

Examples include:

• GE has been harnessing data collected by sensors in its aircraft engines, wind turbines, locomotives, scanners, and other industrial engines.

- A number of B2C companies are mining sentiment and other social network data for customer service and marketing data.
- A number of auto insurers are using telematics data for better risk management.
- Retailers and casinos are starting to leverage facial recognition databases.
- Agencies like LEVA are doing forensic analysis of large video databases.

In a Big Data study, the outsourcing firm TCS reported:

"On the dimension of structure, 55% of leaders' data is unstructured or semi-structured vs. 45% of laggards. And 37% of leaders' data is external vs. internal. For laggards, that percentage is 26%."[106]

With SAP's investments in BusinessObjects, Sybase, and HANA over the last decade, SAP was very well-positioned to lead its customers with analytics of external, unstructured data.

For the most part, though, it has stuck to its ERP comfort zone — internal, structured data. It offers the ERP Suite and Business Warehouse on HANA. It announced Simple Finance at Sapphire Now in 2014 — more internal data. Its major acquisitions — SuccessFactors, Ariba, Concur — are focused on corporate functions. Its social offering — Jam — is focused on work patterns and team collaborations. In Chapter D1 we will see Burberry blend social with point-of-sales data, and John Deere blend sensory and textual data in its HANA

---

[106] http://www.tcs.com/big-data-study/Pages/download-report.aspx

projects, but for the most part, SAP's focus has been internal, structured data.

HANA ecosystem startups like Exa AG, founded by SAP veterans, are also starting to offer solutions that leverage external data. SentryExpress from AlertEnterprise focuses on security intelligence — cyber security; physical access to facilities and assets; and operational technology like SCADA or industrial control systems. At SAP's TechEd event in October 2014, Imaginestics profiled its HANA based image base search engine and AppOrchid showcased a cognitive computing application in the utilities sector.

At the core, though, SAP has been late in leading its customer IT into a world of externalization.

Boardrooming of IT

Karl-Heinz Streibich, CEO of Software AG, the other large German software company, embarked in 2013 on what he called the "search for digital excellence," alluding to Tom Peters' 1982 book, *In Search Of Excellence.*

His driving thought was that digital excellence is reshaping processes in every industry. That will create strategic advantage for some — and disadvantage for others — in spades. And that every boardroom is hungry for guidance as they embark on digital transformation journeys. He invited me to interview several of his customer executives for what became his book, *The Digital Enterprise.*[107]

Talking with over 30 C-level executives at companies around the world (including Allianz, Coca-Cola Enterprises, Daimler

[107] http://www.amazon.com/Digital-Enterprise-Moves-Motives-Leaders-ebook/dp/B00I09E3G0/ref=sr_1_1?s=books&ie=UTF8&qid=1406561491&sr=1-1&keywords=the+digital+enterprise

and Statoil) I found a surprisingly positive sentiment in most of these conversations. The big reason is that their companies have moved past their "systems of record."

To some degree, the digital transformation at these companies is a throwback to the 1960s and 1970s, when we first dreamed of achieving competitive advantage through technology. Remember how Sabre, the airline reservation system, and American Hospital Supply were praised back then for transforming their industries?

Sure, the executives I interviewed are still optimizing their ERP systems (most use SAP) and data centers and moving them to the cloud to manage their costs and risks. But, they didn't dwell on those systems. They're really excited about their "systems of competitive advantage."

Those are what are bringing them differentiation and those are the projects which are getting increasing boardroom attention.

How did so many sophisticated SAP customers get lulled into missing so many major IT trends while continuing to invest so much on that platform? In Section IV, we will look at root causes that have led to such a bloated, failure-prone economy.

In fairness to SAP, many other enterprise vendors like IBM, Oracle, HP, and Microsoft also did not show so well compared to the consumerization, industrialization, etc. at Apple, Google, Amazon, and Facebook.

However, many SaaS vendors did better. Marc Benioff of Salesforce.com admires the pioneers of the consumer web. He has been quoted as saying, "We stand on the shoulders of giants like Jerry Yang [founder of Yahoo!], Pierre Omidyar [of eBay], Jeff Bezos [of Amazon] and Biz Stone [of Twitter]."

In a 2008 debate with Dr. Plattner, Benioff only half-jokingly said:

> "I want to figure out how to get SAP to build on our platform. SAP needs to write its new apps on our platform, and I need to help him do that because there is no way he can figure that out."[108]

You do have to wonder how different SAP's path would have been if the scenario were real.

---

[108] http://www.zdnet.com/blog/btl/a-saasy-sap-vs-salesforce-debate-is-benioff-overestimating-his-platform/8376

Case Studies Group C: Pragmatists

∿→

Chapter C1: Customer Strategy –
Keep Relationship Analytical

"We sat down with our regional SAP team earlier this year, and shared that our Supplier Assessment System (SAS) scores for them had dropped significantly during the course of the last year," says Andre Blumberg, Director — IT at CLP Group, one of the largest power utilities in the Asia-Pacific region.

Headquartered in Hong Kong, CLP operates in a number of Asian markets and in Australia. It is one of SAP's largest adopters of utility industry features including its customized IS-U offering with unique billing and other functionality. CLP serves 2.5 million customers in Hong Kong and has used SAP in a "wall-to-wall" fashion since the early 2000s. In addition to customer care, it uses SAP's plant maintenance for CLP's power plants, and transmission and distribution networks. It also uses Supplier Relationship Management and all back-office functions such as Finance, Procurement, HR, and Payroll.

SAP has long been one of CLP's strategic suppliers. In 2005, the two companies collaborated on SAP's first Mobile Asset Management solution. CLP has won numerous SAP awards for support, highlighting its strong in-house capabilities.

Blumberg has a long history implementing SAP at CLP, first as a consultant in the late 1990s and in a variety of internal roles thereafter. In his current role, his responsibility is to set the company's IT strategy and drive effective implementation.

SAS scores at CLP are a composite of a variety of safety, quality, cost, delivery, and support attributes. They are meant to give a supplier a 360-degree view on how it is performing. It also gives the supplier, in return, an opportunity to score CLP.

Even though SAP is a strategic supplier to many of its customers, it is rare to see the detailed analytical feedback that CLP provides. Says Blumberg:

> "We have an engineering culture at CLP and our operational and other major suppliers get frequent and quantitative feedback.
>
> SAP is a very important supplier, so there was a lot of give and take in that session. We discussed joint projects — like the recent successful rollout of the SAP Business Planning and Consolidation across all of CLP's regional group companies.
>
> But, we also gave very specific feedback. We pointed out several high-severity tickets were open for over 150 days and the most serious one for 275 days. Part of it relates to how SAP sales and support is organized on a global basis."

Even more telling, CLP also shared with the SAP executives the many IT initiatives it had missed out on in the previous couple of years. Mobile enterprise application platform, predictive maintenance, emission management, work clearance, safety document management, and

SAP Nation

advanced analytics opportunities were awarded to other vendors. Fuel and commodity management functionality was custom developed.

Continues Blumberg:

> "We are one of SAP's showcase utilities customers. We are growing significantly across Asia, and we wanted to highlight they can continue to grow nicely with us with regional growth and with newer functionality as our industry evolves. But, SAP needs to keep an edge over alternative solutions. Gone are the days where everything used to be automatically awarded to SAP. We are looking to agile, efficient, and fit-for-purpose solutions, and are not afraid to go best-of-breed or innovate internally."

The analytical bent continued when CLP recently evaluated HANA as a platform to consolidate its sprawl of SAP landscapes. It also wanted to reduce its infrastructure costs compared to the Microsoft SQL Server database environment it currently runs on. The study objective was aligned with SAP's mantra outlined in the 2013 Annual Report:

> "Simplify our products with SAP HANA as the common platform: We will standardize every SAP product on the common SAP HANA platform, and deliver integration across our portfolio. This will drive a simplified suite experience for our customers and partners."

CLP found the total cost of ownership (TCO) would actually be significantly higher with HANA, by a large multiple.

- HANA would require many more servers (especially due to Business Warehouse scale-out requirement).
- HANA licensing and ongoing maintenance is significantly pricier, as SAP positions it as a premium product.
- Significant labor — SAP consulting and CLP's — is required, especially in application regression testing during the landscape migration.
- Additional systems software is required.

Given the unattractive economics and given the significant business risk of the still-evolving HANA product, CLP chose to delay the instance consolidation project.

Blumberg summarizes: "At CLP, we continue to evaluate SAP's solutions, and, of course, take note of their significant investments in HANA. Given our highly efficient as-is platform, however, we could not make a compelling business case. We will consider HANA in other future requirements, but it will have to stack up with a clear benefit on the investment."

Over and over again, CLP has shown a willingness to evaluate new SAP features and innovations, but it analyzes them thoroughly before it adopts them. Conversely, it is always pushing SAP for more innovation and better support, and openly shares its research findings. In many ways, it is a model customer-vendor relationship — one based on fair, fact-based interaction.

Chapter C2: Customer Strategy – Keep Projects Low-Hype

Not too many CEOs take an active role on IT projects. One exception, as we saw in Chapter 1, was how Mike McNamara sponsored the risky Workday project at Flextronics. Daniel Hamburger, CEO of DeVry Education Group, is another executive who takes an active interest in IT projects. I have seen him change in a few minutes the course of stalled technology negotiations. The company reflects his hard-nosed, low-hype approach to technology.

DeVry institutions offer a wide array of programs in business, healthcare, technology, accounting, and finance. Global growth is a significant focus for the company, and, in 2009, DeVry bought a majority stake in a Brazilian higher-education company, Fanor Group. It enrolled 10,000 students in three schools — Fanor, FRB (Faculdade Ruy Barbosa) and Área1, located in two cities, Fortaleza and Salvador in Northeast Brazil.

Daniel Black, Director, IT International and Professional Education, describes the move:

> "We saw significant opportunity for growth, but the manual processes in place when we made the acquisition limited recruiting, customer service, responsiveness, and capacity for growth. Since IT is one of the enablers of such a growth and integration strategy, we put an architecture together around infrastructure and key systems, and called it "IT in a box." We leveraged the Student Information

Systems (SIS) and Salesforce.com systems in the US and then turned our attention to the back office.

The legacy financial systems required hundreds of manual journal entries to close the books and run payroll each period. We decided on SAP, based on its Portuguese-language support, localizations and country support. Our plans were to integrate SAP with the SIS platform and the banks for payroll purposes."

Over six months, the company implemented SAP accounting, finance, and payroll modules with an aggressive budget of $2 million. It was a single instance running at the DeVry Brasil data center in Salvador.

Continues Black:

"We had one major issue during the implementation — actually after the go-live — in the receivables area, which took a while to sort out, but it was more of a data than a software issue. We also had to resist typical user demands to customize the software to mirror old business processes. But, kudos to the local leadership for setting the tone. The President of DeVry Brasil Carlos (Degas) Filgueiras and VP of Operations Geraldo Magela set a deadline and we drove to the date.

We have subsequently greatly expanded SAP to encompass three more acquisitions in three new cities. The subsequent rollouts have been even more successful than the original rollout. We used Neoris as the systems integrator for the first implementation, and then shifted to GFX Consultoria — which is our ongoing partner. We have achieved greater business area leadership as well; they now understand that this isn't an IT project, and have full responsibility for the deliverables along with IT.

With the single instance, all the schools have the benefit of common SAP processes and the robust data model. And, it allows us to handle different HR requirements of six Brazilian states."

Black concludes: "The macro-level results of this one-year investment in this program of IT initiatives was that our Brazil operation grew by 24 percent in revenue, while increasing student satisfaction by 10.6 points, growing our local gross profit by 85.8 percent and operating income by 122 percent in a year."

So, by itself, the implementation was run efficiently, but measured with business metrics, the results look even more impressive.

Chapter C3: Customer Strategy – Rethink the Customer Experience

"We have the best product in the market. Now we have to also make our interface with our customers the easiest," says Jeff Robertson, CIO of DigitalGlobe, a leading provider of earth imagery solutions. Its portfolio includes information products derived from imagery, geospatial analytic software, and expert services that derive insight from the imagery. Figure 1 shows the diversity of DigitalGlobe products in one target market.

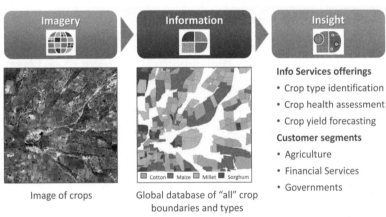

Imagery	Information	Insight

Info Services offerings
- Crop type identification
- Crop health assessment
- Crop yield forecasting

Customer segments
- Agriculture
- Financial Services
- Governments

Image of crops

Global database of "all" crop boundaries and types

Figure 1   Credit: DigitalGlobe

Customers include the U.S. government, international civil authorities (such as airports), location-based service providers, and many in specific industry niches. The acquisition of Spatial Energy makes it a leading provider of geospatial data to the oil and gas industry. The use cases for the company's products keep expanding to include mitigating copper theft for a utility and to assess crop health.

DigitalGlobe's WorldView-1 and 2, GeoEye-1, and the recently launched WorldView-3 Satellites are already market-leading units, with image resolutions under a half meter. With two other satellites, the company collects 1 billion km^2 of quality imagery per year. It covers four times the area, revisits areas three times more and offers 18 times the archive of its nearest competitor.

With a highly competitive product, one of the next phases of investment is focused on improving the customer experience and the consumption model.

Says Bill Begin, Customer Business Solutions Director:

> "We have an ordering process which is ripe for rethinking. Today, some form of manual intervention is needed around orders for 85 percent of our commercial revenues. Ten percent of our orders have to be redone. Fifty percent of our orders need manual pricing. Our product definitions and licensing terms are complex, and pricing is not systemized. There's a lot of babysitting of customer orders."

Adds Aaron Crane, VP of Customer Experience:

> "Training our sales and customer-care agents takes an inordinate amount of time for them to get comfortable with the complexity of our ordering system."

DigitalGlobe had implemented SAP in its early evolution when the U.S. government was its primary customer, and over the years customized it substantially as the revenue mix started to support more diversified commercial sectors, and the creation of many new products and services. The lead-to-order processes have been supplemented with a somewhat stand-alone Salesforce implementation that supports lead and pipeline management, and customer case management for the Customer Care organization. The Salesforce implementation today is primarily internal facing and tactical in nature.

Says Crane:

> "We have an ecosystem of partners and resellers that we are not supporting sufficiently with communications, product information, and easy interactions with DigitalGlobe. Both Salesforce and SAP have plenty of out-of-the-box capability that is not being leveraged yet."

DigitalGlobe brought in a consulting firm earlier this year to see if the SAP customizations could be reversed by moving to more out-of-the-box functionality that has since been delivered by SAP. It also helped evaluate if the new SAP UX of Fiori and Personas could be leveraged to improve the user experience.

The consulting firm recommended a greenfield reimplementation, saying, "Surgical reverse engineering and cleanup while enabling limited new capabilities will be risky and provide a very poor ratio of value versus cost."

Says Robertson:

> "Our product hierarchies have definitely and dra-
> matically evolved, so we need to reflect this in any
> new system. So, I can see some need for some re-
> implementation, but a greenfield implementation is
> intimidating. As a leading-edge, high-tech company,
> our definition of innovation is in next-gen satellites
> and information products, not a large back-office
> re-implementation. That said, a great customer expe-
> rience is strategically important to DigitalGlobe."

So, DigitalGlobe is investing first in "Program EVO"
(Evolution), which is designed to:

- Improve the customer experience and ease of doing
  business.
- Create simple lead-to-order processes.
- Provide better product profitability management
  and reporting.
- Give sales more time back for selling.
- Reduce per transaction costs.
- Accelerate the financial close process.

Says Begin:

> "Much more thought is going into a customer expe-
> rience, product hierarchy definition and product
> pricing analysis before we set a new set of customer
> interactions in stone."

Figure 2 shows some of the design principles being used to rethink the customer experience.

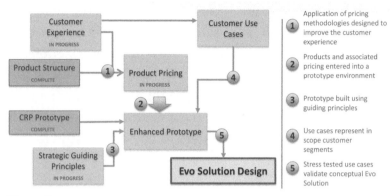

Figure 2   Credit: DigitalGlobe

By starting with the customer first, DigitalGlobe is relooking at all of the core lead-to-order processes. A customer advisory board is helping to define the next generation interactions with the company. In addition, DigitalGlobe is leveraging a more agile, rapid, prototyping approach. Rather than defining the entire end-to-end experience in detail, the team is quickly configuring and defining new experiences. In an effort not to "boil the ocean," the team is also starting with simple-use cases that can be delivered faster and meet a high percentage of the customer need.

Summarizes Robertson:

> "The payback in lower sales and customer care training, less manual cleanup, better reporting, retirement of old customizations, and better integration with Salesforce.com will all help pay for the

SAP reimplementation, but improving our ease of doing business is our ultimate goal. We have taken some time to rethink the customer experience and product hierarchies, and are now looking at how we can iteratively deliver new value in SAP without signing up for another wave of customizations."

It is another example of a pragmatic customer who did not just take SAP's talk of Fiori UX at face value — especially when SAP expected customers to pay a premium for it.

Chapter C4: Customer Strategy – Balance with Open Source and Commodity Technology

I have wanted to interview David Cooper for my earlier books. He arrived as CIO at British Gas from a career in the telecom industry (with experience at BT and Hutchinson 3G among others), and has a mandate to deliver improved IT value. He has undertaken a number of major IT ratio-nalization projects including a data center infrastructure migration. An outsourcing to T-Systems has been replaced with private clouds managed by HP and Fujitsu. That move also involved migrating to open source software like Red Hat and upgrading the Oracle database which was years out of date.

When I heard about Project Slingshot at British Gas, and SAP's role in it, I was eager to profile it in the book. There are so many unique aspects to the project; CRM, industry extensions, the Internet of Things, a systems integrator who delivers on budget — many of which are elusive to find these days in the SAP roadmap where most recent focus has gone to HANA projects.

So, I pursued an interview with Cooper, even delaying the release of the book to include his comments. What I expected was an enthusiastic analysis of the project — instead I got a flattering commentary on the outcomes-based performance by the systems integrator, Cognizant, but also questions about SAP's direction.

British Gas, a subsidiary of the UK energy giant, Centrica, supplies energy and power related services to

11 million homes and 900,000 supply points at small and medium enterprises (such as laundromats), and large industrial and commercial organizations. Like many other progressive utilities around the world, it has been investing in better instrumentation and mobile apps. It has over a million smart meters installed in UK homes, and reports nearly a million-and-a-half downloads of its mobile apps. With this growing customer sophistication, the pressure to improve customer engagement and analytics technology has become even more important.

Project Slingshot delivers a complete business solution for the B2B business, comprising of a CRM system, a Billing system, a digital online solution, a data warehouse, and a complete migration of all the customer data. In turn, this has enabled smart meter reading and customer engagement and analytics for customer service agents. The project driver was to replace over 90 percent of the previous applications estate to provide an improved customer experience. It also seeks to streamline processes by using standard SAP functionality at the core of the solution.

Some of the key benefits expected to be delivered from Slingshot include:

- **Better retention and churn** — A significant improvement in the customer experience and a significantly reduced cost base provide the opportunity to reduce customer prices and result in improved retention and reduced churn.
- **More multiproduct holders** — An integrated customer view where all the products and interactions

are integrated will allow holistic customer services and a digital customer experience.

- **Lower call handling time** — Average handling time should be reduced significantly due to the integrated customer database and the delivery of an enhanced customer experience.
- **Reduced customer service calls** — This should result from a reduction in rebilling activities and in less-fragmented customer interaction.
- **The provisioning of online platform** — This will bring the customer closer to the Business by improving transparency and flexibility. It allows the customers to self-manage their accounts. It also saves considerable costs within the business operations teams.

In the past, Centrica's CRM and billing systems initiatives have been fraught with problems. In 2006, "it had moved its £400m transformation programme in-house, taking back the running of the project from consultancy Accenture."[109] Project Jupiter, as it was called when it was launched in 2002, was focused on the B2C part of the business and aimed to use Siebel software to create a single customer view, and to migrate 17 million domestic energy accounts to one SAP billing platform. System issues and "deteriorating customer service standards caused the defection of approximately a million customers in 2006."[110] The

---

[109] http://www.computing.co.uk/ctg/news/1819523/centrica-takes-it-project
[110] http://www.computerweekly.com/news/2240166485/CIO-interview-David-Cooper-chief-information-officer-British-Gas

previous CIO, Dave Bickerton, was quoted as saying that he had "never seen anything so severe"[111] in his entire career.

Such problems are common with "over customization" of the SAP software. They also reflected SAP's functional immaturity in this industry vertical, when the project was started over a decade ago. Given this track record in the B2C segment, and that a previous B2B implementation had stalled for a number of years, a different approach was called for. Having come from the telecom industry where SAP has not been a significant industry vendor, Cooper evaluated his options for Slingshot with an open mind. He says he decided to stay with SAP because it was the least-costly option providing the project stuck with out-of-the-box functionality.

The systems integration contract was outcome-based with a number of protection mechanisms in place. Cooper says the key was choosing an implementation partner like Cognizant with an appropriate cultural fit and with appropriate governance and senior relationships established between the two companies. Cognizant's fees and payments were tied to specific milestones such as the number of customers migrated. The 18 month implementation has progressed fairly smoothly even though at peak the project had over 350 resources. Nearly 40 percent of the effort exerted in the project focused on testing tasks to prevent the type of problems and the poor press seen in the the previous B2C project (SAP has also had negative publicity with billing issues at another UK utility, Npower).

---

[111] http://www.computerweekly.com/video/Video-British-Gas-CIO-Dave-Bickerton-discusses-massive-IT-transformation

Besides the Red Hat investment, Cooper is a big believer in other open-source software and commodity platforms. From a Big Data perspective, British Gas has a significant commitment to Apache Hadoop. He also likes to use commodity hardware as it is easily swappable and scalable in the form of low-cost servers. The proprietary SAP appliance hardware from its partners around HANA goes against that philosophy. British Gas has evaluated HANA and thinks it is fine for speedier queries. In order to replace its Oracle database, however, HANA would have to match resilience and disaster recovery thresholds needed for heavy transaction processing. When considering the business case for HANA, the years of experience in the team working with the Oracle database and the cost of retraining need to be considered. His conclusion so far is — British Gas does not have a burning performance problem today to justify the risks of moving to HANA as a transaction engine.

SAP does appear to have lagged behind the needs of the Utilities industry. One example Cooper highlights comes from 2012 when "we evaluated a digital interaction platform for our B2B customers. At that point even SAP could not recommend their *own* solution, so instead we developed an internal solution. This year, SAP told us they now have a potential solution, but unfortunately it is a little too late, and I suspect it would cost much more than what the internal solution has."

In many ways, Cooper's comments echo those of Blumberg at CLP profiled in Chapter C1. SAP had a successful run in the Utilities industry, but in the last few years has not led with solutions for the industry. Cooper says he hears a number of his industry executive peers question where their significant maintenance dollars have gone. They would appear to have gone towards HANA as opposed to industry specific applications and business process areas.

Cooper also thinks that the more segmented architecture he saw in the telecoms sector can help speed up organizational change and reduce associated costs. He feels the current SAP application architecture does not support enough segregation of functions. Depending on how the SAP evolves in his industry, he may build some elements of the future architecture "around SAP" where he can leverage the telecoms segmented thinking and open source/cheaper technology solutions.

Root Cause Analysis

CHAPTER 9

SAP's Illusions

∿➤

For any company with decades of history and an active founder, you tend to find plenty of mythology. I have heard from many sources the story of how Dr. Plattner dropped a box of punch cards in a rainy parking lot. He had to dry them for a couple of days, and then sort them. If he had not, the story goes, SAP software could have been lost even before the company took off.

I remember hearing another anecdote about a staff member who went into the stockroom in Walldorf to find a product brochure. (It was the 1990s after all, when we still snail-mailed stuff.) The shelf was empty, even though the online inventory showed a balance. Instead of just accepting the reality that brochures do get misplaced, he dug into the software and found a bug in the code that explained the discrepancy. Next time I heard the story, it got even better — the guilty coder who had written the buggy portion was assigned to the stockroom for a couple of days as punishment.

Both anecdotes left a positive impression on me of the thoroughness of SAP staff. Over the years, however, many of us have fallen into the trap of stereotypes and other illusions about SAP.

Three of them are around simplification, efficiency and the company's "Boy Scout" image.

The Simplification Illusion

At the Sapphire Now conference in Orlando in June 2014, Dr. Plattner introduced the concept of "Simple Finance." He called HANA "minimalist."

McDermott said, with humility:

> "That's why there is a huge chip on my shoulder and on the shoulders of 67,000 employees. We can and we will fight complexity."

The company changed its tagline from "Run like never before" to "Run simple." Prof. Clayton Christensen, widely known for his theories on industry disruptions, joined Dr. Plattner on the stage as if to validate that SAP was truly serious this time about disrupting its past.

You have to compliment SAP for wanting to run lean and simple. As the camera panned away from the keynote stage, however, it showed the exhibit hall where over 200 exhibitors, representing a third of the attendees, were listening intently. They were here to sell a variety of consulting, hosting, upgrade, benchmarking, and other services.

Just two of the bigger exhibitors, Accenture and IBM, are estimated by analysts to have between them 70,000 SAP-focused consultants to feed. Other exhibitors included the major

India-centric outsourcers — TCS, Infosys, Wipro and HCL — with a number of the smaller ones like IGATE and L&T — all of them labor intensive. They included hardware vendors like EMC and HP, and software vendors like Adobe and Microsoft. And, the vendors with booths in Orlando represented just a fraction of the total ecosystem that has mushroomed around SAP over the years.

Simplification could come from automating much of that labor and consolidating/virtualizing much of the infrastructure these partners want to sell, but SAP executives did not discuss that.

Or, they could have focused on reducing the "sprawl" at many SAP customers. Most customers rolled out multiple instances of SAP they customized for subsidiaries in different industries and in locations around the world, or for those inherited after corporate mergers. A 2013 study by HCL showed the average SAP customer (with revenues in excess of $1 billion a year) had five instances.[112] Consolidating those, the study suggested, could drop operating costs per user by 25 percent. Yet only 6 percent of SAP's customers had attempted the consolidation. This should have been a top concern for SAP when it comes to simplification, but Sapphire Now did not address it.

Simplification also needs to stretch to the SAP business model. Joe LaRosa, Vice President of Global Pricing and Commercialization at SAP, was quoted as saying, "Last year, (Treasury) customers could buy seven different applications carrying a variety of license metrics, making for a complicated sale and contract. Now SAP has reduced that application set

---

[112] http://www.computerweekly.com/news/2240183772/HCL-CIO-research-SAP-Hana-prized-for-future-strategy

into two bundles, Treasury Operations and Treasury and Risk, that both use company revenue as a pricing metric."[113]

Adds John Emmitt of Flexera Software, which helps companies with software asset management:

> "SAP license management is very difficult and tedious. SAP requires their customers to assign a named user license type to every user account on every SAP system based on their role, with no hard enforcement to ensure that the correct license type is assigned."[114]

More recently, SAP has allowed trading of older licenses to be applied toward subscriptions on its newer products, but it typically requires increased, multiyear commitments to SAP. That makes the software asset management tasks at customers even more complex.

The Sapphire Now event did not address the license simplification issue, either.

The repeated simplification talk brought snickers from some in the Sapphire Now audience. That's because SAP executives have repeated the mantra for years, probably to atone for a statement attributed to Dr. Plattner in the 1990s:

> "The more complex the better. We Germans would never invent something as simple as Coca-Cola."[115]

---

[113] http://www.pcworld.com/article/2598060/sap-takes-steps-to-simplify-pricing-and-licensing.html?utm_source=dlvr.it&utm_medium=linkedin

[114] http://www.itassetmanagement.net/2014/06/13/sap-licensing-elephant-room/

[115] http://www.amazon.com/SAP-Inside-Secret-Software-Power-ebook/dp/B000QCTOWC/ref=sr_1_1?ie=UTF8&qid=1404354363&sr=8-1&keywords=gerd+meissner

Here is a sampling of the simplification-talk track record:

1998:

Dr. Plattner in a press release:

"Our EnjoySAP initiative is focused on simplifying the software and making it even more intuitive, so that it forms a natural complement to the user's working environment."[116]

Late 1990s:

"There was a team called the Simplification Group, based in Palo Alto and part of SAP Labs. Their mandate was defining methods and documentation to reduce custom configuration in the field, thereby reducing implementation time."[117]

2002:

Dr. Plattner in *InformationWeek*:

"We still need to hide complexities."[118]

2006:

Bullets in an Agassi presentation at Sapphire:

Simplicity at the Core:
- Simplicity in Usage

---

[116] http://www.thefreelibrary.com/SAP+1998+Nine+Months+Sales+Increase+54%25+to+DM+5.9+Billion.-a053098768

[117] http://www.zdnet.com/blog/projectfailures/more-on-simplification-at-sap-sapphire-vienna/107

[118] http://www.informationweek.com/plattner-on-oracle-portals-and-multiple-interfaces/d/d-id/1019552

- Simplicity in Ownership
- Simplicity in Deployment

2009:

Apotheker in *The Local*:

"The ultimate goal is making SAP products simpler and faster."[119]

2011:

McDermott in *Forbes*:

"I've tried to simplify everything. That's the big thing I've done."[120]

2012:

Then-Co-CEO Jim Hagemann Snabe in *Computerworld*:

"We can simplify the pricing…We want a more solution-oriented price list."[121]

2014:

Chief Marketing Officer Jonathan Becher in *USA Today*:

"We want to make the S in SAP stand for "simple"….We haven't gotten there yet."[122]

---

[119] http://www.thelocal.de/20091117/23339
[120] http://www.forbes.com/sites/victoriabarret/2011/01/26/a-chat-with-saps-bill-mcdermott/
[121] http://www.computerworld.com/s/article/9232849/SAP_co_CEO_We_39_re_working_to_fix_software_licensing_pricing_complexity
[122] http://www.usatoday.com/story/tech/2014/08/31/sap-ceo-bill-mcdermott-software-giant-wants-to-simplify-everything/14450519/

Dr. Plattner in a blog post:

"Only with HANA, SAP found a way to really simplify the architecture dramatically."[123]

Tagline in SAP branding campaign launched in October 2014:

"What the world needs now is Simple".

When you talk to SAP executives about its customer base, you typically get a bipolar response. There is humility at having the honor (or burden) of the fact that "SAP systems touch $12 trillion of consumer purchases around the world." And, at times, you get the bragging tone, as in "SAP customers produce 70 percent of the world's chocolate."

What you don't get enough of is comfort that the company is qualified to handle the complexity of this customer base or the ecosystem around it.

In their 2010 book, *SAP Enterprise Support*,[124] two SAP executives, Gerhard Oswald and Uwe Hummel, describe several initiatives and tools SAP has launched over the years to try and tame the complexity. They make simplistic statements like, "In most cases, IT costs can only be reduced quickly by implementing outsourcing and outtasking." The recurring vibe in that book, however, is that of "too little, too late."

ASAP (AcceleratedSAP) was a methodology launched in 1997, after SAP had started selling R/3 years prior. It was a defensive response to growing complaints that SAP implementations were too complex. So, ASAP focused on basic SAP-centric

---

[123] http://www.saphana.com/community/blogs/blog/2014/08/29/the-benefits-of-the-business-suite-on-hana

[124] http://www.amazon.com/SAP-Enterprise-Support-ASAP-Run/dp/1592293492

tasks such as configuration of tables. Its systems integration partners rightly complained that tasks such as data conversion, integration with legacy systems and organizational change management were given short shrift in ASAP.

SAP's next response was to deliver Solution Manager, its automation to control configuration and other tasks in an implementation, and to support other tasks in the ongoing application lifecycle. Again, its focus was product-centric and not focused on the world outside the product that complicates most projects. Besides, it took a while to evolve. An IBM consultant wrote in 2008: "So, no matter what your size and current solution lifecycle management tools, it's time to create an SAP Solution Manager adoption plan — something that the majority of clients I consult with still do not have."[125]

Adds Michael Krigsman:

> "The original vision of Solution Manager was meant to replace AcceleratedSAP. From a technical perspective, replacing ASAP meant that implementation data and documentation could be stored inside Solution Manager, which was tightly coupled to other parts of the SAP system. However, there was also a political dimension, because ASAP was started by the American consulting organization while German developers created Solution Manager.
>
> Rapid Deployment Solutions represent the continued evolution of SAP's attempts to simplify implementations while reducing waste and inefficiency. The RDS program is an evolutionary link in a chain that SAP

---

[125] http://sapinsider.wispubs.com/Assets/Articles/2008/July/Why-SAP-Support-Can-T-Be-An-Afterthought

started during the mid-1990s, with the Simplification Group and then AcceleratedSAP. RDS extends the vision of AcceleratedSAP by offering modular solutions that serve as building blocks for the customer deployment. To a greater or lesser degree, all these approaches use package standard processes to reduce implementation time, cost, and hassle for the customer. Of course, these goals are ideals, but certainly the trajectory is correct.

Unlike Solution Manager, which is an operations management tool, RDS is a set of implementation building blocks. Each RDS package consists of documentation, processes, knowledge, and software tailored to specific corporate functions or processes. Customers can combine multiple RDS packages to create a standardized implementation at lower cost and faster speed than would otherwise be possible."

Starting in 2008, SAP introduced Run SAP as a lifecycle management methodology. It focused on "post-live" activities such as application management and upgrades. An outsourcing partner like Capgemini was finally certified on a global basis as compliant with the methodology in 2012. That was almost two decades after countless SAP customers had already been live on R/3. In the meantime, the industry definition of "continuous improvement" had dramatically evolved.

In a world where Amazon Web Services (AWS) has been reducing cloud storage costs just about every quarter, SAP did not push its hosting partners for similar efficiencies (though more recently it has introduced AWS and Microsoft Azure as options to its customers). While a number of Indian outsourcers were showing Six Sigma and CMM Level 5 certification (which focuses on continuous, metric-driven improvements), SAP application management providers have not been pushed for similar productivity. Even as open source and crowdsourcing communities have shown a different path to software economics, SAP's community, while addressing plenty of first-level queries, has not led to lowered SAP maintenance rates. Surrounded by SaaS customers who are seeing painless and multiple release upgrades a year, SAP's customers are frozen in place petrified by the cost and risk of upgrades in their settings.

SAP executives are clearly not callous about the situation. They just don't appear qualified to tackle the complexity.

Here's a possible explanation: In my book *The New Polymath*, I profiled companies like GE comfortable in blending infotech, cleantech, healthtech, nanotech, and biotech into their solutions. Even in the IT industry, companies like Microsoft have shown the ability to blend a wide range of skills. As it emphasizes its "One Microsoft" message, it highlights ability to blend its strengths around operating systems, high-value apps, hardware/ Nokia, cloud services, machine learning, natural UI, and its comfort in both consumer/enterprise technology markets. HP with EDS and software acquisitions has become a polymath. Oracle, with the acquisition of Sun, diversified its skill set. SaaS companies like Salesforce and Workday learned about hosting and application management services from birth.

SAP, for the most part, has remained an on-premise software company — a "monomath." That hit me when Apotheker took over as CEO at HP. His nine months in the role are widely regarded as disastrous. He tried to rapidly turn HP into a software company with expensive acquisitions and a de-emphasis of its hardware assets (something his successor Meg Whitman is also attempting with an announced split of the company — but after she had been at the helm for four years). On the one hand, you can appreciate the desire to move to much higher-margin software revenues. You could argue, however, that software was the only area Apotheker knew well after a long career at SAP.

Sure, in pockets SAP has hardware and services expertise and it is learning more with its HANA Enterprise Cloud, but for the most part, SAP has not diversified. It has relied heavily on partners for infrastructure and services. It has also not invested in the competency to watch over these partners.

If you reroof your house these days, you could be dealing with Registered Roof Consultant (RRC), Registered Waterproofing Consultant (RWC), Registered Roof Observer (RRO), Registered Exterior Wall Consultant (REWC), and Registered Building Envelope Consultant (RBEC) professionals.

Amazingly, in the SAP ecosystem, even at many, many times the budget of a roofing project, there is little formal certification for consultants. Certification is more common at the firm level, as with the Capgemini mentioned above. SAP has allowed its partners to loosely self-certify individual consultants based on a mere few weeks of classroom training. Most buyers have learned to interview key staff members (often a small fraction of the team) proposed for their projects and to check their references from previous projects. It is a cumbersome process and a regular reminder of how little rigor SAP has put in managing this ecosystem.

Contrast this with the comment in the Prologue about SAP controlling every small detail of their partner's participation at Sapphire Now from signage, to dress code, to professional behavior.

It's tough to simplify when you have little control over your ecosystem.

The Efficiency Illusion

German efficiency is an overused cliché, but most German companies including SAP benefit from the perception. SAP's R&D performance, however, smacks of inefficiency. In data center circles, there is a metric called PUE — Power Usage Effectiveness — which measures the power that comes into the data center and that which is available for computational tasks versus cooling, lighting, and securing the site. If there were a similar metric for labor productivity in R&D shops, SAP would show as being extremely inefficient.

In 2013, SAP reported over $3 billion in R&D expenditure. That was almost *four times* larger than the combined R&D spend of the seven leading SaaS providers — Salesforce, Workday, NetSuite, RightNow, ServiceNow, SuccessFactors and Taleo. (RightNow and Taleo are now part of Oracle, and SuccessFactors part of SAP.)

In the late 1990s, as a Gartner analyst, I made several trips to Walldorf. We would get to meet with grassroots product developers and designers. I would walk away in awe at their command of English, and even more in awe of their understanding of regulatory and other business trends they were codifying into SAP products. Between 1997 and 1999, the R&D employee count had doubled, and you could see signs of bloat. Since then, SAP's R&D headcount has nearly quadrupled, to nearly eighteen thousand.

Stories abound of how much R&D effort is wasted in bureaucracy. Recruiting takes months and is constantly being slowed and sped up again by budget freezes and reallocations. Internal charge-backs are a source of common friction, especially when services staff is used. In an organization where a project with less than 100 staff is not considered strategic, there is considerable politicking for budgets. Dealing with the Works Council in Germany also adds a layer of scrutiny. It is a unique challenge in a nonunionized software industry, and something SAP had to adjust to, after the Council was founded in 2006.

There is a constant tension between the thoroughness Walldorf expects when supporting products across multiple countries and heterogeneous environments, compared with the light, rapid development focus found in development centers in Israel, Palo Alto, and elsewhere.

John Wookey was hired by SAP as Executive VP of Development in 2008. He led SAP's on-demand efforts for three years. He had come from Oracle, and understood the technology challenges of moving to the cloud. He says the business-model change challenge is even more significant. To prepare, he made sure to read the book *Behind the Cloud* by Salesforce.com CEO Marc Benioff on his first trip from California to Walldorf:

> "Cloud Computing has changed the technology consumption model. Customers start small in a specific department or business unit. And, the business has to be won every year — if the software is not being used, they are not going to grow the account. Customers provide instant feedback and expect much faster turnaround. Now at Salesforce.com, I can see how our CEO Benioff constantly listens to customers — via email and social networks — and expects our teams to jump and react to customer issues.
>
> On-premise vendors do not get customer feedback or pressure for new feature requests for years. Software often sits on the customer shelf for a while and the projects tend to be longer. So, they end up having to support

many versions of a product till customers catch up to them. Maintaining multiple releases takes a lot of energy."

Wookey is talking about one product like Business Suite. SAP also has Business One, BusinessByDesign, and many other product code bases to keep up with, including some new ones like Sales On-Demand he helped launch.

The Wall Street Journal in Germany[126] reported that Dr. Plattner's comments in 2013 about Walldorf's need to become more productive were seen as demoralizing and a "slap in the face of those employees."

In fact, Dr. Plattner could have made his comments many years earlier when Ray Wang, a respected industry analyst, outlined "five SAP failures in five years" in a presentation to the U.K. and Ireland SAP User Group:[127]

- NetWeaver
- Duet
- Business ByDesign
- Solution Manager
- Enterprise Support

As we mentioned in Chapter 2, the platform versus application focus has caused some of the distraction. The fragmentation of the R&D function, with sizable contingents in Palo Alto, India, Israel, and elsewhere, has clearly been an issue. Global delivery of software is always tricky, but methodologies developed by Indian outsourcing firms in particular, improved telepresence

---

[126] http://www.wsj.de/article/SB10001424052702304906704579114891072093428.html

[127] http://news.idg.no/cw/art.cfm?id=2BF6B6BD-1A64-6A71-CE101F2DC440BAD7

and increasingly well-traveled software developers have all made it easier. Not so at SAP.

Stories are common of young programmers hired in Bangalore who then spend months in Walldorf to "shadow" more mature staff. That breaks the 20/80 onshore/offshore ratio that predicates the economics of the global delivery model. When benchmarked against leading software development shops that use Agile methods, global delivery models, communities, and other tools effectively, SAP's R&D does not reflect efficiency.

The "Boy Scout" Illusion

Jack Welch, former CEO of GE, was reported to have said, "I had breakfast with a competitor, lunch with a supplier, and dinner with a customer. And, it was the same person."

Welch was talking about the reality of "co-opetition" and "frenemies." By his definition, Dr. Plattner and Ellison of Oracle should also be meeting for lattes and gin and tonics several times a day. To call the relationship tightly woven would be an understatement — there is plenty of interlocked revenues alongside plenty of bad blood between the two companies.

In 2010, Ellison had mocked SAP's talk of in-memory databases: "Yes, SAP is going after this. We [Oracle] missed it and IBM missed it, and it's good that SAP CEO Hasso [Plattner] and his five guys in a garage got it. It's wacko."[128] A few years later, at its annual OpenWorld event, Oracle announced an in-memory switch in its database technology. Co-CEO Hurd told media to "Forget them [SAP]." Sikka, picking on the fact that the feature was still in "pre-Beta," responded, "please come back and talk

---

[128] http://www.channelinsider.com/c/a/Spotlight/Oracles-Larry-Being-Larry-Ellison-313073/

to us when it is available."[129]. And, that is the polite version of their talk about each other.

An SAP salesperson once told me, "If Oracle had sent its sales reps to charm school, the story of enterprise software would be very different today." He proceeded to tell me how SAP salespeople were easy to get along with, how customers tensed up when talking about Oracle, how Oracle was aggressive with its software audits, and on and on.

I have heard similar comparisons to Oracle from countless SAP folks. They are almost coached to use that as a defense mechanism to counter any questions about their own behavior. Ask them about their R&D productivity and they will turn it into a discussion of the slow progress on Oracle's Fusion cloud applications.

It starts at the top.

In 1998, Dr. Plattner told a few Gartner analysts about the time he mooned Ellison's sailing tender because it refused to help his boat in spite of a distress call about an injury. I remember all of us chuckling — any time a grown man talks about "dropping trou," you do so instinctively. However, Dr. Plattner was not trying to amuse us. That was his subtle way of telling us not to trust Ellison or Oracle. A few years later, he told a few analysts that Scott McNealy of Sun Microsystems had called him first before it agreed to sell to Oracle.

It was his "we are cleaner" tone. He made his point well. It was Captain Ahab from the Herman Melville classic talking about the "sea monster," the whale named Moby Dick. Ahab

---

[129] http://www.computerworld.com/s/article/9242610/SAP_HANA_isn_t_even_comparable_to_Oracle_s_in_memory_technology_Hurd_says

held it responsible for the destruction of his ship and the amputation of his leg.

Except that it morphed from "we are cleaner" to "we are whinier" as the mooning legend grew over the years and Dr. Plattner told *Sailing World*:[130]

> "Then it quieted off and then Larry Ellison brought it up in interviews again, two times. In German, when he came to Germany, he made snide comments — one comment was my ass looked so awful that he feared about the mental health of his crew when he sailed by. Another story was that I was so pissed when we lost the race and the World Championships in Sardinia in 1997 in Italy that I came by his boat and mooned him. The day when this should've happened, he had already left, because he didn't race the last race because he was not there."

What started off as a moral victory for Dr. Plattner had deteriorated into a series of irate clarifications and even questioning by many whether the incident ever happened (apparently a videotape still exists). The fact that Ellison's teams have twice won the America's Cup only adds salt to the wound. Defensively, SAP fans point out Ellison missed his keynote at Oracle OpenWorld in 2013 and prioritized sailing over his customers.

The "we are cleaner" talk fades when you consider the SAP application economy is many times larger than the Oracle application economy. Oracle is no angel, but it competes with many of its partners, which in turn have built much bigger business

---

[130] http://www.sailingworld.com/racing/i-never-ever-mooned-larry-ellison

units around SAP (and, as a result, become the largest portion of the customer cost, as we will discuss in the next chapter). Oracle is a small part of the economic landscape around SAP. Its database is a common element in many SAP customers. But, its costs are dwarfed by those of IBM's and HP's services, hosting, hardware, and software charges — as well as IT and business process outsourcing charges, MPLS and other WAN charges. Besides, Oracle did not cause all the spectacular failures and overruns we described in Chapter 7.

And, SAP's own business practices are in many ways just as onerous. Here are a few examples:

Indirect access:
David Blake, analyst at Upper Edge, describes the issue:

> "Indirect access violations occur when an SAP licensee breaches SAP's definition of appropriate "use." ....Through our customers, we have observed SAP use indirect access violations as an excuse for predatorily squeezing fees from their customers, and worse, seizing the opportunity to reduce flexibility and promote an anticompetitive environment." [131]

"Engine" pricing in addition to user pricing:
As it introduced a growing number of industry features in the 1990s, SAP started to bundle them as separate "engines" and licensed them to customers on top of the user-based pricing they

[131] http://www.upperedge.com/2012/05/sap-and-indirect-access-is-sap-taking-advantage-of-its-customers/

had already paid. These engines were priced by metrics such as number of customer meters in the utility industry. Customers grumbled because the engine pricing tiers often appeared arbitrary and there usually was little downward protection to customers when their business declined.

Then SAP started applying the engine concept to many other areas. A glaring example appeared when SAP priced what appeared to be a fix — an accelerator — to documented sluggishness in its Business Warehouse product (also termed BI).

As a user complained:

> "I have some trouble understanding the business logic of selling a tool that fixes one of the major flaws of BI at such a steep price… In a sense we're getting an incomplete product and then are told that if we want it to be efficient, we need to cash out even more…"[132]

Of course, when SAP acquired BusinessObjects, many customers were asked to pay for those business intelligence tools as a front end to BW, and more recently with SAP emphasizing HANA there has been more a move to add that to customer portfolios. As SAP's Steve Lucas says not too subtly in his blog title, "Does SAP HANA Replace BW? (Hint: No.)."[133]

More than a few customers resent being asked to pay for licenses three or four times when their annual maintenance payments were supposed to cover ongoing enhancements.

---

[132] http://scn.sap.com/thread/716197

[133] http://www.saphana.com/community/blogs/blog/2012/06/13/does-sap-hana-replace-bw-hint-no

Maintenance increases:

In a particularly unpopular move, deep in the middle of the global recession, SAP attempted to raise maintenance rates from 17 percent to 22 percent in 2008. It deflected the question of why a 30 percent increase during the deep recession behind various "customer payback" and "we are catching up for years of not raising rates" justifications, but most customers guessed it was to get parity with Oracle, which charges 22 percent. Never mind that SAP had bigger license deals and engine additions.

SAP eventually backed off (after a customer uprising and related firing of Apotheker) — or, more accurately, postponed that increase.

Another recent customer uprising came around its new Fiori user experience (which SAP calls "personalized, responsive and simple user experience across devices and deployment options.").

The UX was long overdue, as we described in Chapter 8, and yet SAP tried to charge for that and ran into another buzz saw. Andreas Oczko, vice chairman of DSAG (German-speaking SAP User Group), which has 49,000 members in Germany, Austria, and Switzerland, was quoted as saying "DSAG's position is clear. We say [Fiori] must be part of standard maintenance."[134]

SAP also backed off that price increase, but the reality is more nuanced.

Chris Kanaracus of *IDG News* reported:

> "Fiori has significant dependencies on Hana, requiring customers to make that additional, and potentially substantial, investment."[135]

---

[134] http://news.idg.no/cw/art.cfm?id=FFA0CC8F-BD51-E422-EC9B547652D23863
[135] http://www.pcworld.idg.com.au/article/547038/sap_after_sapphire_look_ahead/

Doug Henschen at *InformationWeek* reported:

> "It turns out Fiori apps and interfaces aren't that easy to
> install, so SAP's original Fiori strategy was shortsighted,
> according to enterprise software consultant Frank Scavo
> of Strativa. SAP stands to make more money by giving
> these apps and interfaces away and recovering the cost
> through consulting and implementation service fees."[136]

Engines, dependencies, price increases — most customers
have procurement and legal resources to protect themselves,
but SAP seems to be the only party to believe its continued
illusion about being "cleaner."

SAP acquired TomorrowNow, which offered third-party
maintenance to J.D. Edwards and Siebel customers at half the
rate Oracle charged. (Oracle had acquired both the entities.)
While SAP had hoped to convince TomorrowNow customers
to move to its software, it appeared unconcerned about the
optics. It was offering Oracle customers cut-rate support, but
not offering something similar to its own customers. It likely
believed its products were more complex or its customers were
too content to want something similar.

The TomorrowNow unit was shut down in 2008 by SAP after
a lawsuit by Oracle over allegations of illegal downloads and
copyright infringements. The matter continues to be litigated.
In the meantime, Rimini Street (as we described in Chapter A2)
has moved into the vacuum — and claims to provide third-party
maintenance to over 100 SAP customers.

---

[136] http://www.informationweek.com/software/enterprise-applications/saps-
mcdermott-say-goodbye-to-too-complex/d/d-id/1269412

While the "We are cleaner" defense works with some customers (who do tense up when you talk to them about Oracle), you also get the sense Oracle has worked its way under SAP's skin. It's Melville's Captain Ahab and Moby Dick all over again. While the whale was fearsome, many readers would say Ahab was actually the villain with his relentless obsession and reckless use of his ship and crew in chasing the whale.

CHAPTER 10

SAP Partner Collusions

↯

"A Michelangelo should not charge Sistine Chapel rates for painting a farmer's barn," once ruled a U.S. Circuit Court of Appeals. Although the ruling in that case related to lawyer's fees, it might well have related to SAP partners.

In Chapter 7, we presented a long list of SAP failures and write-offs. In most cases, it was not the software that was at fault. It would appear the software was often overhyped and poorly implemented. The track record of many of SAP's partners has been concerning for a while and yet SAP persists with them.

In 1990, (the late) Dr. Michael Hammer wrote his seminal article "Reengineering Work: Don't Automate, Obliterate" in the *Harvard Business Review*[137] in which he described how Mazda needed only five accounts payable employees while Ford needed 400. He called for a rethink of business processes from a customer point of view. If a customer would not pay for

---

[137] http://hbr.org/1990/07/reengineering-work-dont-automate-obliterate/ar/1

a process or a task, consider eliminating it. It was a powerful concept — indeed, his speaking bio used to say, "Dr. Michael Hammer has changed forever how businesses do business." The article and his later books became the foundation for a wave of process reengineering projects across the corporate world.

A few years later, he was keynoting a SAP conference. With his booming voice and entertaining style, he assured the audience the software met his vision of process reengineering nirvana. He said it forced companies to rethink the way they do business — and so it was natural the change was resisted by many employees and managers.

I met him at an event Deloitte and his firm Hammer and Co. were hosting where SAP was being presented as "reengineering in a box." I wanted to ask him if he had seen benchmarks of the cost of processing invoices at SAP sites compared to the powerful Mazda example he had cited in his article. I wanted to ask if he had spoken to customers about their suppliers who were implementing SAP, and if they were happy to pay for the SAP investments.

Instead, we talked about how Gartner research was showing SAP with inconsistent functionality across several process streams in the enterprise — in manufacturing execution, in product design, in the warehouse, and in finite capacity planning. When you left the manufacturing sector, SAP's coverage was even less impressive, and it was risky to suggest companies use it as a reliable reengineering platform. His response was that the software was "good enough," and that the major challenges were organizational resistance to change.

That "good enough" message was communicated by Deloitte and many other consulting firms to clients. The legend grew of this collection of "best practices" that came with the software.

But, when they came to present to me at Gartner, I would ask them what I missed asking Dr. Hammer: did they mean "best practice" based on empirical data, say comparing cost of processing invoices or journals at SAP sites compared to world-class benchmarks like at Mazda? Few knew.

In his book *The Real Story behind ERP: Separating Fiction from Reality*, Shaun Snapp asks the following questions:

"1. Who decided something is a best practice?

2. Was the best practice put to a vote?

3. Was it deemed to be so by an expert?

4. If item three is affirmative, where is the research to support the notion that a way of doing something is a best practice?

What a person who asks these types of inflammatory questions (yes, simply asking for evidence is considered inflammatory with regard to best practices) will find is that in the vast majority of cases, the practice is a "best practice" simply because the proposer declares it to be so. There is no research and no explanation as to how it was determined to be a best practice. Furthermore, if two different ERP systems — both of which are based upon best practices — diverge in some way on how to do things, which one is actually performing the best practice?"

Brad Callahan is a Partner at Fortium Partners. Prior to Fortium, he led Services for Microsoft in the Americas. Before that he was with Lawson Software and was a Partner with Ernst & Young (later Capgemini).

Callahan recalls the ERP world in the 1990s:

> "ERP and Michael Hammer's "reengineering" became the new Holy Grail. They were probably the two biggest enterprise fads in our lifetime. Every CEO read about them on the airplane and wanted some, but his/her (who am I kidding? In 1993 it was his) knowledge of what to do and how to get it was limited. Certainly their internal MIS departments were not capable. The term CIO was not yet commonly used, and data processing managers managed the corporate technology world.
>
> Whether lucky or smart, SAP also realized that the real risk in ERP was in the implementation and integration. If they could move that risk to the Big Eight and specialty firms, they could maintain their pure valuation and stay above the fray of lawsuits, customer dissatisfaction, and day-to-day implementation/integration nuisances."

Even better, customers paid for this insurance!

In the next phase, many of these partners started to convince nonmanufacturing industries SAP was their "enterprise-wide" solution. In some cases, as with Accenture with utilities, Price Waterhouse with upstream oil and gas functionality and Siemens-Nixdorf (later Wincor Nixdorf) with retail, the partner's industry knowledge helped SAP develop deeper vertical functionality. Others like Deloitte developed IndustryPrint, a modeling framework customized with processes for multiple industries.

Stacking the Deck

By now, consultants were not even trying to pretend they were unbiased. They had three, five, even ten times SAP-dedicated resources compared to their Oracle, PeopleSoft, J.D. Edwards, Baan, or other practices. Even when they promised to do independent software evaluations or gap analysis, unless they were explicitly banned from the implementation, the SAP lean was noticeable.

During the U.S. Justice Department action against Oracle in 2003, a document disclosed:

> "Accenture will recommend SAP to the financial service industries for both vertical applications and ERP applications. In return, SAP will recommend Accenture to FSI for ALL enterprise software implementations. It is quite a wholesale endorsement."[138]

Over the next two decades, many of their SAP practices would grow dramatically. A review of Gartner and other analyst archives shows from 1995 to 2013, Accenture went from a SAP headcount of 2,500 to 38,000. Capgemini went from 1,000 to 13,500. IBM (adjusted for PwC Consulting, which it acquired in 2002) grew from 3,500 to 32,000. Indian vendors went from zero to over 10,000 each for TCS, Infosys, and Wipro.

Just as SAP's maintenance revenues grew much larger than its license revenues, the partners made much more from the "long tail" — multiyear application management contracts — than from the initial implementations.

---

[138] http://www.justice.gov/atr/cases/f204100/204148.htm

A firm like Accenture has long been known for its "school buses" of young consultants. They prefer to be compared to U.S. Marines. In the SAP world, where partners are allowed their own self-certification models, many other firms used the pyramid model with a number of younger staff.

Several SAP Mentors conducted a survey and issued a report in 2010 which discussed the loose state of certification. Some of their comments:

- "Until the recent rollout of the three tiered certification levels (Associate, Professional, and the as yet unavailable Master level), SAP certification has remained largely unchanged over many years. Given that SAP is changing its emphasis away from pure code construction to business process, now is a good time to assess the value that SAP Certification delivers and ensure that Certification validates the skills that SAP customers truly need."
- "The SAP ecosystem is outside of SAP Education's direct control, adding to the challenge of enforcing quality and certification standards. Some SIs offer good quality education that turns out people well suited to implementation. Many do not."
- "Publicly aired implementation failures imply at least a level of technical incompetence that should never be part of the implementation equation. That in turn casts doubt on the value of SAP Certification as currently articulated."[139]

An executive who has dealt with SAP consultants both as a client and as a colleague describes her experience as she went

---

[139] http://www.jonerp.com/pdf/sap_certification_from_cert5.pdf

from being an SAP customer to an SAP consultant and back to an SAP customer role:

"Being at one SAP installation a long time was a disadvantage when I was made redundant; during the downturn, hiring managers would have extremely specific and rigid requirements, and every SAP shop has a slightly different SAP landscape. Typical feedback from Recruiter: "They thought you were great, but the other candidate had experience in the latest release of (SAP solution they were about to implement/ upgrade).

One of my ASUG colleagues recommended me for the consulting job. The upside to working at the consultancy is that they are known for hiring smart, and everyone I met was smart and hard-working. The downside was that I was put on my first project before I had any training on their proprietary tools and techniques, which would have been hugely helpful.

There were very few experienced hires; you could easily tell the consultants who never worked in support... Clients seemed to appreciate having someone like me who could relate to their support challenges.

I did not present myself with the smooth-talking bravado of a Big Four consultant, so that was a drawback to my credibility. The young consultants were pretty good at stalling or deferring questions to the engagement manager. The challenge for me was, there were later projects where I was the only consultant onsite, and I probably wasn't as adept at bluffing and stalling.

Back in the corporate world, I worked on a long delayed project. Certainly some of the delays could be attributed to bugginess of the Support Pack we were implementing, and we could have used competent consultants on hand to ride herd on SAP."

Clients constantly complain about inexperienced consultants, but in most evaluations I have seen, they tend to focus on "key staff" like the project manager, and some functional consultants. They tolerate the armies of junior consultants and pay large fees for those staff.

In turn, most SAP partners brag about the hundreds of projects they have worked on, but when you ask for economies of repetition and scale, they have all kinds of excuses.

Innovation Passes Partners By

Few of the SAP partners tried a different delivery model till offshore firms like TCS brought a global delivery model. And, as we discussed in Chapter 6, that model had its own issues in the SAP economy. In the meantime, as we show in the sidebar later in the chapter, other tech markets were starting to benefit from cloud service delivery, crowdsourcing, and other innovations.

Software modeling experts like Capers Jones have been saying for years that specification and configuration make up less than a quarter of most project efforts. Cleansing and converting data, integrating with other applications, developing new reports, training, documentation, testing — unit, stress, acceptance, certification — this is what makes up most project efforts. SAP partners still try to staff projects with too many generalists (and junior ones at that), and expect them to be good at a variety of testing, training, product, and other skills.

This shows up in titles like manager or director and in promotions, compensation, and billing rates based on tenure. They should have more titles like integration specialist and testing manager. Next, you could easily set up remote "factories" organized by project phases — specialist coding, testing, documentation, training, and conversion resources proficient in their specific skill sets and intimately familiar with specialized tools such as the CA testing or Informatica's integration tools.

Western firms could have also shifted their talent base to lower cost models. In many ways, they had pioneered the global delivery model. Accenture (back then, part of the Arthur Andersen family) had helped SGV, an affiliated firm in the Philippines, set up a software development center as far back as 1986. That could easily have been leveraged and expanded as a link in Accenture's global delivery supply chain. The Philippines talent base was used primarily to service its Asian clients. EDS set up a subsidiary in India in 1996, and did business with local branches of Western companies, such as GM. It eventually bought a majority stake in MphasiS, an Indian outsourcer, in 2006.

Most Western firms grudgingly used the global delivery model for the SAP market, and then only as response to the Indian firms. Many have since diversified their talent geographically, with mixed results.

Robert Cringely thinks globalization has had a very negative impact on IBM. He quotes IBM employees in his recent book:

> "The whole idea that people in different time zones, all over the world can deliver on an engagement in Chicago is absurd."

And:

> "Having eliminated what did not seem necessary, the brains and strategy behind the revenue are now gone, leaving only 'do now' perform people who cannot sell. Sales reps have no technical resources and so they cannot be effective."[140]

Consultant travel, related expenses, and productivity impacts have been another facet of the SAP economy. Systems integrator (SI) proposals often estimate travel expenses at 20 percent to 25 percent of the already high fees — just the travel costs on a project can exceed the cost of the SAP software!

The SAP customer-turned-consultant above says:

> "The consulting lifestyle seemed tailor-made for millennials. Of course, week after week at the trendy hotel for months on end would be lovely when you are young and single and live in a condo shared with three other guys, or even still live at home and your mom can do your laundry for you while you are out of town.
>
> The travel took a toll on my health, and upon recommendation from my chiropractor to improve my lifestyle, I decided to make a change at the earliest opportunity."

Besides the financial impact, the traveling consultants' "work week" — what in the trade is called 3/4/5 as in three

[140] http://www.amazon.com/Decline-Fall-IBM-American-Icon-ebook/dp/B00KRHWZ22/ref=sr_1_1?ie=UTF8&qid=1405344823&sr=8-1&keywords=cringely

nights away from home, four days on the client site and five days of work — had significant project impacts. Many consultants arrived late on Monday morning and left on Thursday afternoon (if you have wondered why upgrades on Thursday evening flights are especially tough to come by, it has been a casualty of this consultant economy). So, they tended to work very long days on Tuesdays and Wednesdays, forcing client staff to adjust their schedule. Fridays back at home, few consultants worked on the client SAP project — they ran errands or did training or worked on proposals. In turn, customer staff often asked for a mirrored schedule — to run chores or work on other projects on Fridays.

What unions have tried unsuccessfully to negotiate, the SAP economy delivered — a four-day work week!

I have advised several clients to cap expenses at five percent of fees — not so the consultants have to stay at cheap hotels or fly backbreaking air routes, but more to encourage their consulting firms to staff locally for many of the junior roles. On the 3–4–5 schedule, I have advised clients to stagger the travel so day five is Monday for some and Friday for other consultants so the project as a whole could continue with a fuller week.

Discouragingly, even as telepresence and collaboration technologies have matured, the consultant travel has not abated.

Karen Watts is passionate about streamlining inefficient processes. She's ambitious enough with her new startup. Apparency, to tackle even the hornet's nest of convoluted processes and endless forms at the Veterans Administration. More mainstream, she founded Corefino to offer business process outsourcing (BPO) to financial executives.

Having been a CFO herself, she says:

> "Most CFOs come up through the financial department
> rank and file as accountants, financial analysts, etc. and
> are used to collaborating and being surrounded by "the
> pack." As we work our way up the management chain
> to controller and CFO, we draw comfort from cube after
> cube of head-down workers tirelessly crunching num-
> bers, rechecking compliances and performing "routine
> financials.""

She has seen most BPO vendors basically rebadge "the
pack" at SAP customers when they should have attempted to
run the processes around more efficient SaaS products like
NetSuite or Corefino.

> "With BPO, you should be focused on end results, not the
> platform it runs on. Cost per invoice or time per journal
> entry should be far more important metrics. I have had
> conversations with most of the outsourcers and all of
> them talk about Six Sigma and other efficiency goalposts,
> but it is so easy for the customer and for the outsourcer
> to not attempt to move the platform. It's been a missed
> opportunity for BPO providers to not have moved away
> from a rigid and expensive platform."

In 2006, I worked with a company that was being spun out
into a joint venture. The "life event" allowed us to revisit many
of the technology contracts. I convinced the CIO to combine
the previously separate SAP hosting and application-managed
services contracts and rebid them as one on a utility — pay

per user — model. I called it software-as-a-customized-service (SaaCS).

Even though many SaaS vendors had by then bundled license/apps management/hosting/upgrades in one contract, the SAP outsourcing market was not well-positioned to even combine just two of those elements — application management and hosting. The bidders brought in subcontractors (or not); you could see separate element proposals had been patched together. And, no one wanted to propose a variable cost, utility model.

The client was happy the winning bid came in 65 percent lower than the total of the two previous contracts. I was disappointed that it was still a fixed annual cost. There were many elements I would have liked to have seen. No CapEx — just like in our utility purchases. Fractional resource and shared infrastructure — with other clients in a multitenant-like setting. Flex capacity — for smaller work orders and upgrades and other projects.

Clearly, SAP partners were not ready for the utility computing model in 2006. Heck, Nicholas Carr would not write his best seller on the topic, *The Big Switch,* till 2009. As I researched this book, I asked several outsourcers if they offered the model today. More are starting to offer managed clouds, business process, and HANA-as-a-service, but there are still only a few customer references for such offerings.

Surprisingly, SAP did little to manage its partners through all these warnings. The common defense was it was the same around Oracle, Microsoft, and other ERP projects. As we see in the sidebar, other technology vendors were seeing innovations in their services ecosystem. I have derisively called SAP's its "egosystem":

"I often get the sense SAP likes to brag about its ecosystem. Numbers fly — we have 1,200 SI partners, more than

1,000,000+ SDN members, etc. Justifications abound —
"our partners deserve their premiums because after all
our stuff is complex, demand is always greater than
supply." etc., etc. You want bragging rights, you get an
egosystem."[141]

An example comes from its community — the SCN (previously SDN).

Agassi gushed in 2006:

"500,000 visitors per month. Aggregation of knowledge
that is second to none. slashdot for SAP. SIs in India are
hiring them 500 people at a time and saying for their first
three months they are supposed to participate in SDN.
Aggregation and knowledge and self-categorization has
created an environment where you know the guy who
is giving advice may have a point ranking that shows
they don't have a life, but a lot of knowledge. We are
contributing perhaps 20% of the content. Average time
from Q&A is less than 30 minutes, I wish our support
channels were that effective."[142]

Eight years later, SAP likes to share metrics like 2.5 million
unique SCN visitors a month and 263,000 contributors a month.

If first-level queries are getting resolved in the community,
should not SAP shave its maintenance 2 percent to 3 percent a
year, and should not application management providers show
reduction in SAP tickets?

[141] http://dealarchitect.typepad.com/deal_architect/2007/12/saps-egosystem.html
[142] http://dealarchitect.typepad.com/deal_architect/2006/05/saps_sdn_wheres.html

I was in a meeting with Apotheker when he commented, "I find it shocking people are walking around talking to customers and have no experience on [SAP]....It's annoying, but that's a fact. Let's start by certifying people."[143] This was in 2009, when SAP should have started certifying in 1995 or earlier, but the industry reaction to his honest comment was shock that he would even acknowledge the issue.

I was in a meeting with Howlett in 2011 when he asked McDermott, then Co-CEO, if after acquiring Sybase with its mobile technology SAP would consider moving to an Apple AppStore model. As he blogged, "It would need to largely ditch its addiction to $1+ million deals in favor of business apps priced at $2–5 per user per month."[144] I followed up asking McDermott if he would consider moving his partner focus to mom-and-pop shops similar to those Apple and Google have done well with. McDermott's response, "We will continue to do fine with our current partners."

SAP has tried the smaller partner model around HANA — an ecosystem of start-ups. While it has ramped up the membership nicely — 1,500 startups in over 55 countries — the customer penetration has been slow. It will be tempting to go back to the older model that has worked well for SAP, but not always for customers, for the previous two decades.

Other elements of the SAP partner ecosystem have been just as inefficient. In Chapter 8 we saw how SAP hosting has lagged design, cooling, and other innovations in the data center industry.

---

[143] http://www.zdnet.com/blog/btl/saps-apotheker-takes-on-shoddy-consultants-certifications/12267
[144] http://www.zdnet.com/blog/howlett/can-sap-see-the-win-win-win-pot-of-gold-that-is-sybase/3138

SAP competitor Infor has, in contrast, aggressively aligned with infrastructure from Amazon for its cloud offerings. In the words of its CEO, Phillips, "Friends don't let friends invest in data centers."

Another example comes from the telecom world. In Chapter 8, we described how MPLS costs are expensive in centralized SAP sites. As SAP connects customers to its new HANA Enterprise Cloud, the hookup is expensive. Amazon Web Services with its Direct Connect and Microsoft Azure with AT&T's NetBond have tried to combat the MPLS and WAN costs that carriers charge individual customers. SAP customers would benefit from similar options.

Our model in Chapter 3 shows the economy at an annual run rate of $204 billion. SAP's own charges to customers are a tenth of that amount. The rest is outsourcer/offshore firm fees, consultant travel expenses, customer staff, hosting/other infrastructure, MPLS/WAN charges and other software — many of them for inefficient offerings.

The inefficiencies also apply to non-SAP IT markets, but in many ways the SAP economy has been a magnet for them. While SAP itself is only partially responsible for the bloat, it is the SAP brand which suffers in the end.

How has a company that sells optimization software to sophisticated customers and its partners who claim expertise in such algorithms not explored different models for their own operations, especially given all the project overruns and the lawsuits? Why, after two decades and thousands of projects, are productivity and predictability so elusive in this market? On the infrastructure side, where are the quarter-to-quarter improvements that Amazon has shown it can deliver?

Other Technology Labor Markets

With labor costs making up 70 percent of the SAP economy as our model shows in Chapter 3, it is useful to look at innovations happening in the IT outsourcing world that have (mostly) eluded SAP customers.

The Appirio Success Story

Appirio, a firm founded in 2006, is recognized as one of the most successful cloud integrators, with practices around Salesforce, Workday, Cornerstone OnDemand, DocuSign, Google and Amazon.com.

Cofounder Narinder Singh, with experience at Accenture, WebMethods (now Software AG), and SAP, describes the company's journey:

> "One of the core notions of our original business plan was that the systems integration model had to fundamentally change. Structurally, the services industry hadn't changed over the last 30 years, despite the ever-evolving nature of technology. (Offshore was disruptive, but not to the core model.) Second, the fundamental shift to cloud was much more than a technology shift (like mainframe to client/server); it represented the creation of shared platforms.

> At WebMethods, we made money integrating SAP to SAP, Oracle to Oracle, etc. because

each customer had implemented differently. With the cloud, there was a shared platform, just like the Internet was providing for consumers.

Now, systems integration firms could think about reusability across clients — something services firms had unsuccessfully pursued for years. The cloud also unleashed a step change in the rate of innovation of the underlying apps themselves while eliminating the customer effort in upgrading the application.

So, consulting in this new world couldn't rely on upgrade revenue and also needed constantly learning new capabilities of solutions. And, because the applications were advancing so quickly and the runtime management/ operations were taken care of by the software vendor, the deal sizes were much smaller.

In the early days of cloud implementations, there was heavy integration to on-premise systems. But, over time, as more of the systems went to the cloud, even integration revenue diminished. Cloud-to-cloud integration is not only simpler, it's often packaged into the application by one of the vendors.

Overall, in the cloud world, SIs have to learn to try fast, fail fast — increasing velocity and transaction volume while lessening the possibility of $100 million projects and the failures that often became front page news.

We had to be different from the larger systems integration firms to succeed. We created IP that we could reuse across clients. [Appirio sold PSA functionality it had developed to FinancialForce, a Salesforce partner. Lexmark/Perceptive described in Chapter B3 uses that functionality.] We intentionally lowered deal sizes, especially initial ones, because we knew the large firms couldn't "stoop so low." Finally, we pushed the pace of innovation because we knew the larger firms expected the stability provided by training an army of ABAP or PLSQL programmers and milking that skill set for years. We had to create a game we could compete in, and focusing on the distinct elements of cloud computing let us do that.

The cloud, and mobile and social technologies, had collapsed time and space — a developer in Minnesota or in Bangladesh could get instant access to the same cloud or mobile systems the largest companies in the world were running. In addition, just like the consumer web preceded the enterprise cloud, we saw consumer companies like Uber and

Airbnb show us it was access, not ownership, that really mattered.

We started focusing on creating a community (today known as TopCoder) where we could gather some of the most skilled designers, developers, and data scientists in the world. Today, we have over 665,000 of them. Then, we asked what's the most effective way of creating software in a distributed mode. The answer was open source as a development model. Though it was once looked down upon by enterprises, today everyone acknowledges the ubiquity of Linux, MySQL, and dozens of other community initiatives. Yet, no enterprise had sought to tap into the process that created those solutions because it was considered impossible.

We created TopCoder as a crowdsourcing community that lets us tap into the best talent and motivates their participation by offering financial reward, the opportunity to learn, recognition, social interactions, and control over what they choose to work on.

We are really excited about the exponential combination of clouds and crowds.

We believe the next step is to break down more and more of the consulting services world to be delivered as-a-service, like a utility. We believe crowdsourcing is incredibly powerful, but design/development/data science are only one part of delivering a successful result for a client. Over time, the entire consulting lifecycle will be more and more repeatable — allowing services to be knit together like software components/ services and scaled up and down like cloud technology is today."

The Rural Sourcing Model

Monty Hamilton, another Accenture alum, is CEO at Rural Sourcing, Inc., which offers a "domestic offshoring" model. Founded by the former CIO of Baxter Healthcare, it seeks to offset the hidden cost of offshoring to India, Eastern Europe, and elsewhere. That includes fatigue from red-eye flights and jet lag, the phone calls at ungodly hours with the distant support, and the lost-in-translation factor.

Says Hamilton:

"During the early days of the 1990s and 2000s as offshoring became widely adopted, IT work could be done at one-fifth the cost of the U.S. software developer. Today, that gap has narrowed closer to 30 percent to 40 percent in comparable labor costs. And, this difference is before you take into consideration less productivity due to factors such as time zone and calendar differences, employee turnover, cultural and business context gaps, and an increasing onsite-to-offshore ratio. Once these factors are brought into the discussions, offshore costs versus rural sourcing are in a virtual dead heat on a total cost comparison."

Hamilton is on a crusade to replace offshoring with backyard sourcing in his three U.S. development centers in Jonesboro, Arkansas; Augusta, Georgia; and a new one in Mobile, Alabama. He says about half his SAP-centric customers had previously tried the offshore model. While all current locations are in the U.S. Southeast, he says the next location will likely be in the Midwest or Mountain time zone region. His clients are spread across the country.

A quarter of his business comes from supporting SAP applications for clients like Piolax and Auxilium. RSI also supports Java and .Net custom development, SharePoint, testing/quality assurance, and several vertical applications. Hamilton says he wants a balanced portfolio of services and does not want to be viewed as an SAP-only provider.

He concentrates his location search on U.S. tier 2 or 3 cities. They tend to be two to three hours from major metropolitan areas, and close to universities and/or military bases. He says he finds "highly skilled and loyal professionals who do not want to relocate or commute from their 'high quality of life and low cost of living' locations."

"We looked at a final list of six or seven cities before we chose Mobile, AL. We saw a wide swath of tech talent all the way from Biloxi, MS, to the west and the Florida Panhandle to the east.

Specific to SAP, we help with BW work, upgrades, ABAP development, and small teams with a staff of three or four to supplement a client's steady-state team. We are also seeing quite a bit of interest in "fractional" support for BASIS skills. There is lesser interest for fractional interest in other SAP areas — clients still want to deal with named resources.

With broader adoption, and in some cases mandates to use Agile development methodologies, the rural sourcing model provides clear advantages for those companies who value speed-to-market and want to reduce the risk of outsourcing. Companies today are more interested in smaller, nimble teams who can work on newer technologies enabled by mobile devices and cloud-based solutions. Outsourcing will continue to grow and flourish as a corporate strategy. However, with a multitude of options available, clients will move toward "smarter outsourcing," leading to the growth of domestic sourcing as both a complement to, and in some cases a replacement for offshore outsourcing. Much like finding the vast oil reserves available now through fracking, rural sourcing is finding a whole new reservoir of IT talent hidden in America's tier 2 and tier 3 cities."

A Different Accounting Firm

Baker Tilly Virchow Krause, LLP ("Baker Tilly") is a large public accounting and professional services firm. Bryan Majewski and Ethan Bach, leaders of its Business and Technology practice, started building a new strategy for the practice to provide cloud-based ERP and other software package services in 2010. Having come to the firm from other Big Four Firms, they naturally evaluated opportunities around SAP.

They saw companies frozen after the first wave of massive ERP projects. Their clients did not want to invest again in big CapEx projects, yet the competitive world around them was rapidly changing. In that sense, they were paralyzed.

Majewski says:

> "Cloud apps have allowed them, in the last few years, to break the thaw. We see clients more with three to five year roadmaps and less "Big Bang" thinking. It is the Kaizen

mentality applied to IT — smaller moves faster. And, our projects are more of "operational plan alignment" reflecting this mix of long-term strategy with short-term operating plans. Cloud software is much more intuitive, so change management these days is much more about process standardization and optimization than about end-user training."

Bach also sees a big difference where his clients see value. Even though he lives and works in a still highly industrialized part of the United States, if a young person asks him where to think of a career, without hesitation, he says marketing and the front of the business.

"Supply chain and fulfillment remain important aspects of the customer experience, but the world has beaten supply chain and operations to death and optimized just about every last nickel there. Innovation and value in many manufacturing and distribution based businesses has moved to providing an integrated customer experience where sales, marketing, service, and supply chain and fulfillment work in concert to provide the best customer experience possible."

So, he likes what Oracle has done with its acquisitions and focus on customer-experience solutions, talent management, and third-party data integration.

Baker Tilly is an Oracle partner, focusing around Oracle HCM Cloud, Oracle Eloqua (part of Oracle Marketing Cloud) and a broad set of Customer Experience (CX) and analytics products. It also does well with Plex Systems, and works with other cloud applications such as NetSuite.

All three firms profiled — Appirio, Rural Sourcing and Baker Tilly — have tried different business and delivery models which would be of benefit to the SAP customer base.

CHAPTER 11

SAP Market Watcher Omissions

∿→

Africa has not been known for technology leadership. Yet remarkably, pioneering mobile payment technology in the form of M-Pesa has come from a Kenyan telco. Go to London and you see all kinds of start-ups like The Currency Cloud and Seedrs which are targeting foreign exchange trading, capital raising, and other traditional activities of the banking sector. PayPal supports payments in all kinds of form-factors from credit cards to mobile devices, and facilitates a variety of financial transactions in 26 currencies.

That is the new "bank" — but SAP has not been helping customers with these innovations. (In fairness, Standard Chartered introduced mobile banking in South Africa using SAP technology, but that was years after M-Pesa was introduced.) Check out compliance areas like Basel II or anti-money laundering capabilities, and SAP is very focused.

Regulators have always been good for SAP's business. FDA validation in pharmaceuticals, antimoney laundering in banking and several other industry regulations made SAP a major player in what it calls Governance, Risk, and Compliance (GRC).

Sarbanes-Oxley (SOX) was particularly lucrative for SAP and its public accounting partners. Many SAP customers' executives still have nightmares about SOX, which was enacted as a response to the scandal at Enron. Section 404 of the law enhanced compliance steps and internal control investments.

The Economist summarized:

> "Controversial from the start, SOX came to be despised by many businessmen in America (and beyond, where it has touched big foreign firms). Even its authors have reservations, conceding that its hasty passage into law meant it was badly drafted in parts. "Frankly, I would have written it differently," Michael Oxley, one of the former congressmen who drafted the act said in March. He added that the same was true of his coauthor, Paul Sarbanes. "But, it was not normal times."[145]

SAP benefitted from SOX investments starting in 2002 and even lobbied with the U.S. Congress about the law.[146] SAP's public accounting partners did even better — ironically, the law had been enforced as a reaction to Arthur Andersen's role (and subsequent demise) in the Enron case.

---

[145] http://www.economist.com/node/9545905
[146] http://soprweb.senate.gov/index.cfm?event=getFilingDetails&filingID=49D8AA98-7DD9-4A83-A8C8-64612A0E8AEA&filingTypeID=9

Two Deloitte partners wrote a *Harvard Business Review* article, "The Unexpected Benefits of Sarbanes-Oxley":

> "A few smart companies have stopped complaining about Sarbanes-Oxley, the investor-protection law, and turned it to their advantage — bringing operations under better control while driving down compliance costs."[147]

If you were looking for tangible payback, the title of the Deloitte article was misleading — they provided examples of improved documentation, corporate ethics training, improved software change management, etc.

In January 2006, I wrote:

> "Corporate executives have been muted in their complaints the last couple of years. Nonetheless, the SEC has heard from several quarters. These letters — from the CFO of Ball Corporation, a $5 billion packaging company; from the Chairman of Blyth, a $1.5 billion home expression company; and the U.S. Chamber of Commerce — are respectful but make the point about the burden imposed by 404.
>
> I was trained as a CPA. I realize the importance of controls, but there is no free lunch. More and more companies like Ball will say their costs of $7 million "far exceeds our realized benefits from Section 404."[148]

---

[147] http://hbr.org/2006/04/the-unexpected-benefits-of-sarbanes-oxley/ar/1
[148] http://dealarchitect.typepad.com/deal_architect/2006/01/1_billion_per_w.html

SAP had counted on a similar bonanza around regulations related to climate change. Peter Graf, SAP's Chief Sustainability Officer, invested in a showcase internal program for SAP with elaborate metrics, reports, and websites. Scott Bolick later wrote "During the heady days of 2009, the world was figuratively being painted green. Companies knew they needed to make commitments, launch programs, and issue reports."[149] The UN Climate Summit in Copenhagen in 2009 ended, however, in failure. With a weak global economy, there was little regulatory push for cap-and-trade or carbon taxes. The SAP initiative has lost steam, with four of its sustainability executives (including Graf) departing in the last few months. By itself, SAP's "role model" sustainability program was not enough for customers to adopt its guidance or software.

SAP clearly benefits when regulators drive demand for initiatives.

In contrast, regulators have not scrutinized SAP much. The EU has gone after Microsoft, Intel and Google for anticompetitive complaints. It has even gone after European telcos around mobile roaming charges. In Berlin, Sigmar Gabriel, the German Vice Chancellor and Economics Minister, "is investigating whether Germany can classify Google as a vital part of the country's infrastructure, and thus make it subject to heavy state regulation."[150] None of those vendors have had the financial impact on corporate customers that SAP has had. European regulators have, however, stayed away from SAP, even with its

---

[149] http://www.forbes.com/sites/sap/2012/03/19/sustainability-now-a-strategy-not-just-a-report/
[150] http://www.nytimes.com/2014/10/11/opinion/sunday/why-germans-are-afraid-of-google.html

dominant — estimated at 50 percent — ERP market share in German-speaking Europe.

Regulators tend to react to customer pressure, and in the software vendor world, customers tend to channel their views through user groups. Many customers also believe enterprise software is too esoteric an area for regulators to understand. As an example, the U.S. Department of Justice lost its case against Oracle in 2004 — many say because it argued its case with curious market definitions like "high-function HRM software," a term few in the industry had even heard of.[151]

User Group Network

Most technology vendors encourage formation of user groups. Such groups provide a forum to discuss product enhancements. Their training supplements that of the vendor. They hold events that provide some measure of arms-length content different from what a vendor wants to present.

In the SAP universe, there are over 30 user groups across global regions, as shown in Figure 1. The U.S. and German-speaking ones — ASUG and DSAG — are the largest, with 170,000 members between them. I talked to a few market analysts who have dealt with several of these regional groups. One of them commented, "the user group structure helps SAP divide and rule. A lack of coordination among them is an issue." This remains, even though in 2007, SAP encouraged the formation of an umbrella organization, SAP User Group Executive Network (SUGEN).

---

[151] http://www.mondaq.com/unitedstates/x/31063/Outsourcing/US+v+Oracle+Corporation+Three+Lessons+To+Be+Learned+About+Merger+Review

SAP Major User Groups

FINUG
SBN
SAPSA

AUSAPE
Aused-GUPS
DSAG
GUSP
SAPience.be
USF
VNSG

RSUG
SUSAP

ASUG US/Canada
ASUG Mexico

SUG UK/Ireland

JSUG
KSUG

ASUG Colombia
ASUG Ecuador
ASUG Peru
ASUG Venezuela

SUG-MENA

CSUA
INDUS
STUG
SUGHK
uSAP

AFSUG

ASUG Argentina
ASUG Brasil
ASUG Chile

SAUG
NZSUG

Complied from various SAP sources

Figure 1   Credit: Deal Architect

The analysts' specific comments about the regions:

"Americas — ASUG — is seen as too close to SAP for comfort, but may be changing now that there is a new CEO. Historically, it has been focused more on training and membership activities.

U.K. and Ireland — UKISUG — weird relationship but relatively independent. Leadership can be a pain to work with.

Germany, Austria, and Switzerland — DSAG — fiercely independent, fearless, uses media well.

France — USF — was vocal on the back of DSAG support on licensing, but has been quiet recently.

Australia — SAUG — independent, swashbuckling style.

Netherlands — NSAG — sort of aligned to U.K. — surprisingly large group that speaks freely on occasion.

Japan — JSUG — culturally not likely to be confrontational. Would rather send a back-channel message by showing interest in third-party maintenance. Rimini Street is seeing plenty of direct interest for third-party maintenance in Japan."

With that in background I reached out to ASUG and DSAG for comments for the book.

Geoff Scott has recently taken over as CEO of Americas SAP Users Group (ASUG). While he is new on the job, he brings the credibility of a former CIO with SAP implementations under his belt. When I asked him about well-run SAP shops I should interview for the book, he gave me several names. (I reached out to CIOs at two of them. Both acknowledged my request but given holidays and other travel, I could not interview either on time.)

Scott also pointed out he had pushed SAP to reconsider charging for the Fiori UX — and SAP had agreed. This summer, ASUG issued a fairly comprehensive study of challenges in the customer base that were slowing down adoption of HANA in spite of extensive SAP marketing.

Five years earlier, then ASUG CEO Steve Strout had not pushed back enough on SAP's planned enterprise support maintenance price hike. It was speculated that was one reason why he was asked to leave within a year of taking the position. Strout is also blamed for leaving the organization financially weak. His successor, Bridgette Chambers, was credited with turning around the organization. This meant more on internal ASUG focus rather than customer advocacy. She did help launch services like ASUG Research and Knowledge Builder which with periodic papers and webcasts provide a lens into its members' most critical SAP-related challenges.

Hopefully, Scott can now make the focus more external, and also look at issues in the broader ecosystem his members face, and act as a better interface to SAP and its partners.

DSAG, and its Chairman, Andreas Oczko, have been vocal about SAP maintenance pricing increases on several occasions. Oczko is particularly forceful in pointing out midsized customers (the famed German "Mittelstand") do not tax SAP support much and do not see much value from maintenance.

Angelika Jung of DSAG emailed me other areas where DSAG has successfully lobbied with SAP:

> "1. SAP ERP and SAP Business Suite: DSAG fought successfully for the extension of the maintenance till 2020, so that SAP customers have more time for planning upgrade activities.
>
> 2. SAP NetWeaver: One consolidated portal SAP NetWeaver 7.3; less complexity.
>
> 3. BusinessObjects: Starter Package for SAP Business-Objects with a fixed price for limited functionality,

companies have the possibility to start their BO-activities without buying a full-range license.

4. SAP Solution Manager: functionality like Change Management Database and extended functionality in the fields of central monitoring and alerting is planned for Solution Manager release 7.1.

5. SAP Business Suite: consolidation of Business Suite and harmonization between the different components; less complexity.

6. No additional license costs for SAP Fiori and SAP Screen Personas.

7. Limited runtime license for SAP HANA: Now it is possible to license only a part of Business Suite on HANA or BW on HANA.

8. More transparency of the pricing model.

9. Additional Flexibility gained for software licenses: Under certain, limited conditions, it is possible to partially terminate licenses and their maintenance fees without the corresponding purchase of new SAP applications.

10. Changed cloud licensing option: customers have the option to reallocate parts of their existing investments in on-premise solutions from SAP to investments into respective SAP cloud applications. Specifically, software usage rights for on-premise licenses and respective

maintenance fees can be partially terminated and can be replaced by newly bought cloud solutions for the applications transferred into the cloud."

Howlett cautions:

"The playbook is all too familiar:
- SAP imposes something new that appears to cost customers more money. SAP tries to justify on the back of improved support/features/simplification.
- Disparate user groups grumble about the changes.
- DSAG tries to compromise but ends up creating a ruckus.
- SAP concedes some points but eventually gets its way."[152]

Also, SAP maintenance, which has drawn more of the recent user group focus, only accounts for roughly $10 billion out of $204 billion a year in our SAP economy model in Chapter 3, Neither ASUG nor DSAG have focused much on all the additional "surround costs" in the SAP economy.

Industry Analysts

In 1996, Bobby Cameron, a Forrester analyst, wrote a report which sent shockwaves in the IT industry:

"SAP's R/3 business is booming. The suite promises control over operational mayhem while reducing costs — but only at the risk of implementation failure, missed

---

[152] http://diginomica.com/2014/07/31/dsag-sap-support-survey-skepticism-outweighs-satisfaction/#.U9_CtfldXdQ

opportunities, and internal atrophy. Smart companies will take a prudent approach to managing these risks — including an R/3 exit strategy."[153]

I was at Gartner then, and we thought Cameron was being sensational for asking customers to exit R/3 even before they had deployed it. Looking back, it was a brave statement on his part. In contrast, now even with the runaway SAP economy, it is surprising how few analysts call for an exit strategy.

Many analysts glibly say, "SAP's impact on customer economics is no worse than that of Oracle or Microsoft." They do so in spite of market data which shows that, in the decade from 2001–2010, SAP's base application license revenues were more than twice as large as Oracle's comparable licenses (even after Oracle's significant application acquisition run). They say that even with many of the major outsourcers reporting three to four times as large SAP practices as they do around Oracle applications.

In reviewing two decades of archives for the book research, I realized industry analysis around SAP is inadequate. Some firms have 15–20 analysts covering various aspects of SAP, but have done little integrative modeling of the economy around the vendor.

Liz Herbert, a VP at Forrester, has covered outsourcing and cloud services since 2002. She brings a broad market perspective when she evaluates service providers around SAP. Her current focus is how they support newer SAP products and acquisitions like HANA and hybris. She is looking at how Accenture and Deloitte are blending digital agencies like Acquity and Ubermind with their SAP practices. She sets a filter of at least $1 billion in SAP-related revenue and at least

---

[153] http://www.worldcat.org/title/prudent-approach-to-r3/oclc/81330865

5,000 SAP practitioners to be included in her Wave report on SAP service providers. IDC and Gartner also watch the SAP outsourcing market but their reports also only analyze the top 10–20 firms in that market.

In contrast, my first Gartner report on SAP outsourcers in 1996 analyzed 20 firms and that market size today is at least ten times larger. Over 100 services firms were at the Expo Hall at Sapphire Now this past June, and most are going unanalyzed.

Analysts have for-profit models so you cannot fault them for cherry-picking segments of the market on which to focus. Or maybe you can. Most analysts tend to focus on established vendors that customers most want to hear about. Those vendors also tend to have larger budgets for analyst research and consulting. As analysts, they could be probing and pushing more than just reporting.

Contrast this with a couple of "internal analysts" I know in the technology industry. They work in competitive/sales intelligence for vendors. One is constantly pulling out nuggets from a knowledge base with over 15,000 documents he has been creating since 2000 from public sources. Talk about a "memory" to fact check and help your field. Too bad these "analysts" are not available to the average customer. In my conversations with them, they are frequently appalled at the poor industry analyst coverage they see of SAP and other enterprise software vendors.

Technology Journalists

"'Follow the Money' has always been my maxim," says Chris Kanaracus, a (former) senior correspondent of the IDG News Service, invoking the advice Deep Throat gave the *Washington Post's* Bob Woodward character in the movie *All The President's Men*. "SAP may be unsexy to many other journalists, but I have always considered it hugely important to enterprises and worth my time."

With the turmoil in the media industry, Kanaracus has been one of the few consistent SAP followers since 2007. He has broken many of the SAP failure stories we describe in Chapter 7.

It takes plenty of old-fashioned gumshoe rigor:

> "I tend to be careful of "tips." Usually they are unsubstantiated and have an agenda. I scan a wide range of court filings. I run Boolean searches on SEC and other sites to see if companies are reporting impact of technologies on their financial results. I triangulate from calls with my regular sources.
>
> I am fairly disciplined — I have a daily routine I follow to keep up with my beat. It's like a gardener who weeds and prunes, and notices details on a regular basis.
>
> Failure stories don't make my day cheerful — but they do provide a contrast to all the sunshine and roses talk you hear from software vendors."

But, even Kanaracus does not spend a great deal of his time focusing on the SAP ecosystem, other than when they are involved in failures. He says, "Maybe we should also focus on the channel, but IDG has asked me to focus more on SAP and its customers."

German media is very interested in SAP given its headquarters there, but tends to focus more on its executives and its financial results, rather than its customers. It also reports negatively at times on the growing globalization at SAP. An example of that comes from a blog comment by Peter Färbinger:

"Hello to everyone in the global SAP Community. I am editor-in-chief at the *E-3 Magazine* published in Germany, Austria and Switzerland (www.e-3.de). There are many rumours about an article that describes the current situation within SAP. The focus of the article lies on Jim Hageman Snabe and Bill McDermott. In respect to Vishal Sikka he is a follower of Shai Agassi and an idea of Hasso Plattner. There is nothing wrong with Vishal Sikka but SAP is a German based company. All innovation is coming out of "old Europe" — even Hana was invented in Europe: originally SanssouciDB in Potsdam at the Hasso Plattner Institute (HPI). Every part of the article (http://www.e-3.de/artikel/doppelspitze/) is based on the opinion within the German-speaking SAP community. Maybe we should visit each other to learn from each other. Jim Hagemann Snabe has learned German to understand the roots of SAP. Many comments in the SAP-R/3-Abap-Code are still written in German. Even Vishal Sikka mentions in his blog a German author (Hermann Hesse). Now all executives at SAP are working in Walldorf, Germany — expect CEO Bill McDermott and board member Rob Enslin. Maybe we should talk about the importance of being a board member of a German-based DAX company. I am not sure if Vishal Sikka was realizing this part of his duties. Global is great and important but you should never forget where your roots are. The roots of SAP are in 'old Europe'."[154]

---

[154] http://vishalsikka.blogspot.com/2014/05/words-and-wisdom.html

The fears of the "Americanization of SAP" is a concern with many European SAP customers. Disclosures of NSA's data-mining activities have accentuated it, so it is unsurprising that the German media puts an accent on such fears. Many Germans derogatively call Google an "octopus" with its tentacles collecting all kinds of data. I have also heard some comments that the new CEO McDermott, an American, will be like Stephen Elop who is widely viewed as having gutted the Norwegian company, Nokia. Such gossip is understandable in a global setting. However, that means even more distraction from the focus on customer economics.

SAP Mentors

Jim Spath posted a blog titled "Fast is not a number" in which he asked:

> "When the Business Suite on HANA was recently announced, my question was: what are the numbers?
>
> I've gotten pushback, or no answer. I am a little surprised, though I guess I shouldn't be. Here's what I think may be the reasons this classic benchmark hasn't been made public:
> - The test results are worse than most existing hardware and database combinations.
> - The thing just doesn't scale the way it should.
> - The mantra is "it's really really fast" and you don't need to put a number on "fast"."[155]

---

[155] http://scn.sap.com/community/hana-in-memory/blog/2013/02/20/fast-is-not-a-number

In another post about Sapphire Now (and the ASUG annual conference), he wrote:

> "I will not miss any hyperbole about "cloud," "mobile" and whatever the other alleged key word is this year. Particularly HANA. Will not miss the oversell of a technology that solves few problems in the enterprise except "adding shareholder value" and increasing complexity in an already dense matrix of information services. Won't miss vendor booths solving problems I don't have. Won't miss the global press trying to discern world shattering import from the turn of phrase by a suit."

Spath is not an industry analyst. He is a technical analyst at Stanley Black & Decker. He is also an "SAP Mentor." Mentors are a group of 100 or so "hands-on experts of an SAP product or service, as well as excellent champions of community-driven projects."[156]

Spath says the notes above are a bit atypical. Mentors are not primarily about customer advocacy — though they tend to provide SAP input in private. Mentors are "offered unique opportunities for access to SAP senior management, early access to information on products and programs, and greater visibility in the online communities as well as at SAP events such as SAP Tech Ed," he says. They are well respected in the SAP community for their technical competence.

Spath says Mentors have had an impact making the case for streamlining developer licensing at SAP, especially for

---

[156] http://scn.sap.com/docs/DOC-23155

those in indie settings. A subset of this group wrote a paper on consultant certification we described in Chapter 10. It has also been influential in creating sharing face-to-face forums like the SAP Inside Track.

They also speak up when they feel SAP overmarkets. A blog post by Dr. Plattner drew derisive comments from several Mentors including one from Jelena Perfiljeva:

> "Dior does not even bother advertising their dresses to me. They must have somehow figured out I'm not really their demographics. Most importantly, they also don't try to convince the world that I don't buy their dresses because I'm simply uninformed about how supercalifragilisticexpialidocious they are."[157]

And, another from Gretchen Lindquist:

> "Hasso,
>
> I must be missing something here. Why are you asking the customers for the reason that your organization has failed to convince us to jump on the HANA bandwagon? To me, that is an internal issue for your marketing people to figure out. You want to sell us something but blame *us* for *our* failure to craft a business case? Blaming the customers for failing to embrace your no-longer-so-new solution is scarcely a way to influence people in a positive way."

---

[157] http://scn.sap.com/community/hana-in-memory/blog/2014/09/10/y-u-no-love-hana

In general, though, the Mentors tend to focus on technical topics over economic ones. As Spath says, "I am not the designated negotiator for my company." Besides, only 20 percent to 25 percent of the Mentors work for SAP customers. The rest work for consulting partners or are bloggers who track SAP.

Bloggers

As we mentioned earlier, SAP was a pioneer in conversing with independent bloggers like the Enterprise Irregulars (the author is a member of the group). The growth of social media has created plenty of content especially in the SAP Community Network. Many of the blogs, however, come from SAP partners, which is hardly independent analysis. Many of the bloggers who follow SAP bring little retrospective and many parse and parrot, and tweet statements from SAP executives. So, the simplification messages that came out of Sapphire Now in 2014 were not met with cynicism about the countless previous simplification statements we pointed out in Chapter 9.

There is also peer pressure in the partner community to "conform," as a couple of blog comments suggest:

> "What is never talked about is that there are factions within SAP that will do everything in their power to "punish" a partner if they provide a negative perspective publicly even if it is 100% true and has been mentioned repeatedly in back-channels with no action happening. It puts partners in a tough position as I have heard repeatedly through the years, "I would love to say some of the things you say but it would hurt my business if I did."

And:

> "SAP has also tried to "punish" me for speaking out against them on behalf of customers. It's a sad, sick reality of their new marketing engine. Many of their "community" projects are focused around "cheerleading." It's actually designed this way and provides little to no value to the customers who actually feel the financial pinch of SAP's inefficiencies. They need to take a note from Bill Gates notebook: "Your most unhappy customers are your greatest source of learning." I was hoping we would get back to when they first joined social media and were having "open" discussions in social media. That all but stopped it seems with their new CMO. A clear regression in my eyes. Also, makes the customers tune them out and trust them less."

Academic Research

With an annual economy in the range of the GDP of countries like Ireland, and with investments in SAP one of largest categories of corporate capital expenditures, I had expected to find plenty of academic research around SAP.

In the Summer 2002 issue of *Journal of Management Information Systems*, Lorin M. Hitt, D.J. Wu, and Xiaoge Zhou at Wharton wrote a paper which summarized:

> "While the business value of ERP implementations have been extensively debated in IT trade periodicals in the form of qualitative discussion or detailed case studies, there is little large sample statistical evidence on who

adopts ERP and whether the benefits of ERP implementation exceed the costs (and risks)."

And:

"Due to the lack of mid- and long-term post-implementation data, future research on the long-run impact of ERP is proposed." [158]

Few of their colleagues in academia, however, helped conduct such research over the next several years. I did find an interesting 2009 Senior Honors Thesis: "ERP value: the market response to announcements of enterprise resource planning investments,"[159] by Jacob Craig Case as part of his studies at the David Eccles School of Business, University of Utah.

This paper evaluated the change in a firm's valuation after it announces an ERP system. He listed prior papers he had found in his research — in Figure 2 — and, as we can see, most focus on the impact of an announcement of ERP investments on stock performance, not after the fact analysis of business value from the investment. I reached out to him to see if he had done more recent research — he has not.

---

[158] http://scheller.gatech.edu/directory/faculty/wu/pubs/Hitt_Wu_Zhou_JMIS_2002.pdf

[159] http://content.lib.utah.edu/cdm/ref/collection/etd2/id/1720

Title	Authors	Investment Data	Metrics	Variables	Key Findings
Market Reaction to ERP announcements	David C. Hayes James E. Hunton Jacqueline L. Reck (2001)	Public ERP adoption announcements	Event Study 244 firms in sample 1990-1998	Firm size (large/small) Firm health (healthy/unhealthy) Vendor size.	Reaction is the most positive for small/healthy firms and large/unhealthy firms. Large vendors, such as SAP, Oracle, and Peoplesoft provide the largest returns.
The reaction of financial analysts to Enterprise Resource Planning (ERP) Plans	James E. Hunton Ruth Ann McEwen Benson Wier (2002)	Hypothetical financials that were analyzed by financial analysts	Analyst valuation methods	Firm size (large/small) Firm health (healthy/unhealthy)	Analysts forecast and subsequent valuations increased after learning of the ERP investment. Large unhealthy, and small healthy firms showed higher mean earnings forecasts than small unhealthy firms.
ERP Investments and the Market Value of Firms: Toward an Understanding of Influential ERP Project Variables	C. Ranganathan Carol V. Brown (2006)	Public ERP adoption announcements.	Event Study 116 firms in sample 1997-2001	Physical Scope Functional Scope ERP Provider	Firms with larger physical scope and larger functional scope showed the highest returns. ERP vendor has no influence on market return.
The impact of enterprise systems on corporate performance: A study of ERP, SCM, and CRM system implementations	Kevin B. Hendricks Vinod R. Singhal Jeff K. Stratman (2006)	Public ERP adoption announcements	Event Study. Pooling comparable firms to use as benchmarks at the time of the event. 186 ERP, 140 SCM, and 80 CRM observations 1991-1999	Category of "Enterprise System"	SCM adopters showed positive abnormal stock returns as well as increased profitability. ERP adopters showed increased profitability, particularly in early adopters, but no increase in stock returns. CRM showed no increase in stock returns or profitability.

Figure 2   Credit: Jacob Craig Case

Such a massive SAP economy, and yet, such fragmented coverage. Way too much coverage goes to SAP itself, too much to the gossipy executive revolving door and to nationalistic stereotypes. In the meantime, inefficiencies in the data centers, networks and armies of talent running SAP get little attention.

You have to admire folks like Herbert, Kanaracus, Spath, and others quoted in the book for shining attention on specific elements of the SAP economy. Overall, though, the inconsistent coverage of the SAP economy reminded me of the fable of the blind men around the elephant — one who touched a leg thought it was a pillar, the one who touched the tail called it a rope, and so on.

CHAPTER 12

SAP Customer Permissions

In the previous three chapters we have seen how SAP, its partners, and market watchers have all had roles in helping shape the SAP economy. In the end, though, the buck stops at the customer's desk — or more accurately leaks from the customer's bank.

A colorful, now retired, Andersen Consulting/Accenture partner once told me, "You and your Gartner colleagues can say what you want, but I don't hold a gun to our clients' heads when they write us checks."

He may not have been diplomatic, but he was right. Of course, you could argue he is a vendor and pointing fingers elsewhere.

John Dean agrees with him. He is former CIO of Steelcase, Inc., which is a long-term SAP customer. Since 2008, Dean has been a member of the SAP Independent Executive Advisory Council (IEAC). In that role he advises new and existing SAP customers on how to implement the product successfully to ensure adoption and achieve expected business impact. He says:

> "I spend the majority of my time as a consultant helping people how to be very successful. You can tell right away what their chances are for success. If they fail, pointing fingers at others is the norm. They only have themselves to blame because they simply are not good at big change."

Dean says too many projects are technology-driven when they should be business-results-driven:

> "Projects focused solely on installing the application by the IT organization should not be pursued. For example, I am currently working with two organizations as a member of the executive steering team. The first, a $5 billion company, had only implemented financials (from another ERP vendor) in the decade from the time of purchase. With a new SAP solution and adhering to what it takes to get true value, they have replaced financials and implemented global order fulfillment in eighteen months. With full completion (of other modules) to come in another year. The second was a $2.5 billion global company with obsolete solutions and little experience with major IT initiatives. They started by adhering to the ten key steps we showed them. They will be fully implemented in a little over two years.... They could have gone faster, but chose a more deliberate pace to manage spend. It takes discipline and a cultural change on the business side to achieve success."

The ten key steps Dean talks about are as follows:

1. Business Executive Commitment: Clear executive sponsorship, ownership of the business case, accountable for project success, provides the right resources.

2. Business Pull versus Technology Push: Results should be targeted to achieve key business strategies and objectives. With a focus on differentiation in the customer's eyes. The 20 percent of total business execution, at best.

3. Organizational Readiness for Change: Will the people be prepared when the "switch" goes on? Were the users of the solution fully engaged?

4. Dedicated Team: People will do what they can versus what they should if pressured for time due to an "overflowing plate."

5. Rationalizing Priorities: Need a corporate project portfolio governance process. Balance supply (resources) with demand (initiatives). More will get done through time.

6. Right SI Partner: Cultural fit and size of SI partner with the right level and type of software provider involvement/oversight.

7. Leverage Best Practices: Customization should only be contemplated in cases of very high perceived value where the customer would see it as a differentiator.

8. Time to Value: The longer the project, the greater the chance…for alternative solutions to be pursued and for the business case to change.

9. Solution Creation Process: That correctly controls customization.

10. Strong Initiative Governance: Safeguarding project goals, resources, and services.

Michael Doane, author of *The SAP Green Book — Thrive After Go-Live*,[160] would not disagree with Dean but would say the advice ignores the very long tail that is an SAP implementation. He says few customers think long-term marriage when they commit to SAP. Most of them concentrate on the implementation project (the wedding) and not worry about the long-term deployment (the marriage). Many of the post go-live disappointments can be squarely laid at the doorstep of the implementation project in the vein of "bad wedding, worse marriage." In many projects, a "going live" focus shortchanges proper organizational change management, end-user training, and other issues erroneously viewed as peripheral. There are few SAP divorces (i.e., customers dropping SAP in favor of other applications software). And, those tend to be the result of a merger rather than a rip-and-replace. If, for sunk cost alone, firms that adopt SAP are less inclined to drop it. The life span of an SAP implementation needs to be thought of in the 20–30 year range.

---

[160] http://www.amazon.com/Green-Book-Thrive-After-Go-Live/dp/1575794152/ref=sr_1_2?ie=UTF8&qid=1406899875&sr=8-2&keywords=sap+green+book

Unilever, the global consumer products company, is an example of a marriage in SAP world. In a drive towards "One Unilever," it had Project Orchestra in South America starting in 2001. Over five years, 34 companies in that region were migrated to a single instance. In 2006, Project Sirius focused on integrating 17,000 users at sales organizations and factories across 24 European countries. Similar projects were happening around the globe, and by 2013 Unilever had moved to four regional ERP systems and was deploying SAP HANA "with more than 4.6 billion records." That's one company with over 200 global subsidiaries and over a decade of consolidation and other projects. It's not an uncommon phenomenon with many of SAP's largest customers.

Thinking about 20–30 years would suggest SAP customers should emulate how airlines manage their fleets. The average age of fleet in the airlines industry is over 15 years old, and you can see how airlines are constantly extending asset lives through elaborate maintenance programs, and periodic retrofits (like adding winglets to reduce drag and save on fuel). However, most planning, as Doane points out in the book, in the SAP world is short-term.

The airline industry is constantly thinking of fuel and labor efficiencies — so innovations like fuel hedging, continuous descent landings, moves to two-engine, and two-pilot planes occur with regularity. The industry also provides examples of early exit strategies. Singapore Air, widely respected as one of the best-run airlines in the world, has a fleet which averages under seven years. It continuously benefits from better fuel efficiency and other industry innovations.

The Value of Thinking Small

Sukumar Rajagopal, former CIO of Cognizant, the global out-sourcing firm, and now an entrepreneur and start-up mentor, says one way to do that is to think "small":

> "As a general thumb-rule "keeping the lights on" con-sumes 80 percent of a typical IT budget. Considering the heavy reliance on ERP software in Cognizant — and in general in the Fortune 2000 companies — one could argue that the lion's share of the IT budget is spent in the care and feeding of the ERP systems. From an IT strat-egy perspective, I call this heavy reliance on ERP and other COTS products as the "Big App" strategy. While the other 20 percent of the budget is available for new initiatives, we tend to spend it on rolling out new "Big Apps" using a multiyear, multimillion-dollar program approach. Given the user dissatisfaction around the ERP software (all the Big App vendors are guilty as charged), effective adoption doesn't occur. This leaves IT in a pre-carious spot of not innovating fast enough, preventing IT from being a true business partner. In Cognizant, we used the 20 percent available to conceptualize and execute a "Small Apps" strategy using a Lean Start-up approach. This approach allowed us to roll out apps in eight to ten weeks with feature addition contingent on user adoption and feedback. We started the "Small Apps" platform rollout with just two new apps and 25 connector apps that simply deep-linked inside the ERP systems. In under three years, the App Store had seven hundred plus transactional and analytical apps, with over 60 million app invocations, and had a 97.5 percent

reach across the globe. To boot, we spent next to nothing on change management, which is typically a big drain on costs in a traditional "Big App" strategy. We also had to introduce innovations like Design Thinking, Social Design, Jobs to be Done framework, etc. to develop apps that are much easier to use. Interestingly, this strategy, which focused heavily on transformation, actually had helped us become more efficient by helping us cut IT spend on new apps by 20 percent year over year."

The attitude at many SAP customers is quite defensive; instead of constantly optimizing, they accept the status quo. In win-loss analyses that cloud and other niche vendors conduct, comments such as these from SAP shops are pretty common:

- "IT and end users know SAP. We really don't need to learn about another product and technology."
- "Industry analysts tell us SAP, IBM, and Microsoft will be around forever, and, at our organization, being risk-averse, that is important to consider."
- "Integration is a vendor responsibility in SAP world, but it becomes ours if we adopt other solutions."
- "The big outsourcers do not have much of a practice around cloud vendors."
- "If a project fails with SAP it is somewhat acceptable to executives — there are so many other failures in that world."
- "There's safety in numbers — most of the Fortune 500 uses SAP."

I hear from many customers, "we are in line with industry benchmarks — 1.5 percent or 2 percent of revenues spent on

IT." But, would it not be better to ask, "Can we shave .25 percent or .5 percent off that and beat the industry benchmark?" Most of the case studies in the book are taking risks — some small, some large — and seeing significant payback.

Learning from Financial Services

Many of SAP's larger customers have sophisticated IT, strategic sourcing, and legal resources — so you would expect. But, in reality, the manufacturing, utility, and other industries where SAP has done well often do not have the same rigor of IT procurement as banks, brokerage houses, and other financial services firms.

Michael Laven is CEO of The Currency Cloud in London which has built a payments engine that transforms the way businesses move money around the world. Over the last two decades he has played roles as Chairman, CEO, or COO at several start-ups in the financial services sector including Traiana, Infinity Financial Technology, Cohera, Coronet, and FRS Global. Before this focus on the financial sector, he had executive roles at McCormack & Dodge and ASK Software which dealt more with customers in manufacturing, distribution, and other industries.

Laven contrasts the differences between IT at banks, brokerages, and other financial institutions with that in other sectors:

> "I find that banking core systems are, by definition, always out of date, as regulatory pressure and fiduciary responsibility mean that systems can only change much more slowly than advances in technology. Large banks are under even greater pressure than, say, manufacturing business as their capital markets and retail customers

rapidly adopt technology advances, whether in high-velocity trading or mobile payments, technology always appears to be disintermediating some core business area. I have been working with large and small banks on trading, back office processing, and consumer systems for over 25 years and banking IT always seem in the midst of a 'transformation' agenda."

Financial institutions also tend to have a much more diversified portfolio of technology vendors. It's not uncommon for them to have several hundred software vendors in their IT budget. Banks have built significant integration, testing and change management competencies so they tend to not be as reliant on suites from single vendors as is common in the ERP world.

Continues Laven:

"Business operations, naturally concentrated in high-cost money centers, New York, London, and Hong Kong, increase the cost pressure over other industries. The result of these pressures, I've found, is that banks have taken the lead in offshoring and near-shoring, must meet very high security standards in advance of other industries, and must have better lifecycle management to meet the cost pressure of finding savings in rationalization of existing systems to fund new technologies."

Financial institutions as a result tend to better perform software lifecycle management. Many banks use a sophisticated "sunset" model where they cut off or reduce vendor maintenance after five or six years of going live. They tend to have captive development facilities, and use a wide range of Indian, Israeli, and Eastern European outsourcers. They also do a significant amount of custom development.

Of course, given demands of their trading desks, they tend to be cutting-edge when it comes to data centers and networks. Finally, given the unique security and regulatory needs of their sectors, they also tend to be more demanding when it comes to their due diligence in technology procurement.

Learning from Others' Mistakes

With over three decades of experience, Henry W. Jones III, a software and IT attorney at Intersect Technology Consulting, has represented dozens of software licensors and licensees, and worked full-time inside six tech vendors. He is surprised that more buyer teams do not know enough to mine ERP and other IT litigation filings, especially given the spate of SAP project failures and litigations.

As Jones argues:

"Dozens of ERP and other software litigation documents disclose how high-quality enterprise-application procurement is tough. Detailed courthouse pleadings reveal both subtle glitches and obvious slop: ambiguous and unreconciled contract terms; nonspecialist buyers in over their heads; lost source code; licensors not securing a stable, long-term supply chain for code components; noncompliance with mandatory, increasingly-enforced, open source software licenses; inadequate initial creation or ongoing preservation of technical documents; inadequate ETL (data porting and reformatting, when transitioning to new applications and platforms); old obsolete programming languages; and other IT pain and suffering. Here, ongoing homework is necessary for operational health and safety."

Jones also thinks it helps in SAP and partner negotiations:

"You can reduce the friction of forging a multimillion-dollar deal by both sides referring to detailed documents from prior same-field failures, with no finger-pointing. Future-doctor medical students dig down into cadavers in their first month of professional schooling; world-class software users hunt and study "sick transaction" outputs for their own "preventive medicine" operational interests."

There is an expression, "Fool me once, shame on you; fool me twice, shame on me." In the SAP world, customers appear to have been fooled over and over again. It's easy to blame SAP and its partners, but as Krigsman points out in Chapter 7, SAP customers make up the third dimension to the IT Devil's Triangle.

Case Studies Group D: Committed

∿→

Chapter D1: Customer Strategy –
Align with SAP's Future

John Douglas of Burberry, the U.K. luxury fashion retailer, joked at an SAP event:

> "I am the Chief Technology Officer. I used to be the Chief Information Officer. But, CEO Angela (Ahrendts) changed my job title because I never gave her any information — only technology. With HANA, she may have to change my title back."

Actually, Ahrendts has moved on to manage Apple's retail empire, but Burberry's is an example of a company which is tightly aligned with SAP's past and future. It runs a single instance of the SAP Business Suite. It jointly developed with SAP a point-of-sale (POS) app that puts product and customer information into sales associates' tablets at the store. It uses HANA to blend transactional, customer, POS, and social media data. And, it next plans to swap out its Oracle database and put the Business Suite on HANA.

In his demo, Douglas simulated a customer, Natasha from New York City, visiting Burberry's Orlando store. The salesperson greeted her by name and used HANA to make predictive suggestions based on her transaction history, her Twitter posts, and fashion industry trend data. Natasha looked at products on the salesperson's tablet and then viewed videos of an "eclectic trench coat" she had seen at a runway show. The salesperson used the device to check if the coat was available at the 57th Street store in New York, and arranged for it to be available for in-store pickup. It was a good way to showcase a wide range of SAP technology at Burberry's.

Deere's HANA Vision

John Deere was one of SAP's earliest customers, going back to the mid-1970s. Now, it is aligned with SAP's HANA future. Deere is driven by a goal that the world needs to double its food production by 2050. With shrinking arable land, technology has to help agriculture become much more efficient. In a previous book, I described Deere's FarmSight initiative, which helps farmers in three areas: machine optimization for increased up-time; logistics optimization for better fleet management; and decision support with user-friendly monitors, sensors and wireless networks to enable access to machinery and agronomic data.

With its growing fleet of "smart equipment" in the field, Deere is using HANA for predictive maintenance. It says it can detect potential failures two to three months ahead, perform root-cause analysis quicker, reduce equipment downtime, and keep farmer satisfaction high. Deere mines patterns from telematics data from the equipment, warranty claims data, and textual data from dealer service tickets.

It had previously piloted a HANA "sidecar" for analytics — reports which used to take 16 hours to run were delivered near real-time. It then volunteered to be the first implementation of Business Suite on HANA to support 15,000 users across all time zones.

Both Burberry and Deere fit what Dr. Plattner calls his "radical approach." In an interview, he said "That's because we [SAP customers] were wimps and thought we'd go the easy way and do the read-only [analytical] applications first. My radical approach, if I may say so, scares people, but they're starting to see that they don't have to be scared."[161]

Dr. Plattner is correct — his expectations are radical. Historically, mixed mode — transaction and analytical processing — databases have taken time to mature. So, his customers are careful to try what he calls "read-only" capabilities.

Dr. Plattner should also compliment Burberry's and Deere for using HANA to crunch external data — social, sensory, etc., and unstructured data. They are leading SAP into newer areas whereas SAP itself continues to be focused more on internal, ERP-generated data.

---

[161] http://www.informationweek.com/cloud/software-as-a-service/sap-chairman-hasso-plattner-exclusive-qanda/d/d-id/1269486

Chapter D2: Customer Strategy – Make SAP Dance to Your Business Tune

Endo International plc, with global headquarters in Dublin, Ireland and U.S. headquarters in Malvern, PA, is a $3.5 billion specialty healthcare company with a broad portfolio of products. When Marc Kustoff arrived as CIO at Endo in June 2012 the company had four major divisions — branded products (Endo Pharmaceuticals, with products like the Lidoderm pain-relief patch), generic medications (Qualitest), medical devices (American Medical Systems), and medical data services (HealthTronics).

Upon arriving at Endo, Kustoff reacted to the CFO's question about why there had been no IT synergy savings achieved across acquisitions Endo had made in the previous year. Kustoff saw right away that separate ERP solutions — SAP, MAPICS, Epicor, and J.D. Edwards — across the divisions offered a major opportunity for IT efficiency.

He quickly recommended consolidating to SAP as the logical path. He had previously worked with other pharma companies which had implemented SAP. The other packages at Endo were approaching end of support life or could not scale to support the entire Endo family. Some could not meet validation and other compliance requirements unique to the industry. He realized that to gain approval for a project of such magnitude for the following year would require that a proposal be ready for the next board meeting in September. This gave him just a few weeks to prepare the business case and the consolidation project plan — many companies take a year to conduct similar analysis.

Kustoff wondered why this obvious path had not been previously considered. Migrating data and users from three very different platforms to SAP, managing related parochial objections, and consolidating infrastructure does add up to a complex project. It was an idea, however, whose time had come.

Kustoff relishes complex technology projects — besides SAP projects at other companies, Kustoff has been CIO at several, mid-sized, pharmaceutical companies. He was also CTO and then President at Dendrite International, a software vendor focused on the pharmaceutical industry. At industry events, he presents on his "Ten Commandments" — his rules for success with complex IT projects.

Still, says Kustoff, "I knew I would be proposing the largest IT project Endo has ever undertaken — if not Endo's largest and most expensive project of any kind." As he says, "We needed to deliver an analysis where even the details had details."

A team from Cognizant (which he selected based on a quick review of systems integrators that could also help him conduct the initial assessment and develop the work plan) helped him perform the SAP fit-gap analysis and prepare the business case.

SAP functionality looked attractive across the four divisions, as Figure 1 illustrates.

The business case showed savings in several manufacturing, supply chain, finance, and IT areas. But, the most compelling argument came from showing that the risk and cost of staying with the status quo was higher than the

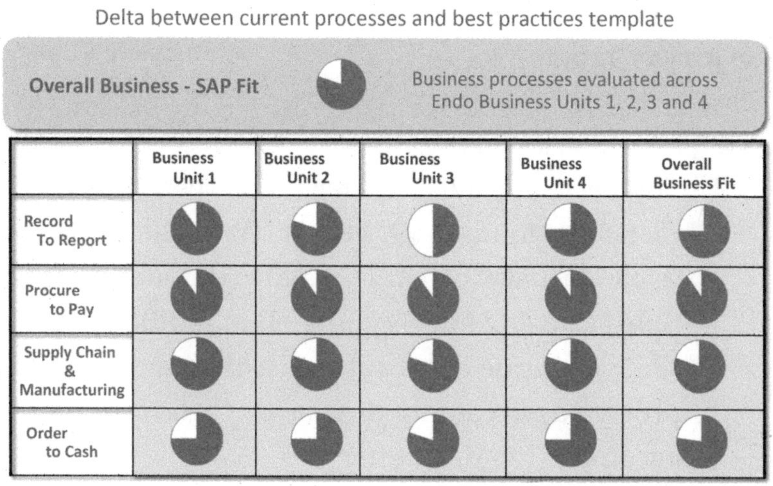

Figure 1 — Credit: Endo International

cost of the proposed consolidation to SAP. The hardware platform support costs across the existing multiple ERPs, as well as the people supports, and the costs for needed software upgrades for multiple systems quickly overshadowed the core cost of replacing the gaggle of systems with a single instance of SAP.

The 186-page analysis — the executive summary had drill-down links into level two (graphs) and level three (raw data, spreadsheets) detail — had to be socialized across the Endo executive suite and pass COO, CFO, and CEO scrutiny. It was approved by the board.

The project itself innovated in a number of areas. Given the range of integration plus end-user training needs across the four ERP environments, they used tools like WebMethods and uPerform (a training platform).

Kustoff describes some of the techniques used to keep the project agile:

> "We kept a separate instance of SAP, copied production back, created a master client, then could copy that client to up to 999 clients. We would load and reload in a new client. This allowed us to have multiple cleansing efforts going on in multiple clients. We were agile and could start the whole refresh process again at any time as the production data became better and better.
>
> For training, we created a separate instance with a master client where we created training data which is a combination of converted data and manually entered data. We locked that client down and then were able to copy and create clients based on training schedules having multiple classes in different clients going on simultaneously.
>
> All data reporting is on HANA for speed, simplicity, and streamlined data environment. But, we did not use HANA for the transaction part of SAP, because it was cost-prohibitive to do so. So, we operate with two databases."

The implementation was well under way when the company brought in a new CEO in April 2013, Rajiv De Silva, with a mandate to reorient the company's strategy and transform its business. De Silva brought in a new COO and CFO, and also froze the SAP project. He wanted to ensure the SAP direction was the appropriate and most efficient one.

Kustoff's team evaluated other "lighter" ERP products available in the market. With the consolidation project already 40 percent completed, with additional SAP licenses procured and not "tradable," a new direction would have actually been more expensive for Endo. De Silva approved the restart, but challenged the SAP implementation with a number of business restructuring moves.

An acquisition of Canadian drug company, Paladin Labs, allowed Endo to redomicile in Dublin. The operating efficiencies, tax savings and corporate flexibility enabled by this redomiciling are expected to be significant, but it required SAP to now accommodate a new set of accounting, tax, and regulatory requirements.

Endo has also divested the HealthTronics unit and is considering other restructuring moves, so the original consolidation project has changed considerably. Such distractions derail many an SAP project, but Endo went live on Phase One of its project in May of 2014. This included the corporate financial functions, all transactions related to the branded pharmaceutical division, and one small manufacturing plant. Phase Two, which covered the generic liquid products plant, went live in July of 2014.

As we have discussed in Chapter 9, consolidating the sprawl of SAP instances has been an attractive optimization strategy for many customers. It is tough work, however, so not many customers have attempted it, and those that have, report multiyear projects. So, when I heard Endo had rapidly consolidated multiple ERP systems, I was interested in profiling them in the book.

As you see, the original consolidation project became more complex with significant strategy changes, spinoffs, and executive changes. A common expression in ERP circles is "Implementing SAP freezes you in place." The Endo story is about not letting SAP constrain you, but instead making it help you adjust to rapidly changing business scenarios.

A New World Beckons

CHAPTER 13

New Customer Priorities — From IT to OT

Michael Lewis' latest book, *Flash Boys*,[162] is a controversial look at high-frequency trading, the use of advanced technologies, and computer algorithms to gain advantage in trading securities. While the practices described in the book have raised a firestorm on Wall Street, and are leading to regulatory reviews of such trading, Lewis does point to a whole new world of IT.

The New York Times, in its review of the book, describes the technology at the start of the book:

> "It involves the stealthy building of an absolutely straight tunnel to run fiber-optic cable through the mountains of Pennsylvania. The firm building the tunnel calls itself Spread Networks, and the job is monstrous. Huge

---

[162] http://www.amazon.com/Flash-Boys-Michael-Lewis/dp/0393244660

mountains need to be drilled through. Every small town needs to grant permission. No one can know what the tunnel is for, and the cost of the digging is beyond astronomical."

And, one that ends the book:

"He ends this book with a trip through the forest, up a mountain and right to the base of a sinister microwave tower with an F.C.C. license number that he provides. Got a computer and a free day? He claims you can track down that license to find another Wall Street nightmare in the making."[163]

Besides the speed of electrons via fiber and microwave, Lewis covers wide technological ground — the mining of competitive intelligence via LinkedIn, colocation of trading servers as close as possible to the exchange's servers, the mindset of Russian coders, and gritty details of trading systems.

The book describes technology that has been around for several years. *Forbes* described Daniel Spivey, the founder of Spread Networks mentioned above:

"In 2007 Spivey contracted with a New York hedge fund to devise a low-latency arbitrage strategy, wherein the fund would search out tiny discrepancies between futures contracts in Chicago and their underlying equities in New York."[164]

[163] http://www.nytimes.com/2014/04/01/books/flash-boys-by-michael-lewis-a-tale-of-high-speed-trading.html?_r=0
[164] http://www.forbes.com/forbes/2010/0927/outfront-netscape-jim-barksdale-daniel-spivey-wall-street-speed-war.html

Think how much further computing power and software algorithms have evolved since 2007. While Lewis focuses on the ethical issues of the unfair advantage from such trading, the reality reflects IT as today's business weaponry. That is the new IT horizon, not just about optimizing the back office.

Bill Ruh, of GE, who we introduced in Chapter 6, likes to say we are transitioning from information technology (IT) to operational technology (OT).

Ruh elaborates:

> "SAP and other ERP transaction architectures served us well when we were looking to pull together islands of custom-built, back-office systems. But, we have evolved to an operational technology world.
>
> In this new world, the UX has to be thought in terms of human-machine interface, not just via a tablet or desktop screen. When you are looking at 120,000 gas turbines around the world generating half-a-terabyte of data a day, you have to evaluate what is processed locally, versus moved to the cloud. Security has to be rethought, with so many distributed processing nodes.
>
> Uptime definitions are much more demanding. When the utility grid is down, you have thousands of angry businesses and consumers, not just a few disgruntled systems users. OT thinking makes you overlay a variety of physical realities on the digital infrastructures we have built in the past."

And, the business model impact is dramatic. Ruh continues:

> "At GE, we think of it in three layers — productivity, what we call 'predictivity' and our Predix platform.

Most of GE's service contracts are outcome-based. As data allows us to improve productivity, we can share more of the gains with customers.

We have been able to launch new services, which we broadly brand as predictivity. You can change gradually the physics of a locomotive or a turbine, but data allows us to tune and generate incremental operational efficiencies. An example is our PowerUp offering. It is an outcome-based, software-enabled platform created to increase a wind farm's output by up to 5 percent. For a typical U.S. wind farm operator using GE's 1.5–77 turbine, a 5 percent increase in energy output translates to up to 20 percent increase in profit per turbine.

While the first two are delivered through GE services, Predix is our software platform for the industrial Internet. GE customers (and soon others) can license and leverage on their own to improve asset performance management, support machine-to-machine communications and optimize operations. It is a collection of embedded technologies, algorithms, and other components. It is meant to deliver consumer-grade mobile experiences for industry-grade control and insights. And, it is meant to be cloud-agnostic — it runs on equipment, in your data centers, or in public clouds."

Paul Maritz, former CEO of VMWare and now CEO of Pivotal, a GE partner, echoes Ruh's sentiments:

"Historically much of the innovation in information technology has originated in the financial services industry. In the last decade it has moved to "consumer internet giants." Now, we are seeing it move to the industrial space, which is taking data to a whole new level." [165]

As Ruh summarizes:

> "OT is about how a business makes money; IT was mostly about the back office. There is a hugely exciting difference."

Rogow's Vision of IT's Evolution

How does the world of *Flash Boys* and operational technology challenge the SAP customer? My former Gartner colleague, Bruce J. Rogow — whom I introduced in Chapter 3 as a keen pulse-taker and trendsetter — likes to look in IT's past eras to project what is coming down the pike.

Here is what he counsels SAP customers:

> In almost any sport, the players know that before the next play, they must do three things aggressively: forget whatever happened in the last play; anticipate and look for signs of where the next play is likely to go; get loose, heads-up, and up on the balls of their feet ready to spring into appropriate action as the next play unfolds. It is not the time to be focused on the last play, missing the clues or being caught flat-footed.
>
> The next big play in IT is under way, but many CIOs and IT leaders are remaining passive; solely consolidating or optimizing the last play; not looking at the likely signs of

---

[165] http://www.enterpriseirregulars.com/63487/the-third-wave/

IT evolution for where the play may go; tightening down and settling in on their heels. In short, instead of doing what is needed for the next era of IT, they are hunkering into the current era of SAP Nation.

An IT era change is under way:

We could argue about the details, dates, and aspects of IT eras, but the critical points are that:

- Each era brought new IT technologies, architecture, applications, business contributions, political drivers/owners, major and minor vendors/players, capabilities required, and management challenges, as shown in Figure 1, Footprints of IT Eras.

- Each era was based on what had been learned and done in the previous one. The previous era was not abandoned, but became a part of the underpinning legacy.

- Players and perspectives came and went within each era as the era went through a lifecycle.

- The dominant player of each era struggled, was dragged through the next era, or became irrelevant.

- The challenges of each new era swept aside the IT leadership and capabilities of the last era as inadequate or improperly focused.

- Waiting for Godot or in the current case, post-SAP, is a bad strategy.

- Assimilation, absorption, IT evolution, and management prowess do not move at the speed of Moore's Law. The future isn't mature or imminent and will take many years, but building the capabilities required must be started.

The extent and status of the SAP Nation is not a new phenomenon. This is a master IT platform change. We have had platform changes before, and there is much to be learned from them to begin the process of becoming aggressive, ignoring the last plays, anticipating the shape of the next play, and getting loose and ready to spring forward.

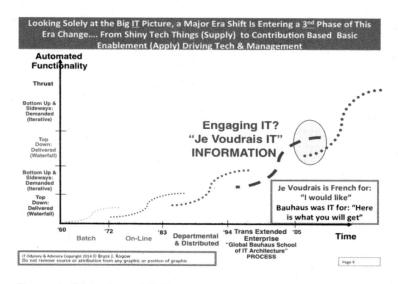

Figure 1: Footprints of IT Eras   Credit: Bruce J. Rogow

Timeframe	ERA	Business Objective	Scope of Applications	Political Driver or Thrust	Dominant Vendors or Players
1960-71	Batch	Basic accounting	Serial File Administration	CFO, DP Manager: Top Down	IBM, Univac, Honeywell
1972-82	On Line and non-serial Databases	Real Time inventory, order entry	Low volume transactions by qualified admin	CFO for Administration; MIS Manager: Top Down	IBM 370 and clones
1982-92	PCs, Minis, Client Server	Departmental & Knowledge Workers	Personal, Office, Departmental Support	Individuals and Departments; Emergence of CIO: Bottom Up	IBM, HP, DEC, PC makers, Lotus, Microsoft
1993-2013	Bauhaus or Global One Size Fits All	Commonization, control, visibility IT technology and business processes	Global reach to operating staff & then customers, staff over web	CIO, Senior Business Execs, Supply Chain Management: Top Down	SAP, Accenture and the Outsourcers
2013-????	Je Voudrais (Users saying "this is what I want"	Best and most appropriate fit to grow the business	Any data to any device & internet of things	Senior execs, individual users, customers, channel partners, the internet masses: Outside-In	To Be Determined

Figure 2   Credit: Bruce J. Rogow

Several factors shape the current and future:

Most pundits talk about how IT change is speeding up. The pace and breadth of new technology change may be increasing. However, contrary to conventional thinking, many believe real IT absorption is slowing down, and not speeding up for established enterprises. These successful legacy businesses must accommodate legacy business models, skills, business processes, products, customers, channels, measurement systems, cultures, and overly complex systems.

Seven Principles
From my over 45 years of watching the IT game, it is the absorption and capitalization aspects of the game that separate the winners and losers. As we move from the SAP Nation to our next IT era, it is critical that today's IT and business leaders understand the factors that

shape the evolution, absorption and capitalization, and use that understanding to drive their strategies and management agendas:

1. *The Collapse of the Current Platform Margin Circus Tent:* Each IT era has had a dominant vendor or vendors who defined not only the common architecture, but also had the most lucrative lasting margins. View them and their architecture and margins as the center poles of a large one- to three-ring circus tent with cables drooping down from the center pole to the sides of the tent. The other vendors and providers hung on bungee cords from those cables with smaller footprints and margins. As long as the supporting/ancillary providers' margin bungee cord didn't hit the ground, they had sustainable businesses.

As the era's master platform dominant vendor was growing and their margins remained high, the whole industry flourished and grew in a symbiotic relationship as long as they had the proper margin bungee. However, as the era matured, the margin pole of the dominant vendor shrunk and the tent got bigger. The dominant vendor tried to pump up their center pole with gimmicks, but found they had less and less resource to change. The ancillary players found their margin bungees were too long and had to find a circus with new characteristics.

Just as IBM lost control and market power in the 1990s, SAP and large outsourcers are losing margin and architectural dominance. The bungee firms are look-ing for new tents, and within the competing circuses the game is on to see who will be the dominant players.

IT strategy implication: Expect that the current dominant players will face diminishing margins and growth from existing customers and products. To delay this impact, they will try to increase pricing, promise "breakthrough extensions" of a last-era platform, add gimmicks, and stay relevant as long as possible. However, the action and investment will be shifting to the new circus tents. So, start shifting plans and resources from the current base, do not expect an answer from the current players and learn as much as possible about the various new circuses, their players, and their evolution.

2. *IT Aspect Dynamics/Evolution Define the Future:* Several of my mentors including Ken Branch, Max Hopper, and Carl Reynolds described that the use and capitaliza-tion of IT evolved in a relatively predictable manner.

- Step 1: A new "raw" technology such as the PC or Internet is introduced. Few folks can initially figure out how to gainfully use it.

- Step 2: After two to four years, someone comes up with a primitive application such as a basic spread-sheet, word processor, or browser. As folks try to use the primitive application, they outgrow the technology's capabilities. Thus, interplay between trying to improve the technology and improve the application goes on back and forth for perhaps three to five more years. Early winners fall by the wayside, new winners emerge, and eventually a few standards emerge. The app and technology spread like wildfire.

- Step 3: Someone in management realizes that this new symbiotic relationship between technology and applications has grown, but is not being managed. In about the seven to ten year timeframe, a series of management tools, processes, and governance emerge.

- Step 4: Around the 10–15 year timeframe, the technology, applications, and management process is solid. There have been episodic benefits that some of the users can cite, but the firm realizes the big, transformational material contributions have not been achieved. Typically, they require new business models and organizational change. As an example, we got PCs and their apps in the 1980s, but it wasn't until the 1990s that firms eliminated secretaries, bookkeepers, middle management, and used email to manage on a more real-time, global basis. The same happened a decade before, as online systems and databases did not profoundly impact inventories for many years.

IT strategy implication: Watch the shiny new technologies such as SMAC [social, mobile, analytics, and cloud] and anticipate how the applications, management processes and material benefits will evolve. Try to stay one step ahead of what is likely to happen next. Do not get overcommitted based on where in the IT evolution cycle you and the industry may be.

3. ***Platform Economics Drive the Trade Winds:*** In each era, the potential users have congregated around obtaining functionality that had apparently positive and easily achieved economics. Their deployment of IT was based on economic elasticity. There has also been a small number of more adventuresome users who have gone beyond the apparent economics and chosen to be functionally elastic. They were prepared to invest more for what they believed would give them clear differentiation. The functionally elastic were willing to spend more and work with not-ready-for-universal-primetime technologies or skills to do what others would see as economically feasible in the next era.

The leaders of the evolving era are already out there.

IT strategy implication: Identify and closely follow the journey of the functionally elastic players in your industry, adjacent industries, and even those in unrelated industries, but who are doing things that might be just over your horizon. Don't fall into the trap of dismissing what they are doing because of cost, troubles they might encounter, or your belief that their firms may fold or fail.

4. **Who Defines the Future, Expectations and Vectors:**
The entrepreneurs, pundits, and emerging vendors would like to think they define the next era. It is actually the political group or audience within or attached to the firm that defines what will be the shape of the next era. The last era was defined by global executives wanting global control and visibility for the optimization of the enterprise. The evolving era is being defined by or being conceptualized to meet individual consumerized expectations for IT.

IT strategy implication: IT and the enterprise must add the technology merchandising, audiencing, IT brand management, and service management functions often seen in media companies.

5. **Each Platform or Era has Dramatically Expanded the Scope of and Possibilities for IT Contribution:** We often hear that each new IT platform expanded what could economically be done with IT by a factor of five to ten times. I'm not sure if that number is correct, but the multiplier over the last five eras and fifty years has been amazing. I remember the outstanding and visionary MIS executive of a Fortune 10 company telling me that he thought his new McCormack & Dodge accounting package would do over 80 percent of what he could envision his firm could ever do with DP.

IT and business organizations become prisoners in capability and vision of their current era platform. Optimizing your

SAP Nation entry may not be any more worthwhile in an era change than optimizing, say, your Dun & Bradstreet (or was that McCormack & Dodge?) accounting package.

IT strategy implication: Resources must now be dedicated to understanding, uncovering, communicating, and socializing what the new era can enable. These efforts should be both within the firm and reach out to customers, partners, and channels.

6. *Experiential Learning Can't Be Bought:* New IT requires the firms, organizations, and markets to adapt and change as well as to learn how to take advantage of the new IT and make money from it. This involves experiential learning versus something taught by a professor, suggested by a consultant, read in a book, delivered by an outsourcer, or brought in by a new hire.

IT strategy implication: Any effective IT strategy and agenda must include consideration of how the required experiential learning needed for the next era will be developed over time.

7. *Seasons of IT:* The new IT era will happen over many economic and philosophic seasons of the firms. These eras take at least a decade, if not more. During the era evolution, the company, view of IT, economy, political environment, and business objectives will change.

IT strategy implication: Prudent leaders are focused on the evolution and outcome of the era, rather than being totally consumed dealing with the season of the business or economy. They adjust to the season.

The IT leadership, challenges, and capabilities must morph if the future is not to be fumbled:

When I started my career, DP managers were all looking for keypunch operators, and Assembler or COBOL programmers. These DP managers were swept away by MIS directors needing analysts, systems management, and capable operators. They were swept away by CIOs looking for relationship managers, business analysts, web developers, governance mavens, SAP implementation firms, vendor benders, and capable outsourcers. This new platform will demand an even bigger change in IT leadership, capabilities, and organization.

We already see situations where the greenfield, new competitor with a digital business model can run rings around the established player mired in their legacy. Yes, it is likely that the greenfield may not survive and will also grind to a halt in mayhem or the mud of its own legacy. But, the key issue is that the industry will not be the same.

Many firms talk of needing to be more lean or agile or responsive, but aren't taking the steps to get beyond their current cultural, process, and IT platforms.

My great regret is that in over 47 years in IT, I've seen too many capable friends swept aside by the next platform change or situation. Not considering or planning for the points above represents an ignorance or arrogance that will bring its own reward. History is rhyming loudly, to paraphrase Mark Twain."

CHAPTER 14

The New SAP Economy

∿→

The week of September 15, 2014, was a significant one for Luka Mucic, the new Chief Financial Officer of SAP.

On Monday, he presented at an event called the SAP Cloud Deep Dive to a group of industry analysts. CFOs usually present to Wall Street analysts, not industry analysts, but his presentation in this session was crisp and confident. "One of the better ones that day," remarked an analyst who was present.

On Thursday, he broke the news of SAP buying Concur for over $8 billion and its fit with SAP's vision of the "network economy." On the conference call, he said,

"For me, the big charm comes in scaling the network. We can make money while we sleep and I like that model a lot. This has the possibility to be very profitable."

The focus on clouds and the network economy reflect a new horizon for SAP. What do the related subscription- and fee-based business models mean for SAP's customers? Has SAP thought about the cost of "managing a cost per terabyte" in the face of exploding data volumes like GE has described in Chapter 6? Will SAP applications be more efficient to manage in cloud settings?

I had invited SAP to provide me up to ten pages and describe how the SAP economy will be different going forward. I told them I would run it unedited — in the company's unfiltered voice.

For two months, they evaluated my request. Several phone calls and emails were exchanged. In the end, with time running out, I invited market observers to speak on their behalf. Each provides a perspective on how they think SAP and its partners may behave differently going forward.

Market Observers Project SAP's Future Economy
Here's Holger Mueller of Constellation Research:

> "HANA and a series of acquisitions have invigorated SAP, and I see that as good for its customers, too. We should see a lot more custom development as enterprise applications catch up to the fast-moving 21st century business realities and enterprises do not want to wait for long vendor delivery cycles that we have seen in the past.
>
> The HANA Cloud Platform (HCP), SAP's cloud platform-as-a-service (PaaS) is exciting from that development perspective. It is also exciting to see SAP heavily leverage open source components like Docker containers and CloudFoundry in HCP. That should make next-generation development a lot easier and economical, rather than being dependent on proprietary tools.
>
> HCP is also moving SAP to the "API economy" with composable business applications as the big promise.

The cloud delivery model should also encourage more remote development and new forms of labor arbitrage and delivery models.

The HANA start-up program with over 1,000 entre-preneurs is also a shift to more IP-based partners, away from the traditional services-based partners. All these trends point to a very different SAP economy, particu-larly the labor components in the future."

Jason Busch at Spend Matters, which focuses on supply chains, has this to say:

"SAP had its back against the financials and enterprise software wall and they've made some very gutsy moves with a string of acquisitions that would make any cor-porate development executive cringe from a valuation perspective — (i.e., betting long-term versus doing anything approaching a DCF model with historical assumptions). The moves to acquire Ariba, and more recently Concur, could eventually transform SAP if they can leverage the concept of a networked business model to create a range of new value propositions for participants of all sizes — payment financing, for one, could prove transformative, in and of itself, for buyers and suppliers globally.

However, the deals raise a number of additional fascinating issues, questions, and prospects including: how might SAP apply its in-memory database technology, HANA, to analyze supplier network data beyond basic buyer/supplier transactional connectivity? What types of metadata flowing through the supplier network will be most interesting to buyers and suppliers? For example, what will the points of intersection be between SAP Supplier InfoNet and the Ariba Supplier Network? How will SAP work to monetize the networks in new ways?"

Jarret Pazahanick, a SAP Mentor who focuses on the HR software sector, says:

"One of the things I am excited about is many of the issues customers have faced in the bloated SAP ecosystem having an opportunity to be streamlined as they move to cloud-based offerings such as SuccessFactors. Areas such as hosting, upgrades, and technical support are now the responsibility of the cloud vendor. Integration is an interesting one, as SAP is living in a hybrid world where this integration remains an important topic for many of their customers. There is an expectation that integration between all vendor-owned offerings such as SAP HCM, SAP Financial, and SuccessFactors, for example, should "just work," but on the ground I see this as a lot more challenging. SuccessFactors, for example, is a combination for four acquisitions and still involves a lot of heavy lifting for customers to interface with SAP's On Premise offering, but SAP has delivered some functionality and more is on the future roadmap.

There is a growing ecosystem of software integrators that understand that you don't deploy SAP's cloud-based offering the same way as the previous generation on-premise model, and are more nimble by using a combination of newer implementation methodologies, remote consulting, and other things to help streamline overall implementation costs, which is a win/win for SAP and their customers. It is important for customers to watch out for consulting firms that continue to use their older methodologies, onshoring/offshoring model, and big teams of on-site consultants as that is not required to successfully deliver cloud implementation. It is more of a case of them trying to make the same revenue they were accustomed to in the past.

As always, it is important that customers are educated about the vendors, consulting firms, and services they are purchasing and I always recommend they use multiple data points, and most importantly, talk to other customers before spending any money."

John Appleby of Bluefin Solutions, Ltd focuses on the impact of HANA and the HANA Cloud in a comment he left on my Deal Architect blog:

"HANA cannibalizes the UNIX/mainframe market and the hardware partners didn't like this, so they have tried to build systems that maintain their lucrative margins. Do remember that companies like IBM, HP and Cisco are much bigger than SAP and have much more influence, both with customers and with partners like Intel. Sometimes SAP is David and not Goliath!

Thankfully, we have seen this change this year. There is now support for VMWare in production; support for IBM POWER is coming, which will provide more competition. There are relaxed requirements for nonproduction systems. Ivy Bridge CPUs and the lowering cost of memory are helping. Improved options for system replication mean we can combine Dev/Test and DR to lower TCO.

On the hardware front, we now see HANA pricing come out at around $80k/TB on a regular basis, and less to customers who are good at negotiating. By the way, I heard IBM are now discounting 40% off HANA pricing as of this month. Now Lenovo are in the game, the TCO will continue to drop.

I told Jim Snabe that the real value in the HANA Cloud is the kick-start of an ecosystem of cloud vendors, and that's what the HANA Cloud Platform has done. You can buy HANA as IaaS for $6,495/month for 1TB or $77k/year. If you compare this to an equivalent powered and sized RDBMS on AWS based on other vendors, you will see that HANA comes out for less money."[166]

It's a new SAP world. Or, so it would appear. The subscription and fee-based business models that SAP is learning through its new products and acquisitions could mean a significant change in future licensing and consumption models.

---

[166] http://dealarchitect.typepad.com/deal_architect/2014/09/hassos-dozen.html

CHAPTER 15

The Long Shadow

∿→

Everywhere you look in SAP world, there appears to be change.

McDermott has been quoted as saying, "I've always been a hustler" as he reminisces about his teenage jobs and entrepreneurial pursuits. He has written about his move from "Corner Store to Corner Office" in his recently released book, *Winners Dream*.[167]

As the new CEO of SAP, he is bringing a sense of energy and optimism to the company. At SapphireNow, this past summer, the presence of a group of young, HANA entrepreneurs and an even younger group of "teen reporters" (sponsored by the GenYouth Foundation) emphasized a company in transition.

CSC, the outsourcing firm, estimates the average CIO today is 57 years old. In five years, they expect the age to dramatically

---

[167] http://www.amazon.com/Winners-Dream-Journey-Corner-Office-ebook/dp/B00IWTWO0K/ref=sr_1_1?s=books&ie=UTF8&qid=1412458361&sr=1-1&keywords=bill+mcdermott

drop to 42. The younger CIO will be more driven by time-based competition and will expect far speedier deliverables from vendors like SAP. SAP has been emphasizing speedier processing via HANA, but its customers will expect quicker releases, rapid implementations and speedier payback on investments. Raised with a new set of social, mobile, sensory, and wearable technology, they will demand SAP's experience and functionality to reflect the new order. Aneel Bhusri, CEO of Workday, has projected, "It's hard for me to see any enterprise not buying HR and finance in the cloud in ten years time."

In July 2014, SAP became a European legal entity — it is now called SAP SE. That reflects the maturing of the European Union and SAP's own evolution from a German to a European phenomenon. SAP's big global opportunities, however, come from BRIC countries and other emerging economies. Many customers in these markets will not support the expensive software licensing and partner model SAP has become accustomed to in the West.

Henrique Pinto of SAP Brazil commented on a blog, "It's a terrifying moment: Will my skills still be relevant?" He is optimistic though: "(Whatever comes next) I'm sure it will be easy-peasy compared to what the mainframe people went through when the client-server architecture came out."

His comment is one of many which forces you to notice signs from SAP's past, even as you think it is changing.

SAP Alumni in New Roles

During "events season" in September and October, when most software vendors have their user conferences (and as I was wrapping up this book), I came across several SAP and partner alumni now in new jobs. Many are trying to create SAP's runaway success in their new environments. Hopefully, they will create a much leaner economy around themselves. The risk, of course, is they could replicate the "bad practices" we described in the SAP economy — the inefficient data centers, double-charging for adjacent functionality, the extensive consultant travel and the related four-day work week, the project failures, and the overpromised benefits.

In the preface, we mentioned the battle to tame SAP is an epic effort to reshape back-office IT, and to refocus resources with attention to product- and customer-centric "front-office" digital technologies. The inefficiencies in the SAP economy apply across many other areas of IT. And, those efficiencies will continue to show up around newer SAP products. Indeed, SAP commissioned an IDC infograph to showcase that its partners will "earn US$220 billion in revenue in the next five years related to analytics and Big Data solutions from the company."[168] That may be music to the ears of its partners, but it should create more caution for its customers.

I ran into a technology strategist, one of the best in the industry, and he looked even further back into the past:

> "HANA in 2014 reminds me greatly of Java in 1997. That is, it's a compelling piece of software that's giving a new level of sex appeal to a major vendor with a maturing core product line. Management at those companies greatly tout it, the technology gets lots of press attention, and some key managers behind the products (read Kim Polese, Vishal Sikka) are given huge personal opportunities. However, there's a problem. Neither product drives

---

[168] http://global.sap.com/corporate-en/news.epx?PressID=21316

much revenue for the vendor. More concerning, neither is able to drive new life into the maturing core product; Java didn't sell many Sun workstations or servers and didn't revitalize the offer, and it seems there's little relation between HANA and new SAP ERP license sales or the core of the ERP offer."

I read in *PC World* in early October of another member of the "billion dollar club" that SAP has become known for:

"The cost of finishing a massive SAP software overhaul at a New York gas utility will rise to nearly US$1 billion from an original estimate of $383.8 million, a newly released audit report has found."[169]

The drumbeat of failures we described in Chapter 7 continues. Their gestation period is measured in years, so there may still be many more such failures lurking.

SAP and market analysts are talking HANA, Ariba, and SuccessFactors. The "old SAP" — Business Suite, Business One, BusinessObjects etc. — still costs customers the best part of $204 billion a year.

Throughout the book, we have seen how the SAP economy has continued to grow in spite of both customer and SAP's own pivots. So, will recent customer and SAP moves change the trajectory of this "old SAP" economy? Will SAP apply newer subscription, variable cost, fee-based business models around the new products to the older products?

---

[169] http://www.pcworld.com/article/2691712/price-tag-for-troubled-sap-project-will-skyrocket-to-nearly-1-billion-audit-says.html

When Oracle had launched its acquisition spree a decade ago, SAP had launched a "Safe Harbor" marketing campaign aimed at customers of the acquired companies. With its own spree of acquisitions, can we be optimistic that SAP itself will help customers optimize their portfolios? It has been offering to trade older licenses for new subscriptions. Will it go further and help them with much larger savings around its partners?

Ginni Rommety, CEO of IBM in announcing in October 2014 the company's tenth consecutive quarterly revenue decline said "Our results also point to the unprecedented pace of change in our industry." Hurd, Co-CEO of Oracle, told the audience at his annual conference in September 2014: "There are no CEOs giving CIOs unlimited checkbooks. IT budgets are flat, if not down. I think being a CIO is probably the toughest job out there, Think of a CIO as rowing a boat with plenty of people around him with megaphones shouting orders. The CIO is getting coached and is under a lot of pressure from business colleagues and vendors."

Dr. Plattner has emphasized SAP is a "trusted advisor" to its customers — can it step up into that role or is it just another party with a megaphone screaming at its customer CIOs to buy HANA and other new products?

Will strategies in the four sets of case studies we have profiled — Un-Adopters, Diversifiers, Pragmatists, and Committed — spread across the SAP community? Will other SAP customers emulate AstraZeneca, CLP, Deere, Endo, Flextronics, Inteva, Schneider Electric, and other customers we have profiled throughout the book? Most of them did not wait for SAP or its partners. They took the initiative on their own to optimize their SAP environments. They also got to know a new set of players — Plex, Kinaxis, Rimini, Workday, and others we have profiled in the book.

Should the broader customer base take the initiative, we will see momentum to reduce the cost footprint with increased focus on value from the investment in older SAP products. Some of our case study customers are reporting better than 50 percent savings and better value in other ways. Let's be more modest and think about shaving just 10 percent from the SAP economy. What could enterprises do with an additional $20 billion a year?

While we drool about what we can do with the potential savings, let's not forget SAP's long shadow. The project failures have been spectacular. The net yield — SAP's product R&D is only around 1 percent of the $204 billion "surround" economy it costs customers. Many of its customers have missed out of waves of industrialization, consumerization and other IT trends. While SAP has been running campaigns about "Run Better" and "Run Simple", the economy around it has been "Runaway".

So, let's end with some caution from George Santayana in *The Life of Reason:*

> "Those who cannot remember the past are condemned to repeat it."

The Eye of the Storm

Towards the end of October 2014 a full-page ad in the *Wall Street Journal* caught my attention. The words could have been a tagline for this book:

"Technology can save us all. Provided it doesn't kill us first."

The imagery in the ad got me more curious. It was a green orb surrounded by shades of brown. Looking closer, I saw the reflection of glass in an eye. I also noticed there was no branding — no logos, no web address, nothing else — on the page. Then I got distracted from the paper and forgot about it.

Couple of days later a friend called and suggested I check out Pages A10 and 11 of the morning's *Journal*. As I flipped through the pages there was the eye again on Page A9. This time I flipped the page and noticed it was part of a three-page spread. And, as I read the text, they were talking about how complexity costs companies over $200 billion a year. I wondered — could they actually be talking about the economy we have described in the book?

So, I walked over and asked my wife about the eye. She said it reminded her of "The Eye of God" — the Helix Nebula. Then I asked her to turn the page. She read the text and smiled. And, like a good Floridian who has seen countless hurricane images she said:

"Actually, I think it is the eye of a storm."

Index

~→

Sybase, 21, 22, 25, 34, 106, 111, 170, 231
Syclo, 22, 106
Syspro, xv

Tablack, George, 47
Tableau, 91
Taleo, 206
Tawakol, Omar, 93
TCS, xxii, 31, 45, 81, 170, 197, 221, 224
Technidata, 106
TechTarget, 21
Tesla, 162
Thiele, Mark, 83
Thomas Manes, Anne, 22
Tidemark, 160
TomorrowNow, 215
TopCoder, 236
TopManage, 75
TopTier, 21
Tradeshift, 108
Traiana, 272
Triversity, 106
T-Systems, xxii, 187
Tungsten, 108
Tupperware, 157
Twitter, 159, 172, 276
Tyler Technologies, 48

Uber, 162, 235
Ubermind, 253
UKISUG, 248
Unilever, xii, 269
Unisource, 138
Unit4, xv, 50–51
United Biscuits, xii, 54–55
Upper Edge, 212

USA Today, 200
U.S. Chamber of Commerce, 245
U.S. CIA, 155
U.S. Circuit Court of Appeals, 217
U.S. Congress, 244
U.S. Department of Justice, 247
U.S. District Court for the District of New Jersey, 147
USF, 248–249
U.S. Government Accountability Office (GAO), 144
U.S. Marine Corps, 222
U.S. Navy, 144
U.S. SEC, 255
U.S. Sugar, 160
U.S. Veterans Administration, 227

Veeva, 116
Virsa, 106
Visiprise, 106
VMware, 155, 290, 307
Volkswagen, 139

Wahl, Paul, 69
Wainewright, Phil, 37
The Wall Street Journal, 19, 72, 74, 136, 208, 315
Wang, Ray, 208
Waste Management, 145, 146
Watts, Karen, 227
WebMethods, 233, 281
Welch, Jack, 209
Wharton, 261
Whirlpool, 139
Whitman, Meg, 112, 114, 204
WH Smith, 140
Wincom, 106
Wincor Nixdorf, 220